# Measure for Measure

edited by Colin Gray

with additional material by John Seely and Ken Elliott

Series Editor: John Seely

Heinemann

Heinemann Educational Publishers
Halley Court, Jordan Hill, Oxford OX2 8EJ
A division of Reed Educational & Professional Publishing Ltd

OXFORD  BLANTYRE  CHICAGO
PORTSMOUTH (NH) USA  MELBOURNE
AUCKLAND  IBADAN  GABORONE  JOHANNESBURG

Introduction, notes and activities
© Elizabeth Seely,  John Seely, Ken Elliott 1997

First published in the *Heinemann Shakespeare Plays* series 1997
Second edition 2000

02  01  00
10 9  8  7  6  5  4  3  2  1

ISBN 0 435 193112

Cover Design by Miller Craig and Cocking

Cover illustration by Nigel Casseldine R. W. A.

Typeset and produced by Celia Floyd, Basingstoke

Additional typesetting by TechType, Abingdon, Oxon

Printed and bound in Great Britain by Biddles Ltd, *www.biddles.co.uk*

# CONTENTS

# How to use this book

This edition of *Measure for Measure* has been prepared
to provide you with several different kinds of information
and guidance.

## The introduction

Before the text of the play there is:
- a summary of the plot
- a brief explanation of Shakespeare's texts.

## The text and commentary

On each right-hand page you will find the text of the play.
On the facing left-hand pages there are three types of
support material:
- a summary of the action
- detailed explanations of difficult words, phrases and
  longer sections of text
- suggestions of points you might find it useful to think
  about as you read the play.

## End-of-act activities

After each act there is a set of activities. These can be
tackled as you read the play. Many students, however, may
want to leave these until they undertake a second reading.
They consist of the following sections:

*Keeping track:* straightforward questions directing your
attention to the action of the act.

*Discussion:* topics for small group, or whole group
discussion.

*Drama:* practical drama activities to help you focus on key
characters, relationships and situations.

*Close study:* a detailed exploration of the act, scene by
scene and in some cases, line by line.

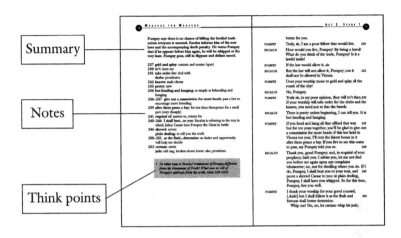

Summary

Notes

Think points

*Imagery:* brief guidance on important themes to look for in the imagery of the play.

*Key scene:* a focus on an important scene in the act. This section applies the thinking you have done in CLOSE STUDY to a key scene within the act and encourages you to think about how the scene fits in to the structure of the play as a whole.

*Writing:* progressive activities throughout the book help you to develop essay writing skills.

## Explorations

At the end of the book there are a variety of different items designed to draw together your thoughts and insights about the play as a whole:
- how to approach thinking about the whole play
- work on character
- work on the themes and issues
- guidance on how to tackle practical drama activities
- advice on preparing for an examination
- advice on essay writing, together with a sample essay written by an A-level student, with comments
- practice essay questions
- glossary of technical terms.

# The plot

## Act 1

As the play begins we see the **Duke of Vienna** handing over his powers before leaving for an unknown destination. He tells **Escalus**, an old and trusted courtier, that he wishes him to act as second-in-command to the young and morally upright **Lord Angelo**. He gives them their commissions and then leaves the city without further ado.

Angelo's interpretation of his instructions soon have their effect. It is clear that Viennese society has for many years been morally lax and even corrupt. Prostitution and venereal disease are rife and although there are strict laws governing sexual morality these have never been enforced. As **Lucio**, a young courtier, and his friends joke about this they learn from **Mistress Overdone**, a bawd (brothel owner), and **Pompey**, a pimp, that Angelo has condemned a young man **Claudio** to death for getting his girlfriend **Juliet** pregnant, even though they had already gone through a civil ceremony which made them man and wife in the eyes of the law. Pompey also reveals that Angelo has ordered all the brothels in the city to be closed and all those in the suburbs to be pulled down. Claudio passes through the streets on his way to prison, escorted by the **Provost**, and asks Lucio to speak to his sister **Isabella**, who is undergoing her probationary period before becoming a nun, to plead with Angelo for his life.

At a friary outside the city, the Duke reveals to **Friar Thomas** (also called Friar Peter in the play) that he is aware of the way in which Viennese society has been corrupted and tells him that he has appointed Angelo to act for him because he believes he will reform the city by enforcing the laws. The Duke argues that having let things slip he cannot now do this himself. Instead he wishes to disguise himself as a friar so that he can travel through the city observing what happens.

At the nunnery Lucio asks Isabella to plead with Angelo for her brother's life and she agrees.

## Act 2

Escalus tries unsuccessfully to persuade Angelo to be merciful
to Claudio, but Angelo argues that the law must be enforced;
Claudio must die the following morning. The comic
**Constable Elbow** brings in two arrested criminals, Pompey
and **Froth**. Elbow has problems with language, constantly
getting words confused, so it is difficult to understand what
he is trying to say, but it appears he has a personal complaint
against Froth because of something he has done to his
(Elbow's) wife. Matters are further confused by Pompey's
interventions and Angelo leaves Escalus to sort things out.
Escalus gives Froth a warning about his behaviour and frees
him. He then warns Pompey that if he continues to pimp
he will be liable to the death sentence under a new law passed
by Angelo.

Isabella and Lucio go to see Angelo. She begs Angelo to
spare her brother's life. Despite his repeated refusals, she
persists. Gradually her passionate pleas begin to affect him,
but not in the way she intends; he begins to find her emotion
and beauty are arousing his desire – despite the fact that he is a
ruler and she is a postulant nun. He tells her to come back the
next day. She leaves and Angelo, alone, wonders what is
happening to him.

The Duke, disguised as a friar, visits Juliet in prison. She
repents her actions, but to her horror he tells her that Claudio
must die the following morning.

Isabella returns to Angelo. He begins by repeating that
Claudio must die because of his wickedness. Then in a lengthy
dialogue about sin and redemption, he reveals to her the only
way in which she can save her brother's life. She must agree to
sleep with him. Horrified, Isabella refuses and says she will tell
everyone what he has proposed. He points out that no one
will believe her. Unless she gives in Claudio will die a painful
death. He leaves her to think about it. Isabella decides to talk
to her brother.

## Act 3

The Duke, in disguise, visits Claudio and tells him to prepare for death. Then Isabella arrives and tells Claudio of Angelo's proposition. Claudio is appalled by the man's hypocrisy, but she says she has done her duty and refused. Terrified at the prospect of death, however, Claudio has second thoughts and begs Isabella to let him live. She is shocked at his selfishness and tells him to prepare for death. Just as Isabella is about to go, the Duke/friar speaks to them. He tells Claudio that Angelo was only testing Isabella, but that he must still die. Claudio goes back to his cell.

The Duke/friar tells Isabella that he has a plan to save Claudio. He says that Angelo was once engaged to a young woman called **Mariana** but rejected her when, because of a family tragedy, it became impossible for her to offer him a dowry. He says that Isabella should agree to Angelo's demands but should arrange to meet him in a dark place at night. Mariana will then go in her place and Angelo will be revealed as a lecher. Isabella agrees to the plan.

Meanwhile Pompey has been arrested by Elbow for theft. He is taken to prison with the threat of appearing before Angelo who will probably condemn him to death as a pimp.

Lucio meets the Duke, hooded and disguised as the friar, and tells him that it is a pity that the old Duke is not in his proper place – he would not agree with all the nonsense about persecuting vice. He (Lucio) is a great friend and knows him as a drinker and nowhere near as wise as people say he is. The Duke/friar challenges Lucio to say all this to the Duke when the Duke comes back. Lucio says he will.

Mistress Overdone is brought before Escalus as a bawd and is condemned to prison.

The act ends with the Duke/friar reflecting on morality and political power and regretting bitterly Angelo's behaviour.

# Act 4

The Duke/friar meets Isabella and Mariana. The plan is explained to Mariana and she agrees to take part.

At the prison the Provost offers Pompey the job of assistant executioner as a way of avoiding further punishment. Pompey agrees and meets **Abhorson**, the chief executioner. The Provost tells them to prepare for the executions of two criminals, **Barnardine** and Claudio. Claudio is brought out, but it appears that Barnardine cannot be roused because he is in a drunken stupor.

A letter arrives, which the Duke/friar hopes will be a reprieve for Claudio, but instead it is a confirmation of the sentence and a demand that Claudio's head be brought to Angelo after the execution. The Duke persuades the Provost to spare Claudio and send Barnardine's head instead.

When the time comes Barnardine refuses to be executed because he hasn't been absolved of his sins and he cannot be absolved yet (even by the Duke/friar) because he is still drunk. The Provost brings news of the death of another prisoner, **Ragozine**, who – remarkably – looks like Claudio. The Provost agrees to take Ragozine's head to Angelo, and tell him it is Claudio's. Meanwhile the Duke prepares to write to Angelo telling him that he is about to return to the city, so Angelo should get ready to give an account of his stewardship. When he sees Isabella, he tells her that despite the plan, Claudio has been executed, but that he will help her get her revenge on Angelo.

When Angelo receives the Duke's letter he is concerned that he will be called to account for his actions. Meanwhile, with the help of the Provost and Friar Peter, the Duke makes his final arrangements. Isabella and Mariana prepare to meet the Duke and confront Angelo.

## Act 5

As the Duke processes through the streets of Vienna with
Angelo and Escalus, Isabella comes forward and asks for
justice. She tells the Duke and the assembled courtiers and
crowd how Angelo made her give in to his desires in
return for her brother's life, but then betrayed her and
executed Claudio. All this was known by a 'Friar
Lodowick', who helped her. The Duke refuses to believe
her and has her arrested and taken away.

Mariana, her face muffled, now comes forward and
accuses Angelo, saying that he has slept with her and that
they were once engaged to be married. When she reveals
her face, Angelo admits that they were once engaged, but
that he broke it off because she was not of good character.
Mariana insists that Angelo has slept with her. Angelo asks
the Duke for the power to investigate this 'conspiracy'
against him. The Duke agrees and then leaves.

Shortly afterwards the Duke/friar returns and Isabella is
brought back. But when the Duke is questioned by
Escalus, he says that the Duke is unjust to leave judgement
to Angelo, the villain. Escalus angrily accuses him of
plotting with the two women, and Angelo calls on Lucio,
who has already accused Lodowick of being a bad
character, to give evidence against him. Lucio obliges with
a string of accusations, which are, of course, untrue.
Escalus orders Lodowick and the two women to be taken
away to prison. The Duke/friar refuses to go and in the
scuffle that ensues his hood is removed and he is revealed
as the Duke.

The Duke orders Lucio to be held to await his
judgement and then commands Angelo to go immediately
and marry Mariana. The Duke apologises to Isabella for
not being able to save Claudio's life. When Angelo and
Mariana return as man and wife, the Duke condemns
Angelo to death for the death of Claudio. First Mariana
and then Isabella – demonstrating her forgiveness of
Angelo – plead with the Duke for his life. The Duke

refuses and turns to accuse the Provost of disobedience. The Provost plays his part in this charade and says that in his remorse for Claudio's death he saved the life of Barnardine. The Duke demands to see Barnardine.

Barnardine is brought in with two others those faces are hidden. Barnardine is freed and Claudio is unmuffled. The Duke forgives this 'Claudio look-alike' for Claudio's crime and turns to Isabella to whom he proposes marriage. He pardons Angelo and turns on Lucio. He sentences him to be beaten and then hanged; any woman wronged by him is to come forward and accuse him. With a swift change of mind, the Duke then says that Lucio must marry any woman who comes forward.

The play ends with the Duke again proposing to Isabella, but again receiving no answer from her.

## The text of Shakespeare's plays

Shakespeare's work is generally treated with such immense respect that it may seem strange to admit that we cannot be certain exactly what he wrote. The reasons for this mystery lie in the circumstances of the theatre and publishing in the sixteenth and seventeenth centuries.

Shakespeare was a professional actor and shareholder in a company of actors, the Lord Chamberlain's Men, for whom he wrote his plays. Since copyright and performing rights did not exist before the eighteenth century there was the risk that, if a play was successful, other companies would perform it and reap the financial rewards. To avoid this, acting companies guarded the handwritten copy of a completed work. It was their most valuable resource and was kept by the prompter: each actor was given only his own lines and cues. None of these manuscripts survives to the present day. The lack of printed texts may seem strange but, like the work of other playwrights of his time, Shakespeare's plays existed essentially as oral, not written, texts. His concern was with what they looked and sounded like on stage.

However, there was money to be made from printed plays

and during his lifetime nearly half of Shakespeare's plays were printed in what are known as quartos: paperback editions of single plays. Some of these, called 'bad' quartos, are pirated editions based on the memories of actors and audience. Others are much more accurate and may have been authorised by Shakespeare or the shareholders in his company, perhaps to capitalize on a popular success which was about to go out of repertory or to forestall a pirate edition. None, however, seems to have been supervised by the playwright and all differ, often considerably, from the key text of Shakespeare's plays, the *First Folio*.

The *First Folio*, published in 1623, is a collected edition of all Shakespeare's plays (with the exception of *Pericles*). It was edited by John Hemming and Henry Condell, two shareholders in the Lord Chamberlain's Men, using 'good' quartos, prompt copies and other company papers to provide an accurate text as a fitting memorial to their partner. They did not start the editing process until after Shakespeare had died and apparently based their editorial decisions on what had happened in the theatre. We cannot be certain how far they represent what Shakespeare's ultimate intentions might have been. Even if Shakespeare had approved the text which went to the printer, it was the custom of writers to leave much of the detail of spelling and punctuation to the printer or to a scribe who made a fair copy from the playwright's rough drafts. The scribe and the printer thus introduced their own interpretations and inaccuracies into the text. The *First Folio* was reprinted three times in the seventeenth century and each edition corrected some inaccuracies and introduced new errors. A modern editor tries to provide a text which is easy to read and close to Shakespeare's presumed intentions. To do this the editor may modernize spelling and change punctuation, add stage directions and scene divisions, and make important decisions about which of several readings in quarto and folio editions is most acceptable. If you are able to compare this edition of the play with other editions, you are likely to find many minor variations between them as well as occasional major differences which could change your view of a character or situation.

## The text of *Measure for Measure*

*Measure for Measure* was probably first performed some time in 1604 and first published in the *First Folio* of 1623. The section of the *First Folio* in which it appears was taken from handwritten versions of the plays prepared by a professional scribe, Ralph Crane. Crane may have worked from three possible sources:

- Shakespeare's original manuscript (sometimes called 'foul papers')
- a copy of this made for use in the playhouse (called 'the Book')
- a later version of 'the Book' with changes made during or after performance.

Crane was known to change scripts he transcribed; for example, he altered and added punctuation, and clarified stage directions. Like all of us, he may also have made mistakes in copying. So may the printers who typeset the pages. In addition, some or all of the papers Crane was working from may have been damaged or difficult to read, nearly twenty years after the play was written.

So it is not surprising that *Measure for Measure* contains some sections where the meaning is not clear and others where it looks as if words or even whole lines have been missed out. The most important of these are commented on in the notes.

The names of some of the characters have meanings as well as being names, and were clearly carefully chosen. It has been pointed out by commentators that although the play is set in Vienna, the names are Italian (Vincentio), Latin (Escalus), or English (Mistress Overdone). Some of the characters listed do not, in fact, speak in the play (Friar Thomas, Francisca, Varrius).

ANGELO: this name is linked to *angel*, meaning both a heavenly being and a gold coin

LUCIO: the Italian word for 'light', in the sense of daylight. He is certainly a bright and breezy character and also 'light' in the punning sense of superficial. He is described as a 'fantasia' or 'fantastic', meaning a person full of wild imaginings and fantastic notions

PROVOST: a person who is responsible for catching and punishing criminals

ELBOW: the name suggests someone who is bony and bent – presumably an old man

FROTH: the name suggests that he is all air (or wind)

POMPEY: Pompey the Great was a famous Roman general. This one's full name is 'Pompey Bum' – which hardly needs any more comment!

ABHORSON: a very evocative name. It suggests both 'abhorrent' and 'son of a whore'

MISTRESS OVERDONE: another name with sexual overtones, that speaks for itself

# MEASURE FOR MEASURE

## *CHARACTERS*

VINCENTIO, the duke
ANGELO, the deputy
ESCALUS, an ancient lord
CLAUDIO, a young gentleman
LUCIO, a fantasia
Two other like gentlemen
PROVOST
FRIAR THOMAS or FRIAR PETER
[JUSTICE]
ELBOW, a simple constable
FROTH, a foolish gentleman
POMPEY, servant to Mistress Overdone
ABHORSON, an executioner
BARNARDINE, a dissolute prisoner
[VARRIUS, a gentleman, friend to the duke]
ISABELLA, sister to Claudio
MARIANA, betrothed to Angelo
JULIET, beloved of Claudio
FRANCISCA, a nun
MISTRESS OVERDONE, a bawd

Lords in attendance, officers, servants, citizens, and a boy

SCENE: *Vienna [and its environs]*

As the play begins we see Vincentio, the Duke of Vienna, hurriedly handing over his power. He tells his elderly courtier Escalus that he trusts his experience, and wishes him to be second-in-command to Lord Angelo in his absence. The Duke summons Angelo, whom he has appointed as his deputy.

> **3–4 Of government the properties...discourse**: if I were to explain to you what is involved in governing the state I should be putting on ('affecting') a style of speaking ('speech and discourse'). The Duke means, of course, that Escalus is an experienced government official who needs no advice from him
>
> **5 put to know**: forced to acknowledge
> **science**: knowledge
>
> **6 lists**: limits, extent
>
> **7–9 Then no more remains...work**: this is obscure. It may simply be a fault in the text, or the Duke may be speaking in a deliberately obscure way. It has been suggested that he is telling Escalus that all he needs to do is to combine the Duke's authority ('My strength') with the skill he already possesses ('your sufficiency') and balance the two ('let them work')
>
> **11–13 y'are as pregnant in...we remember**: you know as much about it as anyone I can recall
>
> **13 commission**: the Duke's written authority
>
> **14 warp**: deviate
>
> **16 What figure of us...bear?**: how well do you think he will perform as my representative?
>
> **17 soul**: intellectual or spiritual power
>
> **18 our absence to supply**: to act on my behalf while I am away
>
> **20–21 given his deputation...power**: granted to him as my deputy all the features ('organs') of my power
>
> **23 undergo**: experience, enjoy

---

*What questions are raised in your mind by:*
- *what the Duke is doing?*
- *the way in which he explains it to Escalus?*

# Act one

## Scene

*Within Vienna*

*Enter* DUKE, ESCALUS, LORDS *and* ATTENDANTS

| | |
|---|---|
| DUKE | Escalus. |
| ESCALUS | My lord. |
| DUKE | Of government the properties to unfold |
| | Would seem in me t'affect speech and discourse, |
| | Since I am put to know that your own science     5 |
| | Exceeds, in that, the lists of all advice |
| | My strength can give you. Then no more remains |
| | But that, to your sufficiency, as your worth is able, |
| | And let them work. The nature of our people, |
| | Our city's institutions, and the terms     10 |
| | For common justice, y'are as pregnant in |
| | As art and practice hath enriched any |
| | That we remember. There is our commission, |
| | From which we would not have you warp. Call |
| |    hither, |
| | I say, bid come before us Angelo.     15 |
| |                   [ *Exit an* ATTENDANT |
| | What figure of us, think you, he will bear? |
| | For you must know, we have with special soul |
| | Elected him our absence to supply; |
| | Lent him our terror, drest him with our love, |
| | And given his deputation all the organs     20 |
| | Of our own power. What think you of it? |
| ESCALUS | If any in Vienna be of worth |
| | To undergo such ample grace and honour, |
| | It is Lord Angelo. |

The Duke tells Angelo that he wishes him to act as his
deputy in his absence and advises him to use his great
personal and moral qualities for the good of all. Angelo
protests that he is not yet ready for such a great
responsibility. The Duke disagrees.

**27 character**: a mark or sign that is clear to anyone, but also with
the secondary meaning of a secret symbol for something
hidden.

**29 belongings**: circumstances connected with you (*OED*)

**30 proper**: exclusively yours. He means that Angelo does not
focus so exclusively on his own situation that he is unwilling
to apply himself and his virtues to others.

**35–36 Spirits are not...issues**: it is only noble matters that
affect our spirits with noble emotions. The references in this
part of the speech are to the minting of gold coins. Gold
coins, also called 'nobles' and 'angels', were checked or
assayed by means of a 'touchstone' and if found to be 'fine'
were marked or 'touched'

**36–40 nature never lends...and use**: like a moneylender,
nature expects people whom she makes good both to give her
thanks and to put their good qualities to good use – she
wants back the principal plus interest

**37 scruple**: the smallest possible measurement

**41 that can my part...advertise**: who knows perfectly well how
he should behave as my deputy

**42 Hold**: not entirely clear. It may be that at this point the Duke
gives Angelo his commission and tells him to take ('hold') it

**46 in question**: under consideration (*OED*). The Duke's
meaning is not completely clear. He may mean that Escalus
was considered first by him (and then passed over), or that
most people would have considered him first (but he did not)

**49 Before so noble...upon it**: a further reference to minting
coins. It is also a pun on his own name, since, as noted above,
an 'angel' was a gold coin

**51 leavened**: tempered – modified and improved by judgement,
as dough is by yeast

**53 of so quick condition**: in such a lively state

**54 prefers itself**: is only interested in itself

**54–55 leaves unquestioned...value**: does not attend to things
that are important

*Enter* ANGELO

DUKE                              Look where he comes.

ANGELO     Always obedient to your Grace's will,                25
           I come to know your pleasure.

DUKE                                        Angelo:
           There is a kind of character in thy life
           That to th'observer doth thy history
           Fully unfold. Thyself and thy belongings
           Are not thine own so proper as to waste             30
           Thyself upon thy virtues, they on thee.
           Heaven doth with us as we with torches do,
           Not light them for themselves; for if our virtues
           Did not go forth of us, 'twere all alike
           As if we had them not. Spirits are not finely
               touched                                          35
           But to fine issues; nor nature never lends
           The smallest scruple of her excellence
           But, like a thrifty goddess, she determines
           Herself the glory of a creditor,
           Both thanks and use. But I do bend my speech        40
           To one that can my part in him advertise:
           Hold therefore, Angelo.
           In our remove, be thou at full ourself.
           Mortality and mercy in Vienna
           Live in thy tongue, and heart. Old Escalus,         45
           Though first in question, is thy secondary.
           Take thy commission.

ANGELO                                Now, good my lord,
           Let there be some more test made of my metal,
           Before so noble and so great a figure
           Be stamped upon it.

DUKE                                No more evasion.            50
           We have with a leavened and prepared choice
           Proceeded to you; therefore take your honours.
           Our haste from hence is of so quick condition
           That it prefers itself, and leaves unquestioned

The Duke says he will leave secretly because he does not like the pomp and ceremony of public leave-takings. He goes. Angelo and Escalus agree to discuss their instructions and how to carry them out.

**55–57 We shall write...with us**: I will send you news of my activities, as time allows, and my business dictates

**59–60 To th'hopeful execution...of your commissions**: I leave you to carry out the duties I have given you and I have high hopes that you will succeed

**63–64 have to do...scruple**: have any doubts about carrying out your duties

**67 I'll privily away**: I will leave quietly, without a lot of fuss

**68 stage me to their eyes**: make a public show

**70 *Aves* vehement**: fierce, enthusiastic farewells

**71 of safe discretion**: sound judgement

**78 To look...my place**: to examine the basis of my official position

- *In this formal exchange between a ruler and his chosen deputy is anything of real substance said about the deputy's fitness for his post? Or is it all just words?*
- *How convincing do you find the Duke's explanation of his speedy and secret departure?*
- *What other reasons might he have for behaving in this way?*

|  | Matters of needful value. We shall write to you, | 55 |
|--|--|--|
|  | As time and our concernings shall importune, |  |
|  | How it goes with us; and do look to know |  |
|  | What doth befall you here. So, fare you well. |  |
|  | To th'hopeful execution do I leave you |  |
|  | Of your commissions. |  |

ANGELO                        Yet give leave, my lord,   60
That we may bring you something on the way.

DUKE     My haste may not admit it;
Nor need you, on mine honour, have to do
With any scruple. Your scope is as mine own,
So to enforce or qualify the laws            65
As to your soul seems good. Give me your hand;
I'll privily away. I love the people,
But do not like to stage me to their eyes:
Though it do well, I do not relish well
Their loud applause and *Aves* vehement;      70
Nor do I think the man of safe discretion
That does affect it. Once more, fare you well.

ANGELO     The heavens give safety to your purposes!

ESCALUS     Lead forth and bring you back in happiness!

DUKE     I thank you; fare you well.         [*Exit*   75

ESCALUS     I shall desire you, sir, to give me leave
To have free speech with you; and it concerns me
To look into the bottom of my place.
A power I have, but of what strength and nature
I am not yet instructed.                80

ANGELO     'Tis so with me. Let us withdraw together,
And we may soon our satisfaction have
Touching that point.

ESCALUS                    I'll wait upon your honour.
                                    [*Exeunt*

Lucio and two friends discuss the reasons for the Duke's departure, which they believe has been caused by reasons of state. They banter about personal morality – or the lack of it.

**1–2 come not to composition**: cannot reach an agreement

**2 King of Hungary**: this is probably a reference to events at the time the play was written and performed. Hungary was divided between the Holy Roman Empire (Roman Catholic) and the Turks (Moslem). The new King of Hungary, a Protestant, was supported by the Turks. The dukes would have been supporters of the Holy Roman Empire

**3 all the dukes...King**: they would unite to attack him

**7 sanctimonious**: pretending to be holy or pious

**9 scraped one out of the table**: erased a commandment from the tablet of stone

**11 razed**: erased

**13 their functions**: their jobs

**21 in metre**: in rhythmic verse

**22 proportion**: in rhythm

**24 Grace...grace**: Lucio is using the word in two senses:
  (a) the prayer said before a meal
  (b) the Christian doctrine that man can only be saved through God's generous mercy, by means of the sacrifice of Jesus Christ

**25 controversy**: there was a debate between two groups of Christian believers:
  (a) those who believed that whatever efforts a person made, there was no possibility of salvation without Grace. So it was enough to believe to be saved
  (b) those who said that it was also necessary to demonstrate belief and the acceptance of God's Grace by doing good works

**27 there went but...between us**: we are both made (cut out) of the same material

- *As you read this scene, think about the characters of Lucio and his friend.*
- *Why do you think Shakespeare begins the scene with talk of religious beliefs?*

# Scene  2

*The same. A public place*

*Enter* LUCIO *and two other* GENTLEMEN

| | |
|---|---|
| LUCIO | If the Duke, with the other dukes, come not to composition with the King of Hungary, why then all the dukes fall upon the King. |
| 1ST GENT. | Heaven grant us its peace, but not the King of Hungary's!                                                  5 |
| 2ND GENT. | Amen. |
| LUCIO | Thou conclud'st like the sanctimonious pirate, that went to sea with the Ten Commandments, but scraped one out of the table. |
| 2ND GENT. | 'Thou shalt not steal'?                                                  10 |
| LUCIO | Ay, that he razed. |
| 1ST GENT. | Why, 'twas a commandment to command the captain and all the rest from their functions : they put forth to steal. There's not a soldier of us all that, in the thanksgiving before meat, do relish   15 the petition well that prays for peace. |
| 2ND GENT. | I never heard any soldier dislike it. |
| LUCIO | I believe thee; for I think thou never wast where grace was said. |
| 2ND GENT. | No? A dozen times at least.                                                  20 |
| 1ST GENT. | What, in metre? |
| LUCIO | In any proportion, or in any language. |
| 1ST GENT. | I think, or in any religion. |
| LUCIO | Ay, why not? Grace is grace, despite of all controversy; as for example, thou thyself art a   25 wicked villain, despite of all grace. |
| 1ST GENT. | Well, there went but a pair of shears between us. |

Their banter becomes increasingly bawdy as they accuse each other of suffering from venereal disease. Mistress Overdone, the local bawd (brothel owner), arrives.

**29 lists**: the selvage, the plain edge of a piece of cloth, produced as part of the manufacturing process. It is cut off when the material is made up into clothing

**31 three-piled**: rich and thick material with a long nap; top quality

**31–32 had as lief**: would rather

**32 English kersey**: coarse woollen cloth

**32–33 piled...pilled**: a play on words – 'piled' means with a long nap like velvet; 'pilled' means bald, with a possible reference to one of the effects of syphilis

**33 French velvet**: expensive cloth from France, but also a reference to the 'French disease', syphilis
**feelingly**: sensibly, with understanding, but Lucio takes the word in the sense of physical feeling (a reference to the pain caused by disease)

**37 thy health**: drinking to your health

**38 forget to drink after thee**: not from the same cup, in order to avoid catching any disease from it

**40–41 tainted or free**: infected or not

**42 Mitigation**: satisfaction – of sexual desires

**47 dolours**: pains – with a pun on 'dollars'

**49 French crown**: a coin, but also a punning reference to the baldness caused by the 'French disease'

**51 error**: mistakes/disease

**56 sciatica**: a disease causing pain in the nerve which runs from the pelvis to the foot, believed at the time to be a symptom of syphilis

> • *What does the way in which these characters discuss sex and disease tell us about them and the society they live in?*

| | |
|---|---|
| LUCIO | I grant: as there may between the lists and the velvet. Thou art the list. |
| 1ST GENT. | And thou the velvet; thou art good velvet;   30<br>thou'rt a three-piled piece, I warrant thee: I had as lief be a list of an English kersey, as be piled, as thou art pilled, for a French velvet. Do I speak feelingly now? |
| LUCIO | I think thou dost: and indeed, with most   35<br>painful feeling of thy speech. I will, out of thine own confession, learn to begin thy health; but whilst I live, forget to drink after thee. |
| 1ST GENT. | I think I have done myself wrong, have I not? |
| 2ND GENT. | Yes, that thou hast; whether thou art tainted or   40<br>free. |

*Enter* MISTRESS OVERDONE

| | |
|---|---|
| LUCIO | Behold, behold, where Madam Mitigation comes!<br>I have purchased as many diseases under her roof as come to – |
| 2ND GENT. | To what, I pray?   45 |
| LUCIO | Judge. |
| 2ND GENT. | To three thousand dolours a year. |
| 1ST GENT. | Ay, and more. |
| LUCIO | A French crown more. |
| 1ST GENT. | Thou art always figuring diseases in me; but   50<br>thou art full of error; I am sound. |
| LUCIO | Nay, not, as one would say, healthy: but so sound as things that are hollow; thy bones are hollow; impiety has made a feast of thee. |
| 1ST GENT. | How now, which of your hips has the most   55<br>profound sciatica? |
| M. OVERDONE | Well, well! There's one yonder arrested and carried to prison, was worth five thousand of you all. |
| 2ND GENT. | Who's that, I prithee? |

Mistress Overdone tells Lucio and his friends that Claudio
has been arrested and will be executed for getting Juliet
pregnant when they are not married. The three young men
go off to find out more about this. Pompey, Mistress
Overdone's tapster (barman), arrives and tells her that
Claudio is being taken to the prison.

**70 since**: ago

**72–73 it draws something...purpose**: it is like the conversation
    we had on this subject. (We have not heard this, but
    presumably it is about Claudio and Juliet, or the new laws –
    or both)

**76 the sweat**: various possible meanings, but most likely a
    reference to the use of a sweating bath to induce sweating as a
    treatment for syphilis

**78 custom-shrunk**: she has far fewer customers; their number
    has shrunk

**84 Groping for trouts**: literally catching trout by tickling them,
    but the sexual innuendo is obvious
    **peculiar**: privately owned

**85 maid**: she is using the word to mean a young (unmarried)
    woman

**86 a woman with maid**: Pompey deliberately misunderstands
    her by taking 'maid' to mean virgin. He corrects 'maid' to
    'woman', i.e. not a virgin, and then uses the word to mean
    'young offspring' – 'maid' was another word for the young of
    certain fish

**89 houses**: brothels
    **suburbs**: the city centre was under the control of the city
    authorities; the built-up areas further out were not

- *Why do you think Shakespeare chooses a brothel as the*
  *setting in which Claudio's crime is revealed?*

M. OVERDONE   Marry sir, that's Claudio; Signior Claudio.          60

1ST GENT.   Claudio to prison? 'Tis not so.

M. OVERDONE   Nay, but I know 'tis so. I saw him arrested: saw
him carried away: and which is more, within these
three days his head to be chopped off.

LUCIO   But, after all this fooling, I would not have it so.   65
Art thou sure of this?

M. OVERDONE   I am too sure of it: and it is for getting Madam
Julietta with child.

LUCIO   Believe me, this may be: he promised to meet me
two hours since, and he was ever precise in          70
promise-keeping.

2ND GENT.   Besides, you know, it draws something near to the
speech we had to such a purpose.

1ST GENT.   But most of all agreeing with the proclamation.

LUCIO   Away! Let's go learn the truth of it.          75

                    [*Exeunt* LUCIO *and* GENTLEMAN

M. OVERDONE   Thus, what with the war, what with the sweat,
what with the gallows, and what with poverty, I am
custom-shrunk.

*Enter* POMPEY

How now? What's the news with you?

POMPEY   Yonder man is carried to prison.          80

M. OVERDONE   Well! What has he done?

POMPEY   A woman.

M. OVERDONE   But what's his offence?

POMPEY   Groping for trouts, in a peculiar river.

M. OVERDONE   What? Is there a maid with child by him?          85

POMPEY   No: but there's a woman with maid by him. You
have not heard of the proclamation, have you?

M. OVERDONE   What proclamation, man?

POMPEY   All houses in the suburbs of Vienna must be

Pompey tells Mistress Overdone about the new law ordering all brothels to be shut. Those in the city suburbs will be demolished. The two leave as the Provost takes Claudio to prison. They are accompanied by Juliet, Lucio, and his two friends. We learn that Claudio is being 'shown off' to the public on his way to prison on Angelo's orders.

**92 stand for seed**: be left to stand to ripen so that the seed can be used for sowing in the future

**93 burgher put in**: citizen made a bid

**94 houses of resort**: brothels

**97 commonwealth**: this has a number of meanings; two that might apply are: (**a**) public welfare; general good or advantage (*OED*); (**b**) the whole body of people constituting a nation or state, the body politic (*OED*). However, she may have in mind a third meaning: (**c**) a body or a number of persons united by some common interest (*OED*)

**99 counsellors**: lawyers acting on behalf of a client

**101 tapster**: barman

**103 worn your eyes...service**: there was often a picture of Cupid, god of love, outside brothels. Cupid was blind, so Pompey says that Overdone has almost gone blind working for prostitutes

**110 where I am committed**: to which I have been sent

**111 in evil disposition**: out of spite

**112 charge**: order

**113 demi-god**: half-god

**114 by weight**: heavily

**115–116 The words of heaven...just**: the meaning is not completely clear, but presumably he means that heaven's justice ('words') falls heavily on some but not on others, but despite this apparent unfairness it is just

**118 Liberty**: two meanings apply: (**a**) free indulgence in sensual pleasure; (**b**) personal freedom, e.g. from prison

**119 surfeit**: excessive self-indulgence
**fast**: abstaining from self-indulgence

- *What contrast is there between the first part of the scene and the way it develops after the entry of the Provost and Claudio?*

|  | plucked down. | 90 |
| --- | --- | --- |
| M. OVERDONE | And what shall become of those in the city? | |
| POMPEY | They shall stand for seed: they had gone down too, but that a wise burgher put in for them. | |
| M. OVERDONE | But shall all our houses of resort in the suburbs be pulled down? | 95 |
| POMPEY | To the ground, mistress. | |
| M. OVERDONE | Why, here's a change indeed in the common-wealth! What shall become of me? | |
| POMPEY | Come: fear not you: good counsellors lack no clients: though you change your place, you need not change your trade: I'll be your tapster still; courage, there will be pity taken on you; you that have worn your eyes almost out in the service, you will be considered. | 100 |
| M. OVERDONE | What's to do here, Thomas tapster? Let's withdraw! | 105 |
| POMPEY | Here comes Signior Claudio, led by the Provost to prison: and there's Madam Juliet.          [*Exeunt* | |

*Enter* PROVOST *and* OFFICERS *with* CLAUDIO *and*
JULIET; LUCIO *and the two* GENTLEMEN

| CLAUDIO | Fellow, why dost thou show me thus to th'world? Bear me to prison, where I am committed. | 110 |
| --- | --- | --- |
| PROVOST | I do it not in evil disposition, But from Lord Angelo by special charge. | |
| CLAUDIO | Thus can the demi-god, Authority, Make us pay down for our offence by weight. The words of heaven; on whom it will, it will; On whom it will not, so; yet still 'tis just. | 115 |
| LUCIO | Why, how now, Claudio? Whence comes this restraint? | |
| CLAUDIO | From too much liberty, my Lucio. Liberty, As surfeit, is the father of much fast; | |

Claudio explains to Lucio that he and Juliet had been
planning to marry, but had been prevented by problems
about the dowry (Juliet is an orphan). While this is being
sorted out, the two lovers have secretly been sleeping
together. Now Juliet is pregnant.

**120–121 So every scope...restraint**: so every liberty leads to
self-restraint if we overindulge it

**121–122 Our natures do...bane**: human nature makes us
behave like rats that gulp down things that are poisonous to
them. The reference is to poisoning rats with arsenic which
makes them thirsty then, when they drink water, they die

**123 A thirsty evil**: the thirst-making evil is liberty which makes
us desire what is bad for us

**135 upon a true contract**: in English common law a couple
could make two kinds of vow to each other:

   (a) *per verba de praesenti* (in the present tense) – this meant
that they became man and wife with immediate effect,
although the church did not accept its validity and could
cause difficulties

   (b) *per verba de futura* (in the future tense) – this meant
that they agreed to marry in the future provided certain
conditions were fulfilled, e.g. the payment of a dowry.

     Claudio is saying that he and Juliet have exchanged
the first type of vows and that they then consummated
their marriage, but kept it all secret, rather than making
it public and, presumably, going through a church
service

**140 propagation**: literally 'breeding' – the idea is that the chest
(coffer) will give birth to the money

**143 Till time had made them for us**: until time had brought
them to accept our relationship

**143–145 But it chances...Juliet**: but it happens that the results
of our secret lovemaking are showing only too clearly in
Juliet's appearance

**148 the fault...newness**: faulty glimpse – Angelo is new to the
job and only sees things faultily. An example of *hendiadys* –
see GLOSSARY on page 272.

**149 the body public**: the government of the city

|          |                                                                                                                 |     |
|----------|-----------------------------------------------------------------------------------------------------------------|-----|
|          | So every scope by the immoderate use                                                                            | 120 |
|          | Turns to restraint. Our natures do pursue,                                                                      |     |
|          | Like rats that ravin down their proper bane,                                                                    |     |
|          | A thirsty evil; and when we drink, we die.                                                                      |     |
| LUCIO    | If I could speak so wisely under an arrest, I would                                                             |     |
|          | send for certain of my creditors; and yet, to say                                                              | 125 |
|          | the truth, I had as lief have the foppery of freedom                                                            |     |
|          | as the morality of imprisonment. – What's thy                                                                   |     |
|          | offence, Claudio?                                                                                               |     |
| CLAUDIO  | What but to speak of would offend again.                                                                        |     |
| LUCIO    | What, is't murder?                                                                                              |     |
| CLAUDIO  | No.                                                                                                             |     |
| LUCIO    | Lechery?                                                                                                        |     |
| CLAUDIO  | Call it so.                                                                                                     | 130 |
| PROVOST  | Away, sir; you must go.                                                                                         |     |
| CLAUDIO  | One word, good friend: Lucio, a word with you.                                                                  |     |
| LUCIO    | A hundred – if they'll do you any good.                                                                         |     |
|          | Is lechery so looked after?                                                                                     |     |
| CLAUDIO  | Thus stands it with me : upon a true contract                                                                  | 135 |
|          | I got possession of Julietta's bed.                                                                             |     |
|          | You know the lady; she is fast my wife,                                                                         |     |
|          | Save that we do the denunciation lack                                                                           |     |
|          | Of outward order. This we came not to                                                                           |     |
|          | Only for propagation of a dower                                                                                 | 140 |
|          | Remaining in the coffer of her friends,                                                                         |     |
|          | From whom we thought it meet to hide our love                                                                   |     |
|          | Till time had made them for us. But it chances                                                                  |     |
|          | The stealth of our most mutual entertainment                                                                    |     |
|          | With character too gross is writ on Juliet.                                                                     | 145 |
| LUCIO    | With child, perhaps?                                                                                            |     |
| CLAUDIO  | Unhappily, even so.                                                                                             |     |
|          | And the new deputy now for the Duke –                                                                           |     |
|          | Whether it be the fault and glimpse of newness,                                                                 |     |
|          | Of whether that the body public be                                                                              |     |

Apparently Angelo has unearthed a number of old laws
which have not been applied for many years and he is
enforcing them strictly. Claudio and Lucio agree that he is
doing this to make himself a reputation. Claudio asks Lucio
to pass a message to his sister, who is about to enter a
nunnery, asking her to plead with Angelo for his life.

**153–155 Whether the tyranny...stagger in**: I cannot work out
whether the tyranny comes from the job itself, or the person
who is doing it

**156 Awakes me...penalties**: has brought back into use all the
old laws and punishments

**157 unscoured**: uncleaned, rusty

**158 nineteen zodiacs**: nineteen years (a complete astrological
cycle)

**161 for a name**: to make his reputation

**162 tickle**: insecure

**167 should the cloister enter**: is due to become a nun

**168 receive her approbation**: begin her period of probation, as
a novice

**171 the strict deputy**: i.e. Angelo
**bid herself assay him**: tell her to speak to him on my behalf

**172–173 in her youth...dialect**: her youthful appearance speaks
louder than words. The word 'prone' is used by Shakespeare
to mean 'eager', but here he may mean 'submissive' –
bearing in mind that Isabella is a modest young woman

**174 she hath prosperous art**: she is very skilful and successful

**175 play with reason and discourse**: take part in a debate

**177–179 as well for the encouragement...imposition**: not
entirely clear. He may mean 'as much because I think such
qualities should be encouraged, or else they will be
repressed.' An alternative reading is 'as much because I
think people like her should be encouraged, or else they will
be accused'. (Being Claudio's sister, Isabella might come
under some criticism because of her brother's behaviour)

**181 tick-tack**: an early version of backgammon, a gambling
board game involving both luck and skill, but there is an
obvious sexual innuendo

A horse whereon the governor doth ride, 150
Who, newly in the seat, that it may know
He can command, lets it straight feel the spur;
Whether the tyranny be in his place,
Or in his eminence that fills it up,
I stagger in – but this new governor 155
Awakes me all the enrolled penalties
Which have, like unscoured armour, hung by th'
   wall
So long, that nineteen zodiacs have gone round,
And none of them been worn; and for a name
Now puts the drowsy and neglected act 160
Freshly on me: 'tis surely for a name.

LUCIO   I warrant it is: and thy head stands so tickle on thy
shoulders, that a milkmaid, if she be in love, may
sigh it off. Send after the Duke, and appeal to him.

CLAUDIO   I have done so, but he's not to be found. 165
I prithee, Lucio, do me this kind service:
This day my sister should the cloister enter,
And there receive her approbation.
Acquaint her with the danger of my state:
Implore her, in my voice, that she makes friends 170
To the strict deputy: bid herself assay him.
I have great hope in that. For in her youth
There is a prone and speechless dialect
Such as move men; beside, she hath prosperous art
When she will play with reason and discourse, 175
And well she can persuade.

LUCIO   I pray she may: as well for the encouragement of
the like, which else would stand under grievous
imposition, as for the enjoying of thy life, who I
would be sorry should be thus foolishly lost at 180
a game of tick-tack. – I'll to her.

CLAUDIO   I thank you, good friend Lucio.

LUCIO   Within two hours.

CLAUDIO   Come, officer, away.                    [*Exeunt*

The Duke explains to Friar Thomas that he has pretended to leave the city because he is concerned at the way in which he has allowed the strict laws about morality to fall into disuse. As a result he is responsible for the decline in people's morals.

**2 dribbling**: either 'falling short of its target' or 'inconsiderable'; made up of petty or trifling items (*OED*)

**3 complete bosom**: well-protected heart

**4 To give me secret harbour**: to hide me

**8 removed**: solitary, like a hermit

**9–10 held in idle price...keeps**: had a low opinion of going around with the gang spending a lot of money and flaunting it

**12 stricture**: strictness

**15 strewed it in the common ear**: let it be known publicly

**20 headstrong jades**: badly trained and worthless horses

**28 Dead to infliction**: never having been enforced

> • *Look at the imagery the Duke uses to describe government and the behaviour of those governed. What does this tell us about him?*

# Scene  3

*A FRIAR'S cell*

*Enter* DUKE *and* FRIAR THOMAS

| | |
|---|---|
| DUKE | No. Holy father, throw away that thought; |
| | Believe not that the dribbling dart of love |
| | Can pierce a complete bosom. Why I desire thee |
| | To give me secret harbour hath a purpose |
| | More grave and wrinkled than the aims and ends   5 |
| | Of burning youth. |
| FRIAR | May your Grace speak of it? |
| DUKE | My holy sir, none better knows than you |
| | How I have ever loved the life removed, |
| | And held in idle price to haunt assemblies, |
| | Where youth, and cost, witless bravery keeps.   10 |
| | I have delivered to Lord Angelo – |
| | A man of stricture and firm abstinence – |
| | My absolute power and place here in Vienna, |
| | And he supposes me travelled to Poland; |
| | For so I have strewed it in the common ear,   15 |
| | And so it is received. Now, pious sir, |
| | You will demand of me, why I do this. |
| FRIAR | Gladly, my lord. |
| DUKE | We have strict statutes and most biting laws, |
| | The needful bits and curbs to headstrong jades,   20 |
| | Which for this fourteen years we have let slip; |
| | Even like an o'er-grown lion in a cave |
| | That goes not out to prey. Now, as fond fathers, |
| | Having bound up the threatening twigs of birch, |
| | Only to stick it in their children's sight   25 |
| | For terror, not to use, in time the rod |
| | Becomes more mocked than feared: so our decrees, |
| | Dead to infliction, to themselves are dead, |

Because it would seem unfair and too severe to reimpose the laws himself, the Duke has handed over power to Angelo. He knows that Angelo is firm and unemotional and will apply all the laws strictly. But power can change people and he is interested to see how Angelo will cope.

**30–31 quite athwart...decorum**: all decent and proper behaviour is abandoned

**35 Sith**: since

**36 gall**: harass

**37–39 for we bid this...punishment**: because we order this to be done when we have allowed wickedness to go unpunished

**41 in th'ambush of my name**: lying in wait behind the power of the Duke's authority

**42–43 And yet my nature...slander**: Angelo can do the dirty work and the Duke will keep his hands clean

**43 sway**: rule

**47–48 formally in person...friar**: behave so that I really seem to be a friar

**48 Moe**: more

**51 Stands at a guard with**: maintains his defence against
**Envy**: one of the Seven Deadly Sins. The Duke goes on to refer also to Lust and Gluttony, two more of the seven, the other four being Pride, Anger, Avarice, and Sloth

**52–53 his appetite...stone**: he prefers bread to a stone, i.e. he cares about food at all. This is presumably a reference to Christ's question in St Matthew's Gospel chapter 7 verse 9, 'What man is there of you, whom if his son ask for bread, will he give him a stone?'

**54–55 Hence we shall see...seemers be**: From this we shall be able to find out – if the power he now has changes his attitudes – what is the reality behind outward appearances

> • *In his final speech the Duke explains why he has not reimposed order and morality in the city. Consider how convincing you find his arguments.*

And Liberty plucks Justice by the nose,
The baby beats the nurse, and quite athwart          30
Goes all decorum.

FRIAR                              It rested in your Grace
To unloose this tied-up justice when you pleased;
And it in you more dreadful would have seemed
Than in Lord Angelo.

DUKE                              I do fear, too dreadful.
Sith 'twas my fault to give the people scope,          35
'Twould be my tyranny to strike and gall them
For what I bid them do : for we bid this be done,
When evil deeds have their permissive pass,
And not the punishment. Therefore indeed, my
    father,
I have on Angelo imposed the office;          40
Who may in th'ambush of my name strike home,
And yet my nature never in the fight
To do in slander. And to behold his sway,
I will, as 'twere a brother of your order,
Visit both prince and people. Therefore, I
    prithee,          45
Supply me with the habit, and instruct me
How I may formally in person bear
Like a true friar. Moe reasons for this action
At our more leisure shall I render you;
Only this one: Lord Angelo is precise;          50
Stands at a guard with Envy; scarce confesses
That his blood flows; or that his appetite
Is more to bread than stone. Hence shall we see
If power change purpose, what our seemers be.
                              [ *Exeunt*

Isabella is being instructed by one of the sisters about the
duties of a nun. Lucio arrives and asks to speak to Isabella.

**4–5 wishing a more strict...stood**: wishing that the sisters were
even more strictly disciplined

**5 the votarists of Saint Clare**: those who follow the rule
established by Saint Clare. This order of nuns, also known as
the Poor Clares, was founded in Assisi, Italy, in 1212

**9 yet unsworn**: have not yet taken the vows (see note on line
19 below)

**16 cheek-roses**: she has blushed out of modesty when she
discovers it is a man

**17 stead**: help

**19 novice**: a person who wishes to become a monk or nun and
who is undergoing a period of probation before taking their
final vows of poverty – to have no personal possessions at all,
chastity – to abstain forever from sexual intercourse, and
obedience – to the religious order and to the prior or prioress

> • *Another contrast: compare the Duke's desire to pretend
> to be a friar, with Isabella's attitude to her vocation to
> become a nun.*

# Scene  4

*A nunnery*

*Enter* ISABELLA *and* FRANCISCA *a Nun*

ISABELLA    And have you nuns no farther privileges?

NUNNERY    Are not these large enough?

ISABELLA    Yes, truly; I speak not as desiring more,
But rather wishing a more strict restraint
Upon the sisters stood, the votarists of Saint
    Clare.                                                5

LUCIO    [*Within*] Hoa! Peace be in this place!

ISABELLA                                                    Who's that
    which calls?

NUNNERY    It is a man's voice! Gentle Isabella,
Turn you the key, and know his business of him;
You may, I may not; you are yet unsworn:
When you have vowed, you must not speak with
    men                                              10
But in the presence of the prioress;
Then, if you speak, you must not show your face;
Or if you show your face, you must not speak.
He calls again: I pray you, answer him.    [*Retires*

ISABELLA    Peace and prosperity! Who is 't that calls?    15

*Enter* LUCIO

LUCIO    Hail virgin, if you be – as those cheek-roses
Proclaim you are no less – can you so stead me
As bring me to the sight of Isabella,
As novice of this place, and the fair sister
To her unhappy brother Claudio?                  20

ISABELLA    Why 'her unhappy brother'? Let me ask,
The rather for I now must make you know
I am that Isabella, and his sister.

Lucio tells Isabella what has happened to her brother. He explains to her that Juliet is pregnant and that in the Duke's absence his place has been taken by Angelo.

**30 make me not your story**: don't spin me a yarn

**32 lapwing**: a bird that is known as a trickster; it pretends to be injured, flying low to the ground and drawing predators further and further away from its nest

**34–35 enskied and sainted...renouncement**: made into a saint because you have given up everything to enter the nunnery

**39 Fewness and truth**: I will be brief and tell you the truth

**42 seedness**: sowing the seed

**bare fallow**: land that has been lying empty without crops

**43 teeming foison**: luxurious growth

**44 tilth**: cultivation

**husbandry**: literally cultivating the ground, but with a double meaning

**47–48 Adoptedly...apt affection**: they are only 'pretend cousins' – but it makes the point that they are close friends

**51–52 Bore many gentlemen...action**: it led a lot of people, including me, to think that there was going to be military action

**53 the very nerves of state**: what's really going on in the government

**54–55 His giving out...design**: what he said was very different from what he meant

> - *Think again about Lucio's behaviour – in particular the way in which he talks to Isabella and the words he uses to describe what has happened to Juliet and Claudio.*

| | |
|---|---|
| LUCIO | Gentle and fair. Your brother kindly greets you. |
| | Not to be weary with you, he's in prison. 25 |
| ISABELLA | Woe me! For what? |
| LUCIO | For that which, if myself might be his judge, |
| | He should receive his punishment in thanks: |
| | He hath got his friend with child. |
| ISABELLA | Sir, make me not your story. |
| LUCIO | 'Tis true. 30 |
| | I would not, though 'tis my familiar sin, |
| | With maids to seem the lapwing, and to jest |
| | Tongue far from heart, play with all virgins so. |
| | I hold you as a thing enskied and sainted |
| | By your renouncement, an immortal spirit, 35 |
| | And to be talked with in sincerity, |
| | As with a saint. |
| ISABELLA | You do blaspheme the good, in mocking me. |
| LUCIO | Do not believe it. Fewness and truth; 'tis thus: |
| | Your brother and his lover have embraced; 40 |
| | As those that feed grow full, as blossoming time |
| | That from the seedness the bare fallow brings |
| | To teeming foison, even so her plenteous womb |
| | Expresseth his full tilth and husbandry. |
| ISABELLA | Someone with child by him? My cousin Juliet? 45 |
| LUCIO | Is she your cousin? |
| ISABELLA | Adoptedly, as schoolmaids change their names |
| | By vain though apt affection. |
| LUCIO | She it is. |
| ISABELLA | O, let him marry her! |
| LUCIO | This is the point. |
| | The Duke is very strangely gone from hence; 50 |
| | Bore many gentlemen – myself being one – |
| | In hand, and hope of action : but we do learn, |
| | By those that know the very nerves of state, |
| | His giving out were of an infinite distance |
| | From his true-meant design. Upon his place, 55 |

Angelo has revived an old law which means that Claudio will be executed. Lucio begs Isabella to plead with Angelo to have mercy on her brother. She agrees to do so.

**58 snow-broth**: melted snow

**59 The wanton stings...sense**: the wicked urges of the flesh

**60 rebate**: make dull or blunt

**62–64  give fear to...lions**: to frighten habitual freedom and self-indulgence, which have for a long time skipped past the terrifying laws, as mice do past lions

**65 sense**: meaning

**70 pith**: sum total

**72 censured**: sentenced

**76 assay**: try

**80 sue**: plead

**82–83  All their petitions...owe them**: they can have whatever they ask for, as if it belonged to them anyway

> •  *Why do you think men might 'give like gods' 'when maidens sue'?*

And with full line of his authority,
Governs Lord Angelo; a man whose blood
Is very snow-broth; one who never feels
The wanton stings and motions of the sense;
But doth rebate and blunt his natural edge          60
With profits of the mind, study and fast.
He, to give fear to use and liberty,
Which have for long run by the hideous law
As mice by lions, hath picked out an act
Under whose heavy sense your brother's life          65
Falls into forfeit: he arrests him on it,
And follows close the rigour of the statute
To make him an example. All hope is gone,
Unless you have the grace by your fair prayer
To soften Angelo. And that's my pith of
   business                                                   70
'Twixt you and your poor brother.

ISABELLA                          Doth he so,
Seek his life?

LUCIO                 Has censured him already;
And, as I hear, the Provost hath a warrant
For's execution.

ISABELLA    Alas, what poor ability's in me          75
To do him good!

LUCIO               Assay the power you have.

ISABELLA    My power? Alas, I doubt.

LUCIO              Our doubts are traitors,
And makes us lose the good we oft might win
By fearing to attempt. Go to Lord Angelo,
And let him learn to know, when maidens sue,          80
Men give like gods; but when they weep and kneel,
All their petitions are as freely theirs
As they themselves would owe them.

ISABELLA    I'll see what I can do.

LUCIO               But speedily.

Isabella says that she will send a message to Claudio explaining the situation.

**86 Mother**: the Mother Superior, head of the nunnery
**89 certain word of my success**: definite news of how I get on

ISABELLA      I will about it straight;                                    85
              No longer staying but to give the Mother
              Notice of my affair. I humbly thank you.
              Commend me to my brother: soon at night
              I'll send him certain word of my success.

LUCIO         I take my leave of you.

ISABELLA                                      Good sir, adieu.             90

                                          [*Exeunt severally*

# ACTIVITIES

## Keeping track

### Scene 1

1 What is the Duke's opinion of Escalus?
2 What powers is he handing over to Angelo and Escalus?
3 How does Angelo respond?
4 What reasons does the Duke give for leaving so suddenly and secretly?

### Scene 2

5 What do Lucio and his friends think is the reason for the Duke's departure?
6 What are they talking about up to the point when Mistress Overdone enters, and what impression do you have of them?
7 What news does Mistress Overdone give them?
8 What does Pompey tell her when he arrives, and how does he react?
9 What does Claudio add to Lucio's understanding of what has happened?
10 What does Claudio ask Lucio to do for him?

### Scene 3

11 What further information are we given to explain the Duke's behaviour?
12 What is he planning to do now?

### Scene 4

13 Why does the nun ask Isabella to deal with their visitor?
14 How does Isabella react initially to Lucio's news?
15 What argument does Lucio use to persuade her that it is worthwhile trying to persuade Angelo to change his mind?

## Discussion

In the first act of any play we are concerned to a greater or lesser extent
with the **exposition**: the information that the writer has to set before us
so that we can understand and become involved in the characters and the
plot. In some plays this is a lengthy and complicated process; in others
the writer is able to throw us in at the deep end and gradually feed in the
necessary information.

### Scene 1

1  What should we assume has happened just before this scene?
2  What do we learn in the scene about the characters and 'pasts' of the
   Duke, Escalus, and Angelo?
3  What impression are we given of:
   • the state in which the Duke is leaving Vienna?
   • the importance of the position of the Duke?
   • the powers the Duke has?

### Scene 2

4  What impression do lines 1–106 give you of the state of Viennese
   society? (Remember that although Mistress Overdone and Pompey
   are 'low life' characters, Lucio and his friend are 'gentlemen'.)
5  In this scene we begin to see how Angelo has reacted to the situation
   he found when he took over the government of the city. What do you
   think of the severity with which he has acted?

### Scene 3

6  Here we get the first explanation of the Duke's reasons for acting in
   the way he has and the first indication of his intentions. How do you
   react to these:
   • are they believable?
   • are they to his credit?
7  What impression of Lucio do you gain from these two scenes?

### Scene 4

8  What does the whole scene tell us of the character of Isabella?

## Drama

### 1 Scenes 1 and 2

In groups of 3 to 5, you are teams of designers who have been asked
to design the set, costumes, props and lighting for these two scenes.
The director of the play is particularly concerned to emphasise:

- the Duke's description of Vienna's decadence (scene 3 lines
  19–31)
- the money imagery in scene 1 lines 27–50
- Claudio's description of the results of too much liberty
  (scene 2 lines 121–123).

2 Discuss the different ways the scenery, lighting and costume
  could contribute to the overall impact of these two scenes. Make
  notes of your ideas.

3 Write a detailed description of:
- the scenery (and any furniture and props) for each scene
- how each scene should be lit
- how the main characters should be costumed.

You could think about the different possibilities offered by some of
these approaches:

- making the setting very simple and doing everything with
  lighting
- setting the play in the present day
- experimenting with the idea that the whole thing is like a giant
  puppet play manipulated by the Duke.

### 4 Commissioned portraits

You have been commissioned to produce life-size portraits of the
Duke and Angelo.

- Using one member of the group for each statue, compose the
  images that best fit the two personalities.
- Use these lines as reference points:
  Duke: scene 3 lines 1–12, 35–40
  Angelo: scene 3 lines 50–53, scene 4 lines 55–61.
  Compose statues that reflect these lines.
- Try to find other lines in this act that will produce different
  images.
- Decide which images best reflect your impressions of these two
  characters so far.

### *Claudio*

**5 Scene 2 lines 135–145, 146–161**

In pairs, take it in turns to try these two speeches in different ways to express how Claudio is feeling. Is he:

- angry?
- sad?
- distraught?
- puzzled?
- resigned?

6 Now improvise the scene between Claudio and a tabloid press reporter looking for scandal. Before you start, think about:

- What questions would be asked?
- What answers might Claudio give?
- Would the reporter try to 'buy' Claudio's story? How? How would Claudio respond?

Finish by writing the headline and the first paragraph of the story.

## Close study

### Scene 1

1 Almost the whole of this scene (until the departure of the Duke) is a formal exchange between the Duke and his two deputies. The speech is stylised and the sentences complicated and lengthy. Look carefully at lines 3–14. Practise reading the speech aloud. Try performing it in two different ways:

- with gravity, meaning every word you say
- as a boring formality that has to be got through as quickly as possible – said by someone who is in a hurry to leave.

Which is better and why?

2 Look at the many references in lines 27–50 to gold and money and the ways in which the Duke uses them to talk about personal and moral qualities. What does this tell us about him, the society which he rules and the way in which things may develop in the play?

3 Look at these speeches by the Duke:

- '*No more evasion...*' (lines 50–60)
- '*My haste may not admit it...*' (lines 62–72)

(a) How do the language and tempo of these compare with his earlier speeches? Does this tell us anything about him and his intentions?

(b) Why is the Duke leaving so hurriedly and secretly and how clearly do you think he has worked out what he is going to do?

4 Angelo and Escalus '*withdraw together*' to discuss the situation in which the Duke has left them. How do you think their conversation might develop? Write their dialogue as a continuation of Act 1 scene 1.

### Scene 2

5 Lucio (whose name means 'light') is described in some versions of the list of characters as a 'fantastia', which is defined by the *Oxford English Dictionary* as a person 'Having a lively imagination; imaginative; fanciful, impulsive, capricious'. His companions are described as 'Two other like gentlemen'. What is there in the early part of this scene to justify those descriptions?

6 What attitude towards moral rules and real life actions is suggested by lines 7–16?

7 How many references to Christian beliefs and practices can you find in lines 7–26?

8 In lines 27–34 they are talking about morality and sexual disease, but where are their images taken from? Is this appropriate? If so, why?

9 The stage direction '*Enter MISTRESS OVERDONE*' comes fifteen lines before the character mentioned actually speaks. Why is this, and how should this section be staged?

10 Mistress Overdone adds two different but equally important kinds of information to our understanding of what has happened. The most obvious (lines 57–68) concerns Claudio and Juliet. But equally important is what she says while alone on stage in lines 76–78. What can we deduce from this short speech about the state of Viennese society?

11 Lines 89–96 tell us of a major action taken by Angelo:
   • what is it?
   • why do you think Shakespeare chooses to reveal it to us in this way rather than having Angelo proclaiming it to his subordinates in a more formal setting?

12 Claudio's speech '*From too much liberty...*' (lines 118–123) is a comment not just on his own behaviour but also on that of the society in which such behaviour flourishes. Read it carefully. Do you agree with his reasoning?

13 Make sure that you understand clearly the legal relationship between Claudio and Juliet described in lines 135–145. Assuming that a law banning sexual intercourse outside marriage is just, is the sentence on Claudio also just? What does the sentence tell us about Angelo's character and attitudes? What

does Claudio's next speech (lines 146–161) add to your
understanding of Angelo?

## Scene 3

14 Read lines 1–3 and think carefully about their implications:
   • What do you suppose that Friar Thomas has just said to the Duke?
   • What might have led him to say it?
15 The Duke's third speech (lines 19–31) describes what has been
   happening for the last fourteen years under his rule.
   • What has happened?
   • Why did he let it happen?
   • What does it suggest about his ability and character as a ruler?
16 When the Friar asks him – quite reasonably – why he did not do
   something about the situation, the Duke tries to justify himself (lines
   35–43)
   • What is the explanation?
   • If it is true, in what ways does it add to or change your assessment
     of his character?
17 The next sentence tells us of his intentions (lines 43–45). Given your
   current assessment of the Duke, what do you think of this plan?

## Scene 4

18 What do we learn about the characteristics of the life of a nun and
   Isabella's attitude towards them in the opening lines of this scene?
19 Into this scene of purity and serenity comes Lucio – about whom we
   have already learned a great deal in scene 2. How would you describe
   the manner in which he addresses Isabella in his first three speeches
   (lines 16–20, 24–25, 27–29)? How does Isabella react?
20 In his next speech Lucio talks briefly about himself and his attitude
   when speaking to Isabella (lines 30–37). She believes he is ridiculing
   her: 'You do blaspheme the good, in mocking me.'
   • Is she right?
   • If so, how should the words be spoken?
   • If not, how should the speech be delivered?
21 Consider his next speech (lines 39–44) in the same way.
22 Read Lucio's description of Angelo in lines 57–61. It contrasts the
   life of the sensual man (like himself) with that of Angelo, and implies
   that the sensual life is the norm. Compare this with Claudio's
   reflections on the same topic in scene 2 lines 118–123. How would
   you sum up the contrasting attitudes towards human nature
   presented by the two men?

## Imagery

An important part of the impact of poetic drama is the way key images build up in our imaginations as we watch and listen, almost without our being aware of it. There are a number of themes in the imagery of *Measure for Measure* and it is valuable to start to 'tune in' to these as early as possible in your reading of the play, and begin to list what you consider to be powerful images. In Act 1 you could think about:

- money, coinage, precious metals (scenes 1, 2)
- religious beliefs (scenes 2, 4)
- tailoring, fashion, clothing (scene 2)
- physical control and punishment (scene 3)
- nature, animals and birds, growth, fertility (scene 4).

## Key scene

After each act you will be asked to think about one scene or part of a scene that is particularly important in our understanding of the play. The questions and comments in KEY SCENE assume that you have at least worked through the CLOSE STUDY questions relating to that scene. You will find it useful to make notes on your thoughts, ideas and questions, as you study each key scene.

### Scene 2

Although scenes 1 and 3 give us an account of the Duke's character and intentions, scene 2 contains the seeds of much of the action of the rest of the play, despite the fact that two of the central characters involved – Angelo and Isabella – are absent.

As you read the scene again, think carefully about the following points.

1 The nature of Viennese society, especially concerning:
   - luxury
   - sex
   - war
   - moral values
   - the law.

2 Angelo's attitude towards:
   - getting (apparently unlimited) power
   - the society he is ruling
   - the idea of justice
   - the idea of mercy.

3 The views of human nature, law and morality contained in this scene.

# Writing

1  Write two brief and contrasting descriptions of the Vienna that is presented in this act:
   - for inclusion in a racy tourist guide aiming to attract people like Lucio
   - by a visitor from another country which is strictly puritanical.
2  You are going to direct a production of the play. In readiness for the first meeting with the actors you have decided to prepare brief descriptions of two of the characters who appear in the first scene. Your actors are young and inexperienced, so you want to make these characters seem as 'modern' as possible by using contemporary parallels from the media:
   - television and film actors
   - characters from recent films and television programmes
   - media personalities
   - other famous people.
   You could also describe how the characters might dress today and what their lifestyles might be.

   Using these parallels, plus ideas of your own, write descriptions of the Duke and Lucio.

The scene opens in mid-discussion. Angelo argues that the law must be carried out strictly so that it is not held in contempt. Escalus argues for a more merciful approach, because judges are as human as the guilty. Angelo disagrees, saying it is not a personal matter: if someone is caught, the judge and jury must punish.

2 **fear**: frighten
3 **keep one shape**: remain unchanged
  **till custom make it**: until it becomes so familiar it is made
4 **terror**: cause of terror
5 **keen**: careful, sharp, precise
6 **fall**: chop down, fell
9 **strait in virtue**: strictly moral
10 **affections**: desires
11 **Had time...wishing**: if time and place had given you the opportunity, or a place presented itself in line with your desires
12 **resolute acting**: determined carrying out
  **blood**: passion
13 **attained th'effect**: achieved the aim
15 **censure**: condemn
19 **passing on**: passing sentence on
21 **What's open made to justice**: whatever is able to be tried by law
23 **pregnant**: full of significance

> • *What do we learn about Escalus' relationship with Angelo and what he wants say to him, from the long sentence in lines 8–16?*

# Act two

## Scene 1

*A courtroom*

*Enter* ANGELO, ESCALUS *and* SERVANTS, *a* JUSTICE

ANGELO We must not make a scarecrow of the law,
Setting it up to fear the birds of prey,
And let it keep one shape till custom make it
Their perch, and not their terror.

ESCALUS                                    Ay, but yet
Let us be keen, and rather cut a little,                        5
Than fall, and bruise to death. Alas, this gentleman,
Whom I would save, had a most noble father.
Let but your honour know –
Whom I believe to be most strait in virtue –
That in the working of your own affections,          10
Had time cohered with place, or place with wishing,
Or that the resolute acting of your blood
Could have attained th'effect of your own purpose,
Whether you had not sometime in your life
Erred in this point, which now you censure him,  15
And pulled the law upon you.

ANGELO 'Tis one thing to be tempted, Escalus,
Another thing to fall. I not deny
The jury passing on the prisoner's life
May in the sworn twelve have a thief, or two,       20
Guiltier than him they try. What's open made to
     justice,
That justice seizes. What knows the laws
That thieves do pass on thieves? 'Tis very pregnant,
The jewel that we find, we stoop and take 't,
Because we see it; but what we do not see,            25

Angelo argues that if a judge is found to be guilty, he must take the prescribed punishment. Angelo tells the Provost to execute Claudio, after confession, by 9.00 the next morning. Escalus asks for heaven's forgiveness for him. Elbow, the constable, enters with two arrested criminals, Pompey and Froth.

**27 extenuate**: play down
**30 judgement**: sentence
    **pattern out my death**: determine when I die
**31 nothing come in partial**: let no arguments be put on my side
**36 that's the utmost of his pilgrimage**: that is the end of his life
**39 run from brakes...none**: brakes = 'breaks' – often escape from guilty situations and never pay the penalty – people who are able to break the ice several times but still avoid falling into the water
**41–42 good people in a commonweal**: law-abiding citizens
**42–43 use their abuses in common houses**: regularly fornicate in brothels
**48–49 lean upon justice**: put my faith in the law
**50 benefactors**: he means 'malefactors'

> - *We already know that Claudio is sentenced to death. What is the effect of the repetition of this order in lines 34–35? Note how this fact continues to be referred to right through until Act 4. Why?*
> - *What is the significance of Elbow's confusion of 'benefactor' and 'malefactor'? He is the constable, entrusted with enforcing the law. How do you think his problems with important words (and in this case his confusion of two words with exactly opposite meanings) contribute to the themes of the play?*

We tread upon, and never think of it.
You may not so extenuate his offence
For I have had such faults; but rather tell me,
When I that censure him do so offend,
Let mine own judgement pattern out my death,    30
And nothing come in partial. Sir, he must die.

*Enter* PROVOST

ESCALUS    Be it as your wisdom will.

ANGELO                              Where is the Provost?

PROVOST    Here, if it like your honour.

ANGELO                              See that Claudio
Be executed by nine tomorrow morning;
Bring him his confessor, let him be prepared,    35
For that's the utmost of his pilgrimage.
                              [*Exit* PROVOST

ESCALUS    Well, heaven forgive him; and forgive us all.
Some rise by sin, and some by virtue fall.
Some run from brakes of ice and answer none,
And some condemned for a fault alone.    40

*Enter* ELBOW *and* OFFICERS *with* FROTH *and* POMPEY

ELBOW    Come, bring them away. If these be good people
in a commonweal, that do nothing but use their
abuses in common houses, I know no law. Bring
them away.

ANGELO    How now sir, what's your name? And what's    45
the matter?

ELBOW    If it please your honour, I am the poor Duke's
constable, and my name is Elbow. I do lean upon
justice, sir, and do bring in here before your good
honour two notorious benefactors.    50

ANGELO    Benefactors? Well, what benefactors are they? Are
they not malefactors?

ELBOW    If it please your honour, I know not well what they

Despite his many errors of expression, we can tell that Elbow
thinks Froth has done something criminal to Elbow's wife.
Pompey, who works in the brothel, is implicated. Escalus
tries to establish some sense.

**54 precise**: certain, definite

**55 void of all profanation**: free of all corruption. He means the
opposite; 'profanation' may be another of his mistakes – for
'profession'

**59 quality**: status, job

**61 out at elbow**: without the brains to answer

**63 tapster**: barman
**parcel bawd**: part-time pimp

**64 bad woman**: madam – a woman who runs a brothel

**66 professes a hot house**: operates under cover of being a bath
house

**69 detest**: he means either protest or attest

**75–76 it is a pity of her life**: it will be the end of everything if
she's wrong
**naughty**: corrupt, wicked

**79 cardinally given**: he means 'carnally'; selling her body

**81 means**: pimp, assistant

**82–83 she...him**: Elbow's wife...pimp (Pompey)

**85–86 varlets...honourable man**: he means the opposite
**varlets**: criminals

> • *Elbow misuses more words. Which words has
> Shakspeare chosen and why? Despite his mistakes
> what is Elbow sure of?*

|          |                                                                                                       |    |
| -------- | ----------------------------------------------------------------------------------------------------- | -- |
|          | are. But precise villains they are, that I am sure of, and void of all profanation in the world, that good Christians ought to have. | 55 |
| ESCALUS  | [*To* ANGELO] This comes off well: here's a wise officer. |    |
| ANGELO   | Go to. What quality are they of? Elbow is your name? Why dost thou not speak, Elbow? | 60 |
| POMPEY   | He cannot, sir: he's out at elbow. |    |
| ANGELO   | What are you, sir? |    |
| ELBOW    | He, sir? A tapster, sir; parcel bawd; one that serves a bad woman; whose house, sir, was, as they say, plucked down in the suburbs; and now she professes a hot-house; which I think is a very ill house too. | 65 |
| ESCALUS  | How know you that? |    |
| ELBOW    | My wife, sir, whom I detest before heaven and your honour – | 70 |
| ESCALUS  | How? Thy wife? |    |
| ELBOW    | Ay, sir: whom I thank heaven is an honest woman – |    |
| ESCALUS  | Dost thou detest her therefore? |    |
| ELBOW    | I say, sir, I will detest myself also, as well as she, that this house, if it be not a bawd's house, it is a pity of her life, for it is a naughty house. | 75 |
| ESCALUS  | How dost thou know that, constable? |    |
| ELBOW    | Marry, sir, by my wife, who, if she had been a woman cardinally given, might have been accused in fornication, adultery, and all uncleanliness there. | 80 |
| ESCALUS  | By the woman's means? |    |
| ELBOW    | Ay, sir, by Mistress Overdone's means; but as she spit in his face, so she defied him. |    |
| POMPEY   | Sir, if it please your honour, that is not so. |    |
| ELBOW    | Prove it before these varlets here, thou honourable man, prove it. | 85 |

Pompey tries to obscure the investigation with a series of distracting speeches until Escalus starts to get impatient. Pompey says he's coming to the point.

**89 stewed prunes**: common brothel food, possibly because of a belief that as a laxative they might be used to procure an abortion

**90–97 sir...right**: Pompey's apparently meaningless and time–wasting talk is full of sexual innuendo, e.g. 'stood', 'dish'

**91 distant time**: instant

**96 not a pin**: it's of no importance

**103–104 not give you three-pence again**: not give you any change; he's stressing that Froth paid over the price

**110–111 such a one...wot of**: certain people were beyond treatment for venereal disease

**112 good**: healing

**115 fool**: Escalus' comment implies both that Pompey is stupid and that he is talking like a clown (fool), i.e. wittily

**117 Come me to**: tell me

**119 nor I mean it not**: he is being ironic; he means the opposite

> • *Angelo does not speak and has not spoken since line 62. Why not? How do you imagine him behaving and why?*

ESCALUS   [*To* ANGELO] Do you hear how he misplaces?

POMPEY   Sir, she came in great with child; and longing,
saving your honours' reverence, for stewed prunes;
sir, we had but two in the house, which at that   90
very distant time stood as it were in a fruit-dish, a
dish of some three pence, your honours have seen
such dishes, they are not china dishes, but very
good dishes, –

ESCALUS   Go to, go to: no matter for the dish, sir.   95

POMPEY   No indeed, sir, not a pin : you are therein in the
right : but at the point. As I say, this Mistress
Elbow being, as I say, with child, and being great-
bellied, and longing, as I said, for prunes; and
having but two in the dish, as I said, Master   100
Froth here, this very man, having eaten the rest, as
I said, and, as I say, paying for them very honestly;
for, as you know, Master Froth, I could not give
you three pence again –

FROTH   No, indeed.   105

POMPEY   Very well: you being then, if you be remembered,
cracking the stones of the foresaid prunes –

FROTH   Ay, so I did indeed.

POMPEY   Why, very well: I telling you then, if you be
remembered, that such a one and such a one   110
were past cure of the thing you wot of, unless they
kept very good diet, as I told you –

FROTH   All this is true.

POMPEY   Why, very well then –

ESCALUS   Come, you are a tedious fool. To the purpose:   115
what was done to Elbow's wife that he hath cause
to complain of? Come me to what was done to her.

POMPEY   Sir, your honour cannot come to that yet.

ESCALUS   No, sir, nor I mean it not.

POMPEY   Sir, but you shall come to it, by your honour's   120

Pompey insists on Froth's honesty and innocence. Angelo can stand no more and leaves, hoping that Escalus will have them whipped. Pompey continues to insist on Froth's good nature.

**122 fourscore pound a year**: a considerable amount of money

**123 Hallowmass**: All Saints' Day (November 1)

**125 All-hallond Eve**: Eve of All Saints' Day

**127 lower**: best

**128 Bunch of Grapes**: a tavern

**130 open**: public

**132 I hope here be truths**: he's playing the barrister: 'we're on to something here'

**133 This will last...Russia**: storytelling to pass the time on a long winter's night

**147 mark**: notice

- *Angelo finally speaks, only to exit immediately. What do this and his hope that there will be good cause to whip them all tell us about him?*
- *How does Pompey 'take over' the investigation?*

leave. And I beseech you, look into Master Froth
here, sir; a man of fourscore pound a year; whose
father died at Hallowmas – was't not at Hallowmas,
Master Froth?

FROTH      All-hallond Eve.                              125

POMPEY      Why, very well: I hope here be truths. He, sir,
sitting, as I say, in a lower chair, sir – 'twas in the
Bunch of Grapes, where indeed you have a delight
to sit, have you not?

FROTH      I have so, because it is an open room, and good 130
for winter.

POMPEY      Why, very well then: I hope here be truths.

ANGELO      This will last out a night in Russia
When nights are longest there. I'll take my leave,
And leave you to the hearing of the cause;      135
Hoping you'll find good cause to whip them all.

ESCALUS      I think no less: good morrow to your lordship.
                                      [*Exit* ANGELO
Now, sir, come on. What was done to Elbow's wife,
once more?

POMPEY      Once, sir? There was nothing done to her once. 140

ELBOW      I beseech you, sir, ask him what this man did to
my wife.

POMPEY      I beseech your honour, ask me.

ESCALUS      Well, sir, what did this gentleman to her?

POMPEY      I beseech you, sir, look in this gentleman's face. 145
Good Master Froth, look upon his honour; 'Tis for
a good purpose. – Doth your honour mark his face?

ESCALUS      Ay, sir, very well.

POMPEY      Nay, I beseech you, mark it well.

ESCALUS      Well, I do so.                                   150

POMPEY      Doth your honour see any harm in his face?

ESCALUS      Why, no.

One of Elbow's mistakes – 'respected' instead of 'suspected' – enables Pompey to suggest that it is Elbow's wife who is the suspicious character. Elbow erupts, and Escalus decides that facts will not be established by Elbow's approach and takes over himself.

**153 be supposed upon a book**: swear on the Bible
**159 and it like you**: if it pleases you
    **respected**: he means suspected (of being a brothel)
**162** Pompey turns '*respected*' back on Elbow
**169 Justice or Iniquity**: stock characters from traditional morality plays – Escalus is asking whether Elbow (Justice) or Pompey (Iniquity) is the cleverer, implying that because of Elbow's errors, it is Pompey
**171 caitiff**: rogue
**172 Hannibal**: he means 'cannibal'
**176 have mine action of battery**: place a charge of physical assault on you (he means slander)
**177–178 If he...too**: Escalus replies ironically, pointing out the misuse by doing the same himself

> • *What are the implications of Escalus' question: 'Which is the wiser here?'? Pompey certainly seems to be 'cleverer'. How does this show? What are Elbow's errors?*

POMPEY   I'll be supposed upon a book, his face is the worst
         thing about him. – Good, then: if his face be the
         worst thing about him, how could Master Froth 155
         do the constable's wife any harm? I would know
         that of your honour.

ESCALUS  He's in the right, constable; what say you to it?

ELBOW    First, and it like you, the house is a respected
         house; next, this is a respected fellow; and his   160
         mistress is a respected woman.

POMPEY   By this hand, sir, his wife is a more respected person
         than any of us all.

ELBOW    Varlet, thou liest! Thou liest, wicked varlet!
         The time is yet to come that she was ever          165
         respected with man, woman, or child.

POMPEY   Sir, she was respected with him, before he married
         with her.

ESCALUS  Which is the wiser here, Justice or Iniquity? Is this
         true?                                              170

ELBOW    O thou caitiff! O thou varlet! O thou wicked
         Hannibal! I respected with her, before I was
         married to her? If ever I was respected with her, or
         she with me, let not your worship think me the
         poor Duke's officer. Prove this, thou wicked        175
         Hannibal, or I'll have mine action of battery on thee.

ESCALUS  If he took you a box o' th' ear, you might have your
         action of slander too.

ELBOW    Marry, I thank your good worship for it. What
         is't your worship's pleasure I shall do with this   180
         wicked caitiff?

ESCALUS  Truly, officer, because he hath some offences in him
         that thou wouldst discover if thou couldst, let him
         continue in his courses till thou know'st what they
         are.                                               185

ELBOW    Marry, I thank your worship for it. – Thou seest,

Escalus lets Froth off with a warning about not keeping the company of tapsters, i.e. Pompey. Escalus turns his attention to Pompey to get him to admit his real trade, pimping.

**188 continue**: Escalus has decided that Froth should be left to continue in his supposed crimes until it becomes clear what they are, Elbow having failed to define them. Ironically Elbow mistakes the word 'continue' itself and assumes it is some kind of punishment

**199 Overdone by the last**: sexually worn out by the last of the nine husbands

**202 draw**: two meanings apply:
(a) lead you on
(b) as in hanging, drawing and quartering

**207 drawn in**: see line 202, note (a)

**213 Bum**: two meanings apply:
(a) petty official, bailiff
(b) backside (Escalus takes up this sense)

**217 colour**: cover

> * *What do you make of Escalus' judgment of Froth – bearing in mind that Angelo wanted him whipped?*

|         | thou wicked varlet now, what's come upon thee. Thou art to continue now, thou varlet, thou art to continue. |     |
|---------|---------|-----|
| ESCALUS | Where were you born, friend? | 190 |
| FROTH | Here in Vienna, sir. | |
| ESCALUS | Are you a fourscore pounds a year? | |
| FROTH | Yes, and 't please you, sir. | |
| ESCALUS | So. [*To* POMPEY] What trade are you of, sir? | |
| POMPEY | A tapster, a poor widow's tapster. | 195 |
| ESCALUS | Your mistress' name? | |
| POMPEY | Mistress Overdone. | |
| ESCALUS | Hath she had any more than one husband? | |
| POMPEY | Nine, sir; Overdone by the last. | |
| ESCALUS | Nine! – Come hither to me, Master Froth. Master Froth, I would not have you acquainted with tapsters; they will draw you, Master Froth, and you will hang them. Get you gone, and let me hear no more of you. | 200 |
| FROTH | I thank you worship. For mine own part, I never come into any room in a tap-house, but I am drawn in. | 205 |
| ESCALUS | Well: no more of it, Master Froth: farewell. | |
| | *[Exit* FROTH | |
| | Come you hither to me, Master tapster. What's your name, Master tapster? | 210 |
| POMPEY | Pompey. | |
| ESCALUS | What else? | |
| POMPEY | Bum, sir. | |
| ESCALUS | Troth, and your bum is the greatest thing about you; so that, in the beastliest sense, you are Pompey the Great. Pompey, you are partly a bawd, Pompey, howsoever you colour it in being a tapster, are you not? Come, tell me true, it shall be the | 215 |

Pompey says there is no chance of killing the brothel trade unless everyone is unsexed. Escalus informs him of the new laws and the accompanying death penalty. He warns Pompey that if he appears before him again, he will be whipped at the very least. Pompey goes, still in flippant and defiant mood.

**227 geld and splay**: castrate and neuter (spay)
**230 to't**: have sex
**231 take order for**: deal with
 **drabs**: prostitutes
**232 knaves**: male clients
**233 pretty**: new
**234 but heading and hanging**: as simple as beheading and hanging
**236–237 give out a commission for more heads**: pass a law to encourage more breeding
**239 after three pence a bay**: for less than threepence for a small part (very cheaply)
**241 requital of**: answer to, return for
**245–246 I shall beat...to you**: Escalus is referring to the way in which Julius Caesar beat Pompey the Great in battle
**246 shrewd**: severe
 **plain dealing**: to tell you the truth
**250–251 as the flesh...determine**: as desire and opportunity will help me decide
**252 carman**: carter
 **jade**: old nag, broken-down horse: also, prostitute

> • *In what ways is Escalus' treatment of Pompey different from his treatment of Froth? What can we tell of Pompey's attitude from his aside, lines 250–253?*

better for you.

POMPEY    Truly, sir, I am a poor fellow that would live.    220

ESCALUS    How would you live, Pompey? By being a bawd?
What do you think of the trade, Pompey? Is it a
lawful trade?

POMPEY    If the law would allow it, sir.

ESCALUS    But the law will not allow it, Pompey; nor it    225
shall not be allowed in Vienna.

POMPEY    Does your worship mean to geld and splay all the
youth of the city?

ESCALUS    No, Pompey.

POMPEY    Truly sir, in my poor opinion, they will to't then.230
If your worship will take order for the drabs and the
knaves, you need not to fear the bawds.

ESCALUS    There is pretty orders beginning, I can tell you. It is
but heading and hanging.

POMPEY    If you head and hang all that offend that way    235
but for ten years together, you'll be glad to give out
a commission for more heads: if this law hold in
Vienna ten year, I'll rent the fairest house in it
after three pence a bay. If you live to see this come
to pass, say Pompey told you so.    240

ESCALUS    Thank you, good Pompey; and, in requital of your
prophecy, hark you: I advise you, let me not find
you before me again upon any complaint
whatsoever; no, not for dwelling where you do. If I
do, Pompey, I shall beat you to your tent, and    245
prove a shrewd Caesar to you: in plain dealing,
Pompey, I shall have you whipped. So for this time,
Pompey, fare you well.

POMPEY    I thank your worship for your good counsel;
[*Aside*] but I shall follow it as the flesh and    250
fortune shall better determine.
    Whip me? No, no, let carman whip his jade;

Escalus tells Elbow that he has shouldered an unfair burden as constable – seven and a half years without anyone else taking a turn. He invites Elbow to bring him the names of possible successors. Escalus is left pondering sympathetically Claudio's fate.

**256 place**: position, rank, post
**258 readiness in the office**: confidence and efficiency in carrying out the job
**263 put you so oft upon't**: put the burden of responsibility so often upon you
**263–264 Are there not...serve it**: Escalus refers to the fact that the post of constable was supposed to be shared by the community
**264 sufficient**: of high enough status and competence
**267 some piece**: a small amount
**267–268 go through with all**: do it all
**280 Mercy is not...so**: real mercy does not always look like mercy
**281 still**: always
**nurse**: a person who fosters life

- *What evidence is there of Escalus' tact and diplomacy in dealing with Elbow?*
- *What is the effect of the section with the Justice after Elbow's departure?*

The valiant heart's not whipt out of his trade.

[*Exit*

ESCALUS    Come hither to me, Master Elbow: come hither,
Master constable. How long have you been in     255
this place of constable?

ELBOW    Seven year and a half, sir.

ESCALUS    I thought, by the readiness in the office, you had
continued in it some time. – You say seven years
together?     260

ELBOW    And a half, sir.

ESCALUS    Alas, it hath been great pains to you: they do you
wrong to put you so oft upon't. Are there not men
in your ward sufficient to serve it?

ELBOW    Faith, sir, few of any wit in such matters. As     265
they are chosen, they are glad to choose me for
them; I do it for some piece of money, and go
through with all.

ESCALUS    Look you bring me in the names of some six or
seven, the most sufficient of your parish.     270

ELBOW    To your worship's house, sir?

ʻESCALUS    To my house. Fare you well. [*Exit* ELBOW] What's
o'clock, think you?

JUSTICE    Eleven, sir.

ESCALUS    I pray you home to dinner with me.     275

JUSTICE    I humbly thank you.

ESCALUS    It grieves me for the death of Claudio,
But there's no remedy.

JUSTICE    Lord Angelo is severe.

ESCALUS                         It is but needful.
Mercy is not itself, that oft looks so;     280
Pardon is still the nurse of second woe.
But yet, poor Claudio! There is no remedy.
Come, sir.                         [*Exeunt*

The Provost tries to make Angelo think again about
Claudio's fate. Angelo refuses, taking full responsibility and
ordering Juliet's removal to somewhere suitable.

**1 hearing of a cause**: trying a case
**4 He hath but...dream**: he has acted as if he was
not fully awake or alert, as if daydreaming
**5 sects**: kinds of people
**smack of this vice**: have a taste for this sin
**8 Hadst thou not order?**: have you not already been given the
order?
**10 correction**: teaching, instruction
**12 doom**: sentence
**mine**: my responsibility
**15 groaning**: heavily pregnant
**16–17 Dispose of her...place**: move her to a more suitable
place

> • *With what tone and intention does Angelo answer the*
> *Provost's question (line 7)?*
> • *What more do we learn of Angelo's attitude from lines*
> *12–14?*

# Scene 2

*An ante-room to the same*

*Enter* PROVOST *and a* SERVANT

SERVANT He's hearing of a cause: he will come straight;
I'll tell him of you.

PROVOST                                    Pray you, do. [*Exit* SERVANT
I'll know
His pleasure, may be he will relent. Alas,
He hath but as offended in a dream;
All sects, all ages smack of this vice, and he
To die for't!

*Enter* ANGELO

ANGELO                          Now, what's the matter, Provost?

PROVOST Is it your will Claudio shall die tomorrow?

ANGELO Did I not tell thee yea? Hadst thou not order?
Why dost thou ask again?

PROVOST                                    Lest I might be too rash.
Under your good correction, I have seen          10
When, after execution, judgement hath
Repented o'er his doom.

ANGELO                                    Go to; let that be mine;
Do you your office, or give up your place,
And you shall well be spared.

PROVOST                                    I crave your honour's
pardon.
What shall be done, sir, with the groaning Juliet? 15
She's very near her hour.

ANGELO                          Dispose of her
To some more fitter place; and that with speed.

*Enter* SERVANT

The servant announces Isabella, who is about to become a nun. Angelo is prepared to see her, also ordering that Juliet be given basic necessities. As Isabella enters with Lucio, the Provost hopes she will persuade Angelo. She begins by asking him to condemn Claudio's fault but not Claudio.

**24 needful...means**: the bare essentials for living
**25 There shall be order for't**: I will give official instructions for this
**27 suitor**: person who pleads for something
**28 Please but**: I only ask that
    **suit**: request
**29 abhor**: hate
**35–6 let it be...brother**: let it be the fault that is condemned and not the person who committed it

> • *Is Isabella's distinction between the fault and he who commits it convincing (lines 35–36)? Why does she begin with this?*

| | |
|---|---|
| SERVANT | Here is the sister of the man condemned, |
| | Desires access to you. |
| ANGELO | Hath he a sister? |
| PROVOST | Ay, my good lord, a very virtuous maid;  20 |
| | And to be shortly of sisterhood, |
| | If not already. |
| ANGELO | Well, let her be admitted. |

*[Exit* SERVANT

See you the fornicatress be removed;
Let her have needful, but not lavish means;
There shall be order for't.

*Enter* LUCIO *and* ISABELLA

| | |
|---|---|
| PROVOST | Save your honour!  25 |
| | *[Going* |
| ANGELO | Stay a little while. |
| | [*To* ISABELLA]  Y'are welcome: what's your |
| | will? |
| ISABELLA | I am a woeful suitor to your honour; |
| | Please but your honour hear me. |
| ANGELO | Well: what's your |
| | suit? |
| ISABELLA | There is a vice that most I do abhor, |
| | And most desire should meet the blow of justice; 30 |
| | For which I would not plead, but that I must; |
| | For which I must not plead, but that I am |
| | At war 'twixt will and will not. |
| ANGELO | Well: the matter? |
| ISABELLA | I have a brother is condemned to die; |
| | I do beseech you, let it be his fault,  35 |
| | And not my brother. |
| PROVOST | [*Aside*]  Heaven give thee moving |
| | graces! |
| ANGELO | Condemn the fault, and not the actor of it? |
| | Why, every fault's condemned ere it be done: |

Angelo dismisses this scornfully and Isabella is resigned and turns to go. Lucio persuades her to be more impassioned. She establishes that Angelo does have the power to change his decision, out of mercy, but he remains adamant. Lucio again advises a more fiery approach. She argues that mercy is the greatest attribute of great men, pointing out that, if the roles were reversed, Claudio would show mercy.

**39 cipher of a function**: pointless job
**40 fine**: punish
　　**stands in record**: is written down in law
**43 Give't not o'er so**: don't give up so easily
**45 pin**: something very small. He goes on to comment on how tamely she has pleaded so far
**54 remorse**: pity, compassion
**58 call it again**: take it back
**59 longs**: belongs
**60 deputed sword**: sword of justice (symbolising divine justice)
**61 marshal's truncheon**: officer's baton (symbol of authority)

---

- *What is there in Lucio's words that stops Isabella leaving?*
- *What does Angelo indicate by 'will' (line 52)? Why is this a significant choice of word?*

|  | Mine were the very cipher of a function |  |
|---|---|---|
|  | To fine the faults, whose fine stands in record, | 40 |
|  | And let go by the actor. |  |
| ISABELLA |                             O just but severe law! |  |
|  | I had a brother, then : heaven keep your honour. |  |
|  | *[Going* |  |

ISABELLA                             O just but severe law!

LUCIO [*To* ISABELLA] Give't not o'er so. – To him again, entreat him,
Kneel down before him, hang upon his gown;
You are too cold. If you should need a pin,   45
You could not with more tame a tongue desire it.
To him, I say.

ISABELLA   Must he needs die?

ANGELO                         Maiden, no remedy.

ISABELLA   Yes: I do think that you might pardon him,
And neither heaven nor man grieve at the mercy. 50

ANGELO   I will not do't.

ISABELLA                 But can you if you would?

ANGELO   Look what I will not, that I cannot do.

ISABELLA   But might you do't, and do the world no wrong,
If so your heart were touched with that remorse
As mine is to him?

ANGELO               He's sentenced, 'tis too late. 55

LUCIO   [*To* ISABELLA] You are too cold.

ISABELLA   Too late? Why, no. I that do speak a word
May call it again. – Well, believe this:
No ceremony that to great ones longs,
Not the king's crown, nor the deputed sword,   60
The marshal's truncheon, nor the judge's robe,
Become them with one half so good a grace
As mercy does.
If he had been as you, and you as he,
You would have slipped like him, but he like you 65
Would not have been so stern.

Angelo asks her to go. She stays, wishing he were in her situation and she were in his. Lucio applauds her attempt to make Angelo 'feel' the experience. Although Angelo says she's wasting her time, she persists by pointing out that if he were to be judged by his own law he would see the need for mercy. Angelo denies personal involvement: it is the law that condemns Claudio. Isabella pleads for a delay so that Claudio may prepare himself, adding what a common offence he's committed and how few have died for it.

**70 touch**: involve him

> **there's the vein**: that's the right route

**71–73 forfeit...forfeit**: Angelo insists on Claudio's guilt in the eyes of the law; Isabella reminds him that by the doctrine of Original Sin, we are all born guilty of sin. She points out that Christians believe in the possibility of redemption through Christ

**74 He...took**: God, who is in the best position to judge all

**79 Like man new made**: and you will recreate yourself – as a more compassionate man

**93 edict**: law

> • *Is Isabella's analogy – comparing sending Claudio unprepared to heaven with serving out of season poultry appropriate (lines 85–88)?*

ANGELO                                                    Pray you be gone.

ISABELLA    I would to heaven I had your potency,
            And you were Isabel! Should it then be thus?
            No; I would tell what 'twere to be a judge,
            And what a prisoner.

LUCIO       [*To* ISABELLA]              Ay, touch him: there's the
                vein.                                          70

ANGELO      Your brother is a forfeit of the law,
            And you but waste your words.

ISABELLA                                          Alas, alas!
            Why, all the souls that were, were forfeit once,
            And He that might the vantage best have took
            Found out the remedy. How would you be        75
            If He, which is the top of judgement, should
            But judge you as you are? O, think on that,
            And mercy then will breathe within your lips,
            Like man new made.

ANGELO                           Be you content, fair maid;
            It is the law, not I, condemn your brother;      80
            Were he my kinsman, brother, or my son,
            It should be thus with him. He must die tomorrow.

ISABELLA    Tomorrow? O, that's sudden
            Spare him, spare him!
            He's not prepared for death. Even for our
                kitchens                                      85
            We kill the fowl of season: shall we serve heaven
            With less respect than we do minister
            To our gross selves? Good, good my lord, bethink
                you:
            Who it it that hath died for this offence?
            There's many have committed it.

LUCIO       [*To* ISABELLA]                  Ay, well said.  90

ANGELO      The law hath not been dead, though it hath slept:
            Those many had not dared to do that evil
            If the first that did th'edict infringe

Angelo says the law has slept but is now fully roused and re-establishing itself. He argues that he shows pity with his justice – for the victims of crime. Isabella sees this as a tyrannous use of his power and launches into an impassioned speech about human pride.

**94 answered**: paid the penalty
**96 glass**: crystal ball
**97 by remissness new conceived**: newly thought of as a result of leniency
**98 and so...born**: and consequently on the way to birth and life
**99 successive degrees**: further growth
**100 ere**: before
**101 justice**: exact the legal penalty
**103 dismissed offence**: a crime not punished
  **after gall**: later harm
**104 do him right**: give justice to
  **answering**: paying for
**108 that suffers**: the first to be punished
**111 thunder**: cast thunderbolts like Jupiter
**111–114 Could great men...nothing but thunder**: if the powerful in society could produce thunderbolts like Jove (Jupiter, the greatest of the gods of Classical times), then there would be nothing *but* thunder; every petty official would use heaven for this and nothing else
**117 unwedgeable**: not able to be split
**118 myrtle**: a sweet-scented shrub, sacred to Venus (the Classical goddess of beauty and love), the emblem of love
**120 most assured**: most certain of in his life
**121 glassy essence**: soul
  **ape**: image of vanity and imitation
**123 spleens**: source of laughter and anger
**124 laugh mortal**: laugh themselves into a human (mortal) state

---

- *What is Angelo's definition of pity (lines 101–105)? Is he convincing?*
- *How does Isabella explore and develop the idea of the giant (lines 109–110) in her next speech (lines 111–124)?*

Had answered for his deed. Now 'tis awake,
Takes note of what is done, and like a prophet          95
Looks in a glass that shows what future evils,
Either new, or by remissness new conceived,
And so in progress to be hatched and born,
Are now to have no successive degrees,
But ere they live, to end.

ISABELLA                                           Yet show some pity.     100

ANGELO     I show it most of all when I show justice;
For then I pity those I do not know,
Which a dismissed offence would after gall,
And do him right that, answering one foul wrong,
Lives not to act another. Be satisfied;                105
Your brother dies tomorrow; be content.

ISABELLA   So you must be the first that gives this sentence,
And he, that suffers. O, it is excellent
To have a giant's strength, but it is tyrannous
To use it like a giant.                                110

LUCIO      [To ISABELLA] That's well said.

ISABELLA                                      Could great men
           thunder
As Jove himself does, Jove would ne'er be quiet,
For every pelting petty officer
Would use his heaven for thunder; nothing but
           thunder.
Merciful Heaven,                                       115
Thou rather with thy sharp and sulphurous bolt
Splits the unwedgeable and gnarled oak,
Than the soft myrtle. But man, proud man,
Dressed in a little brief authority,
Most ignorant of what he's most assured –             120
His glassy essence – like an angry ape
Plays such fantastic tricks before high heaven
As makes the angels weep; who, with our spleens,
Would all themselves laugh mortal.

Lucio and the Provost see that Angelo can be moved. Angelo begins to wonder why she is characterising him as a tyrant. Secretly, he wants her to view him warmly because he has discovered his desire for her. Ignorant of this, she pleads with him to examine his conscience. Aside, he admits his arousal. He advises her to return the next day. She promises to 'bribe' him; he misunderstands, believing she is offering herself.

**126 coming**: coming round
**127 weigh**: judge
    **brother**: fellow man
    **with ourself**: by the standards we apply to ourselves
**128 jest**: argue playfully
**129 foul profanation**: disgusting defilement
**131 choleric**: angry
**133 Art avised o'**: do you know about
    **More on't**: keep going
**137 skins the vice o'th'top**: covers over the sins it commits. The metaphor is of a sore place healing on the surface with a new skin – but remaining corrupt underneath
    **Go to your bosom**: consider in your heart
**140 natural guiltiness**: guilt that is in human nature
**142–3 sense**: two meanings apply:
    **(a)** good argument
    **(b)** sensuality, sexual responses
**146–7 bribe...Bribe me**: Angelo, in his aroused and confused state, takes her to mean with her body
**148 gifts**: blessings
**149 marred all else**: ruined your case otherwise

> • *What earlier comments in the play, by herself and other characters, are summed up in Isabella's words 'A natural guiltiness' (line 140)?*

| LUCIO | [*To* ISABELLA] O, to him, to him, wench! He will relent;     125 |
| | He's coming: I perceive't. |
| PROVOST | [*Aside*]                    Pray heaven she win him. |
| ISABELLA | We cannot weigh our brother with ourself. |
| | Great men may jest with saints: 'tis wit in them, |
| | But in the less, foul profanation. |
| LUCIO | [*To* ISABELLA] Thou'rt i' th'right, girl; more o' that.     130 |
| ISABELLA | That in the captain's but a choleric word, |
| | Which in the soldier is flat blasphemy. |
| LUCIO | [*To* ISABELLA] Art avised o' that? More on 't. |
| ANGELO | Why do you put these sayings upon me? |
| ISABELLA | Because authority, though it err like others,     135 |
| | Hath yet a kind of medicine in itself |
| | That skins the vice o'th'top. Go to your bosom, |
| | Knock there, and ask your heart what it doth know |
| | That's like my brother's fault. If it confess |
| | A natural guiltiness, such as is his,     140 |
| | Let it not sound a thought upon your tongue |
| | Against my brother's life. |
| ANGELO | [*Aside*]                    She speaks, and 'tis such sense |
| | That my sense breeds with it. – Fare you well. |
| | [*Going* |
| ISABELLA | Gentle my lord, turn back. |
| ANGELO | I will bethink me. Come again tomorrow.     145 |
| | [*Going* |
| ISABELLA | Hark, how I'll bribe you: good my lord, turn back. |
| ANGELO | How! Bribe me? |
| ISABELLA | Ay, with such gifts that heaven shall share with you. |
| LUCIO | [*To* ISABELLA] You had marred all else. |

Isabella's bribe will be prayers. Angelo repeats his invitation, admitting, aside, how he is yielding to temptation. She leaves, and he begins to explore his feelings in a tortured way: how can he be tempted to sin by the attractions of an innocent?

**150 fond sickles**: coins that are foolishly valued

**151 stones**: precious stones

**151–152 whose rate...them**: which are either worth a lot or a little according to passing fashion or individual taste

**154 preserved souls**: the souls of those who have been saved from sin and death

**155 dedicate**: dedicated

**156 temporal**: on this earth

**159–160 For I...crossed**: Angelo feels himself led into temptation despite the plea in the Lord's Prayer

**160 Where prayer's crossed**: where prayer is contradicted

**162 From thee...virtue**: he is responding to 'Save your honour'; it is her virtue that has aroused him

**165–168 The sun**: the light of virtue – it shines on violets and makes them bloom – it makes dead flesh (carrion) rot – Angelo feels that Isabella's virtue corrupts him

**169 betray our sense**: stir up our passion

**170 lightness**: flirtatiousness

**170–172 Having...there**: since we have enough ground for rotting carcasses, why should we desire to pull down a holy place and deposit our corruption there?

> - *Why does Isabella think her prayers for Angelo would be especially effective (lines 154–156)?*
> - *What prayer does Angelo have in mind (lines 158–159)?*
> - *How does Angelo's soliloquy (lines 162–187) follow up what we already know he's thinking?*

| | |
|---|---|
| ISABELLA | Not with fond sickles of the tested gold,        150 |
| | Or stones, whose rate are either rich or poor |
| | As fancy values them : but with true prayers, |
| | That shall be up at heaven and enter there |
| | Ere sunrise : prayers from preserved souls, |
| | From fasting maids, whose minds are dedicate  155 |
| | To nothing temporal. |

ISABELLA   Not with fond sickles of the tested gold,                                150
          Or stones, whose rate are either rich or poor
          As fancy values them : but with true prayers,
          That shall be up at heaven and enter there
          Ere sunrise : prayers from preserved souls,
          From fasting maids, whose minds are dedicate     155
          To nothing temporal.

ANGELO                          Well: come to me
             tomorrow.

LUCIO     [*To* ISABELLA] Go to: 'tis well; away.

ISABELLA  Heaven keep your honour safe.

ANGELO    [*Aside*]                     Amen.
          For I am that way going to temptation,
          Where prayer's crossed.

ISABELLA                          At what hour
             tomorrow                                      160
          Shall I attend your lordship?

ANGELO                          At any time 'fore
             noon.

ISABELLA  Save your honour.          [*Exeunt all but* ANGELO

ANGELO                     From thee : even from thy
             virtue!
          What's this? What's this? Is this her fault, or mine?
          The tempter, or the tempted, who sins most, ha?
          Not she; nor doth she tempt; but it is I          165
          That, lying by the violet in the sun,
          Do as the carrion does, not as the flower,
          Corrupt with virtuous season. Can it be
          That modesty may more betray our sense
          Than woman's lightness? Having waste ground
             enough,                                        170
          Shall we desire to raze the sanctuary
          And pitch our evils there? O fie, fie, fie!
          What dost thou, or what art thou, Angelo?
          Dost thou desire her foully for those things

Impulsively, Angelo thinks of letting Claudio live. He does not understand the powerful desires loosed in him – he has previously wondered how other men got into this emotional state.

**180 cunning enemy**: devil
**183 strumpet**: literally, prostitute, but used to distinguish sexual allure from moral quality
**184 double vigour**: false efforts
    **art and nature**: artificial allure and natural sexual attractiveness
**187 fond**: foolishly infatuated

- *What troubles Angelo especially about his desire for Isabella (lines 183–186)?*

The Duke enters the prison, only just remembering to act the friar. He says he wants to minister to the inmates. The Provost indicates he would let him do more (presumably thinking of Claudio) when Juliet appears. The Provost begins sympathetically to describe her situation.

**3 charity**: vow to do good
    **blessed order**: brotherhood of friars
**5 common right**: right of all clerics to visit the afflicted
**11 flaws of her own youth**: failings of youthful desire
**12 blistered her report**: damaged her reputation
**13–14 a young...offence**: a man in his prime for whom it would be more appropriate to repeat the 'offence'

That make her good? O, let her brother live!     175
Thieves for their robbery have authority,
When judges steal themselves. What, do I love her,
That I desire to hear her speak again?
And feast upon her eyes? What is't I dream on?
O cunning enemy, that, to catch a saint,     180
With saints dost bait thy hook! Most dangerous
Is that temptation that doth goad us on
To sin in loving virtue. Never could the strumpet
With all her double vigour, art and nature,
Once stir my temper : but this virtuous maid     185
Subdues me quite. Ever till now
When men were fond, I smiled, and wondered
   how.     [*Exit*

## Scene

*A prison*

*Enter severally* DUKE *disguised as a* FRIAR
*and* PROVOST

DUKE      Hail to you, Provost – so I think you are.

PROVOST   I am the Provost. What's your will, good Friar?

DUKE      Bound by my charity, and my blessed order,
I come to visit the afflicted spirits
Here in the prison. Do me the common right     5
To let me see them, and to make me know
The nature of their crimes, that I may minister
To them accordingly.

PROVOST   I would do more than that, if more were needful –

*Enter* JULIET

Look, here comes one : a gentlewoman of mine,     10
Who, falling in the flaws of her own youth,
Hath blistered her report. She is with child,
And he that got it, sentenced: a young man

As the friar, the Duke tests Juliet as to the state of her soul. She accepts responsibility, says that the sin was mutual, and repents. The Duke confirms that Claudio must die the next day. Juliet is horrified at the irony of what love has brought.

**18 conducted**: taken to your designated place

**19 the sin you carry**: carrying on her shoulders the weight of her sin of unlawful sex

**21 arraign**: test, put on trial

**30–34 'Tis meet...in fear**: it is right that you should do so; but if you repent because of shame which you feel on your own behalf rather than heaven's, this shows that we do not refrain from troubling heaven with our prayers because we love it, but because we fear for ourselves

**as**: because

**38 instruction**: the teaching and advice of a priest

**41 respites me a life**: allows me to have my life back

**comfort**: ironic

- *Shakespeare continues to remind us of Claudio's imminent execution (line 16). Why?*
- *What do you think of the Duke's judgement that Juliet's sin is greater than Claudio's (line 28)?*

|          | More fit to do another such offence, |    |
|----------|--------------------------------------|----|
|          | Than die for this.                   | 15 |
| DUKE     | When must he die?                    |    |
| PROVOST  | As I do think, tomorrow. |    |
|          | [*To* JULIET] I have provided for you; stay a while, |    |
|          | And you shall be conducted.          |    |
| DUKE     | Repent you, fair one, of the sin you carry? |    |
| JULIET   | I do; and bear the same most patiently. | 20 |
| DUKE     | I'll teach you how you shall arraign your conscience |    |
|          | And try your penitence, if it be sound, |    |
|          | Or hollowly put on.                  |    |
| JULIET   | I'll gladly learn. |    |
| DUKE     | Love you the man that wronged you?   |    |
| JULIET   | Yes, as I love the woman that wronged him. | 25 |
| DUKE     | So then it seems your most offenceful act |    |
|          | Was mutually committed?              |    |
| JULIET   | Mutually. |    |
| DUKE     | Then was your sin of heavier kind than his. |    |
| JULIET   | I do confess it, and repent it, father. |    |
| DUKE     | 'Tis meet so, daughter; but lest you do repent, | 30 |
|          | As that the sin hath brought you to this shame, |    |
|          | Which sorrow is always toward ourselves, not heaven, |    |
|          | Showing we would not spare heaven as we love it, |    |
|          | But as we stand in fear –            |    |
| JULIET   | I do repent me as it is an evil,     | 35 |
|          | And take the shame with joy.         |    |
| DUKE     | There rest. |    |
|          | Your partner, as I hear, must die tomorrow, |    |
|          | And I am going with instruction to him. |    |
|          | Grace go with you: *Benedicite!*     | [*Exit* |
| JULIET   | Must die to-morrow! O injurious love, | 40 |
|          | That respites me a life, whose very comfort |    |

**42 dying**: deadly

Angelo agonises over how his desire to pray is overwhelmed by his desire for Isabella. He reflects on the false dignity of the trappings of authority. When Isabella is announced, he is almost suffocated by mounting desire.

**2 several**: different, various
**3 invention**: imagination
**4–7 Heaven...conception**: Angelo is tortured by the fact that while his mouth may go through the motion of eating the bread of the body of Christ, his heart is lusting evily after Isabella
**7 conception**: passionate intention
**state**: process of law and government
**9 sere**: dried up
**gravity**: seriousness
**11 boot**: advantage
**idle plume**: mere feathers on a helmet
**12 vain**: vanity
**place**: status
**form**: outward appearance
**13 case**: outward shape
**habit**: clothing
**15 seeming**: appearance
**blood**: passion that cannot be denied
**17 crest**: heraldic shield
**20 muster to**: gather around
**22 dispossessing**: taking power from
**24 swounds**: faints

> • *What is the dramatic effect of the servant announcing Isabella in such a brief and impersonal way (line 18)?*

Is still a dying horror!

PROVOST                                    'Tis pity of him.   [*Exeunt*

# Scene 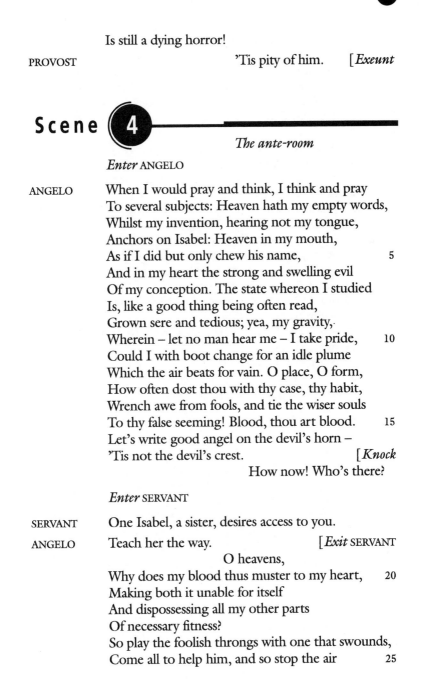 4

*The ante-room*

*Enter* ANGELO

ANGELO      When I would pray and think, I think and pray
            To several subjects: Heaven hath my empty words,
            Whilst my invention, hearing not my tongue,
            Anchors on Isabel: Heaven in my mouth,
            As if I did but only chew his name,                          5
            And in my heart the strong and swelling evil
            Of my conception. The state whereon I studied
            Is, like a good thing being often read,
            Grown sere and tedious; yea, my gravity,·
            Wherein – let no man hear me – I take pride,               10
            Could I with boot change for an idle plume
            Which the air beats for vain. O place, O form,
            How often dost thou with thy case, thy habit,
            Wrench awe from fools, and tie the wiser souls
            To thy false seeming! Blood, thou art blood.              15
            Let's write good angel on the devil's horn –
            'Tis not the devil's crest.                    [*Knock*
                              How now! Who's there?

*Enter* SERVANT

SERVANT     One Isabel, a sister, desires access to you.

ANGELO      Teach her the way.                   [*Exit* SERVANT
                              O heavens,
            Why does my blood thus muster to my heart,              20
            Making both it unable for itself
            And dispossessing all my other parts
            Of necessary fitness?
            So play the foolish throngs with one that swounds,
            Come all to help him, and so stop the air                25

Isabella comes to know his 'pleasure', a greeting which
further inflames him as he reveals in an aside. He seems to
suggest a possible delay of execution for Claudio, but,
questioned further, attacks Claudio's vice. It is soon clear to
the audience that he is preparing to blackmail Isabella – sex
for Claudio's life – though he does not state it directly.

27 **general subject**: common people
28 **Quit their own part**: leave their own jobs
   **obsequious fondness**: foolish, mindless worship
32 **it**: his pleasure
   **please**: Isabella has come to ask what Angelo has decided (his
   'pleasure'); Angelo (aside) shows how his mind is working by
   saying that he would be more pleased if she experienced
   (knew) his pleasure (sexual) instead of asking what it is
39 **reprieve**: time before execution
40 **fitted**: prepared for death
43–44 **from nature...made**: murdered a living man
44 **remit**: acquit
45–46 **coin...forbid**: bring bastards into the world
48 **mettle**: value
   **restrained**: forbidden
50 **'Tis set down...earth**: this may be what religion tells us but it
   goes against normal human feeling
51 **pose**: test
52 **had you rather**: would you prefer

- *Note that no other characters are present at this second
  meeting.*
- *What does Angelo mean by his words in lines 35–36?
  How does Isabella seem to understand them?*
- *Is Angelo changing his argument by shifting from
  'good' (line 42) to 'easy' (line 46)?*

By which he should revive; and even so
The general subject to a well-wished king
Quit their own part, and in obsequious fondness
Crowd to his presence, where their untaught love
Must needs appear offence.

*Enter* ISABELLA

How now, fair maid? 30

| | |
|---|---|
| ISABELLA | I am come to know your pleasure. |
| ANGELO | [*Aside*] That you might know it, would much<br>            better please me,<br>Than to demand what 'tis. – Your brother cannot<br>            live. |
| ISABELLA | Even so. Heaven keep your honour. |
| ANGELO | Yet may he live a while; and, it may be,                35<br>As long as you or I; yet he must die. |
| ISABELLA | Under your sentence? |
| ANGELO | Yea. |
| ISABELLA | When, I beseech you? That in his reprieve,<br>Longer or shorter, he may be so fitted              40<br>That his soul sicken not. |
| ANGELO | Ha? Fie, these filthy vices! It were as good<br>To pardon him that hath from nature stolen<br>A man already made, as to remit<br>Their saucy sweetness that do coin heaven's<br>            image                                            45<br>In stamps that are forbid. 'Tis all as easy<br>Falsely to take away a life true made,<br>As to put mettle in restrained means<br>To make a false one. |
| ISABELLA | 'Tis set down so in heaven, but not in earth.       50 |
| ANGELO | Say you so? Then I shall pose you quickly.<br>Which had you rather, that the most just law<br>Now took your brother's life; or, to redeem him,<br>Give up your body to such sweet uncleanness |

Isabella, not understanding Angelo's intentions, engages in an argument about whether it is a sin or charity to commit a sin to save a brother's life. This drives Angelo to speak more grossly.

**56 I had...soul**: Isabella has misunderstood Angelo

**57–58 our compelled...accompt**: sins we are forced to commit are counted but not held in the balance against us

**59 not warrant**: not argue for – he is giving up this line of argument

**65 take it as a peril**: take the responsibility of your sin (in releasing Claudio) on my soul

**68 Were equal poise of**: would be a balance of

**73 nothing of your answer**: none of your responsibility

**74 Your sense pursues not mine**: you do not understand me

**77 But graciously**: through God's grace

**79 tax**: test, examine

**black masks**: two meanings apply:

(a) nuns' veils

(b) masks of women in the audience

**80 encieled**: shaded, covered

**82 gross**: crudely

- *Note the repeated occurrences of the words 'soul' and 'sin' (lines 55–73). How are they being used?*
- *What is the irony of 'Your sense pursues not mine' (line 74)?*

As she that he hath stained?

ISABELLA                                Sir, believe this:    55
I had rather give my body than my soul.

ANGELO    I talk not of your soul: our compelled sins
Stand more for number than accompt.

ISABELLA                              How say
    you?

ANGELO    Nay, I'll not warrant that: for I can speak
Against the thing I say. Answer to this:    60
I – now the voice of the recorded law –
Pronounce a sentence on your brother's life:
Might there not be a charity in sin
To save this brother's life?

ISABELLA                     Please you to do 't,
I'll take it as a peril to my soul;    65
It is no sin at all, but charity.

ANGELO    Pleased you to do't, at peril of your soul,
Were equal poise of sin and charity.

ISABELLA    That I do beg his life, if it be sin,
Heaven let me bear it; you granting of my suit,    70
It that be sin, I'll make it my morn prayer
To have it added to the faults of mine,
And nothing of your answer.

ANGELO                   Nay, but hear me;
Your sense pursues not mine: either you are
    ignorant,
Or seem so, crafty; and that's not good.    75

ISABELLA    Let me be ignorant, and in nothing good,
But graciously to know I am no better.

ANGELO    Thus wisdom wishes to appear most bright
When it doth tax itself: as these black masks
Proclaim an encieled beauty ten times louder    80
Than beauty could, displayed. But mark me;
To be received plain, I'll speak more gross.
Your brother is to die.

Angelo asks Isabella whether she would give her body to save her brother. She takes this hypothetically and argues that Claudio's death would be a cheaper price to pay than her loss of chastity which would lead, because of her nun's vows, to eternal damnation. Redeeming Claudio by foul means is out of the question. Angelo catches her out, reminding her that she has been playing down Claudio's vice as mere mischief.

**86 Accountant...pain**: liable to that penalty by law
**89 subscribe**: guarantee
**90 But in the loss of question**: unless there is no issue to answer to
**92 great place**: high rank
**97 this supposed**: this hypothetical person
**him suffer**: Claudio die
**100 terms of death**: death sentence
**101 impression**: marks
**keen**: sharp
**103 longing...for**: have been sick with desire for
**105 'twere the cheaper way**: it would be a lower price to pay
**111 Ignomy**: shame
**112 of two houses**: two completely different things
**114 of late**: earlier
**115 sliding**: slipping into sin

> * *How does Angelo think he has caught Isabella out (lines 114–116)?*

| | |
|---|---|
| ISABELLA | So. |
| ANGELO | And his offence is so, as it appears,      85 |
| | Accountant to the law upon that pain. |
| ISABELLA | True. |
| ANGELO | Admit no other way to save his life – |
| | As I subscribe not that, nor any other, |
| | But in the loss of question – that you, his sister,  90 |
| | Finding yourself desired of such a person |
| | Whose credit with the judge, or own great place, |
| | Could fetch your brother from the manacles |
| | Of the all-binding law; and that there were |
| | No earthly mean to save him, but that either    95 |
| | You must lay down the treasures of your body |
| | To this supposed, or else to let him suffer: |
| | What would you do? |
| ISABELLA | As much for my poor brother as myself; |
| | That is, were I under the terms of death,     100 |
| | Th'impression of keen whips I'd wear as rubies, |
| | And strip myself to death as to a bed |
| | That longing have been sick for, ere I'd yield |
| | My body up to shame. |
| ANGELO |                  Then must your brother |
| | die. |
| ISABELLA | And 'twere the cheaper way.     105 |
| | Better it were a brother died at once, |
| | Than that a sister, by redeeming him, |
| | Should die for ever. |
| ANGELO | Were you not then as cruel as the sentence |
| | That you have slandered so?     110 |
| ISABELLA | Ignomy in ransom and free pardon |
| | Are of two houses: lawful mercy |
| | Is nothing kin to foul redemption. |
| ANGELO | You seemed of late to make the law a tyrant, |
| | And rather proved the sliding of your brother  115 |
| | A merriment than a vice. |

Isabella claims that it was frailty born of a desire to put Claudio's case that made her offer this 'wrong' view. Angelo seizes on the idea that women are frail (Isabella agrees) and suggests that she should be true to her nature and give herself to him as he loves her. She reminds him, now fully realising his motives, that he has condemned Claudio for just such a crime.

**121–123 Else...weakness**: if there is no-one else but my brother who has this weakness or will ever have, let him die. A feodary (from feudary) means a feudal tenant, a peasant who was 'tied' to the land and paid for his holding by serving his lord. The implication is that if even such a lowly person can avoid committing such a crime, then Claudio – who should know far better – should die

**125 forms**: images, reflections

**126–127 Men...by them**: men spoil their image of being made in god's likeness by taking advantage of women

**129 credulous to false prints**: easily accept false images (from men)

**133 arrest**: accept

**134 if you...none**: if you behave as if more than a woman, then you are not a woman

**136 external warrants**: outward evidence

**137 destined livery**: the character that it is your fate to have

**139 the former language**: the argument you were offering earlier

**144–6 your virtue...others**: I know that in your position as a virtuous lawyer you are allowed some licence to lure guilty people on, which seems more sinful than it is

> • *What is the effect of Isabella's image of women's frailty (lines 124–125)? Does she conform to her own description?*

| ISABELLA | O pardon me, my lord; it oft falls out |
| | To have what we would have, we speak not what |
| | we mean. |
| | I something do excuse the thing I hate |
| | For his advantage that I dearly love. 120 |
| ANGELO | We are all frail. |
| ISABELLA | Else let my brother die, |
| | If not a feodary but only he |
| | Owe and succeed thy weakness. |
| ANGELO | Nay, women are |
| | frail too. |
| ISABELLA | Ay, as the glasses where they view themselves, |
| | Which are as easy broke as they make forms. 125 |
| | Women? – Help, heaven! Men their creation mar |
| | In profiting by them. Nay, call us ten times frail; |
| | For we are soft as our complexions are, |
| | And credulous to false prints. |
| ANGELO | I think it well; |
| | And from this testimony of your own sex – 130 |
| | Since I suppose we are made to be no stronger |
| | Than faults may shake our frames – let me be bold. |
| | I do arrest your words. Be that you are, |
| | That is, a woman; if you be more, you're none. |
| | If you be one – as you are well expressed 135 |
| | By all external warrants – show it now, |
| | By putting on the destined livery. |
| ISABELLA | I have no tongue but one; gentle my lord, |
| | Let me entreat you speak the former language. |
| ANGELO | Plainly conceive, I love you. 140 |
| ISABELLA | My brother did love Juliet, |
| | And you tell me that he shall die for 't. |
| ANGELO | He shall not, Isabel, if you give me love. |
| ISABELLA | I know your virtue hath a licence in't, |
| | Which seems a little fouler than it is, 145 |
| | To pluck on others. |

Angelo repeats his purpose. Isabella accuses him of hypocrisy and declares that unless he pardons Claudio she will tell the world of his blackmail. He replies that his reputation is such that no-one will believe her. Without restraint, he promises a lingering death for Claudio unless she gives in to him by tomorrow. He goes. Isabella collapses and reflects on her impotence. She decides to go to Claudio.

**149 pernicious**: wicked, villainous
**150 proclaim**: make public
   **look for't**: be warned
**155 vouch**: word
**157 stifle...report**: go to jail because of what you're saying
**158 calumny**: slanderous lies
**159 sensual race**: the drive of my passions
   **the rein**: free rein
**161 nicety**: politeness
   **prolixious**: excessive delaying
**162 banish what they sue for**: drive away the nicety in me
**167 affection**: desire, passion
**170 Did I**: if I were to
**171 perilous**: dangerous
**173 approof**: approval
**174 make curtsey**: obey
**176 as**: wherever
**177 by prompture of the blood**: by following his desires' prompting

> • *In her hour of need, Isabella does not pray to God (lines 170–186). What do you make of this?*

ANGELO                          Believe me, on mine honour,
                My words express my purpose.

ISABELLA        Ha? Little honour, to be much believed,
                And most pernicious purpose! Seeming, seeming!
                I will proclaim thee, Angelo, look for't.            150
                Sign me a present pardon for my brother,
                Or with an outstretched throat, I'll tell the world
                    aloud
                What man thou art.

ANGELO                          Who will believe thee, Isabel?
                My unsoiled name, th'austereness of my life,
                My vouch against you, and my place i'th'state      155
                Will so your accusation overweigh,
                That you shall stifle in your own report,
                And smell of calumny. I have begun,
                And now I give my sensual race the rein:
                Fit thy consent to my sharp appetite;               160
                Lay by all nicety and prolixious blushes
                That banish what they sue for. Redeem thy brother
                By yielding up the body to my will;
                Or else he must not only die the death,
                But thy unkindness shall his death draw out         165
                To ling'ring sufferance. Answer me tomorrow,
                Or, by the affection that now guides me most,
                I'll prove a tyrant to him. As for you,
                Say what you can: my false o'erweighs your true.
                                                            [*Exit*

ISABELLA        To whom should I complain? Did I tell this,        170
                Who would believe me? O perilous mouths,
                That bear in them one and the self-same tongue
                Either of condemnation or approof,
                Bidding the law make curtsey to their will,
                Hooking both right and wrong to th'appetite,        175
                To follow as it draws! I'll to my brother.
                Though he hath fall'n by prompture of the blood,
                Yet hath he in him such a mind of honour,

Isabella convinces herself that Claudio will die for her, since her chastity is more valuable than his life. She decides to tell him of Angelo's demand.

**182 abhorred:** dreadful, vile

That had he twenty heads to tender down
On twenty bloody blocks, he'd yield them up        180
Before his sister should her body stoop
To such abhorred pollution.
Then, Isabel live chaste, and brother, die:
More than our brother is our chastity.
I'll tell him yet of Angelo's request,                      185
And fit his mind to death, for his soul's rest.    [*Exit*

# ACTIVITIES

## Keeping track

### Scene 1

1 What are Angelo and Escalus debating at the start? How do their points of view differ?
2 What is Constable Elbow's complaint? What happens about it? What is Pompey's role?
3 What are Angelo's and Escalus' approaches to judging the issue?

### Scene 2

4 What attitudes do Angelo and Isabella have to Claudio's 'crime' at the start of the scene?
5 What are the main arguments used by Isabella? How does Angelo reply to them?
6 What parts do Lucio and Provost play in this debate?
7 What different hopes do Isabella and Angelo have of their next meeting?

### Scene 3

8 What seem to be the Duke's aims in this first scene of his disguise?
9 What do you learn about Juliet and her attitude in this her only speaking appearance? To what effect does Shakespeare use her?
10 What vital information emerges for the Duke and Juliet?

### Scene 4

11 What tactics does Angelo employ to persuade Isabella to go to bed with him?
12 Why does she misunderstand him?
13 How does he turn the tables on her and what is her response?
14 With what words does he declare himself? How does she answer?

# Discussion

## Scene 1

1  In the main part of the scene, we watch Angelo and Escalus judging the case brought by Constable Elbow against Froth. How does this relate to the preliminary discussion between Angelo and Escalus before the others enter?
2  What is your final view of Escalus as a man and a judge?

## Scene 2

3  At the end of the scene Angelo is shocked at himself. What is he discovering about himself? How sympathetically do you regard him?

## Scene 3

4  What is the dramatic function of this scene? You might like to consider it from these angles:
   • as the first appearance of the Duke in disguise.
   • as the only occasion in the play when Juliet speaks. (Her other appearances are a brief one in Act 1 and then at the end of the play, but on neither occasion does she say anything.)
   • as a necessary 'bridge' between Isabella's two visits to Angelo.

## Scene 4

5  How has Angelo's state of mind changed between the end of scene and the beginning of this scene?
6  How would you describe the thoughts and feelings of the two characters at the end of this scene?

# Drama

1  Isabella says: '*Hark, how I'll bribe you:*' (scene 2 line 146)
   • Use FORUM THEATRE techniques to analyse this moment of tension. Remember that Lucio and the Provost are still on stage.
   • Try to expose these sub-textual thoughts in your positioning, facial expressions, and gestures.

2 In pairs look at Angelo's soliloquy, scene 4 lines 1–17.
Angelo needs help. A range of people might offer him varying
advice:

| Duke | Duke in disguise as a friar |
| Provost | Lucio |
| Isabella | A psychiatrist |

You can probably think of others.
Take it in turns to represent Angelo and an adviser. How does he
respond to each new adviser?

3 There are many moments of tension and passion in this scene. In
pairs:

 • choose a line and produce a **photograph** which sums up the
 power of the moment.

 • compare yours with those of other pairs in the class.

 • each of these photographs could be the starting point for a
 complex piece of FORUM THEATRE.

4 In a group of four to six, one person represents Isabella and the
others become different but equally unpleasant Angelos. Choose
from:

 • cold

 • violent

 • sarcastic

 • laughing

 • indifferent.

Choose which lines from this scene are most appropriate to your
version of Angelo. All the Angelos gather round and speak to
Isabella. Try different interpretations until you find the one that
best expresses her situation.

## Close study

### Scene 1

1 In his opening words, Angelo echoes the Duke in Act 1 scene 1
lines 16–21 and Act 1 scene 3 lines 19–31. What similar images
does he offer? What highly significant word appears in all three
passages? What is its significance?

2 Read lines 1–31. At this point the debate is mainly hypothetical.
Study it carefully and pinpoint all those aspects of the argument
which will sound very ironic and not at all hypothetical by the
end of Act 2.

 Why does Shakespeare include the details in lines 33–36 at
this point?

## Scene 2

1 Consider Shakespeare's use of the Provost:
   (a) in lines 1–25:
      – to affect the audience's sympathies
      – to focus the dramatic situation
      – to show Angelo's authority in action
      – to continue the debate about punishment
   (b) in line 26:
      – as the man Angelo asks to stay (Why does he ask?)
   (c) in the remaining lines:
      – to highlight the drama of Angelo and Isabella.
2 Isabella enters as reluctant suitor. Between lines 26 and 156 she changes into a person who is speaking with fluency, commitment and conviction. She has unintentionally wrought a dramatic change in Angelo. Pinpoint the key stages in this process.
3 What is it that provokes Isabella's most powerful language in lines 107–156? What are the special qualities of this poetry?
4 What is ironic about Lucio's language of encouragement? Contrast it with that of the Provost.
5 Consider Angelo:
   • how would you portray him at the start in the role of judge and governor?
   • where and how would you want an actor to pinpoint the changes in him between lines 106 and 142? You need to think about what he says in lines 142–143, 158–160 and in the final soliloquy (lines 162–187) to understand where her power over him lies.
   • the final soliloquy shows Angelo in a confused state:
      – how is he confused about his view of himself?
      – how is he confused about his view of Isabella?
      – what is his problem with virtue now?
      – what ideas, images and features of style give this speech its impact?

## Scene 3

1 How convincingly does the Duke play the friar? What do his motives seem to be for visiting the prison?
2 How do you view Juliet on the evidence of this sole speaking appearance?
3 Why does she interrupt at line 35?

## Scene 4

1 Contrast Angelo's opening soliloquy (lines 1–17) with that which ended scene 2.
   - What is his state of mind now?
   - Make a list of 'oppositions' in the speech, e.g. '*Heaven in my mouth*' (line 4)/'*in my heart...swelling evil*' (line 6). How many of Isabella's ideas from Act 2 scene 2 lines 107–156 are now obsessing him?
   - Note Angelo's use of '*seeming*' (line 15), the Duke's usage in Act 1 scene 3 line 54, ('*seemers*'), and Isabella's later use of the same word as Angelo (line 149).
   - How does the servant's message (line 18) affect him? Note the sexual connotations of the message and his reply.
   - What is the impact of the extended image related to blood constricting the heart (lines 20–30)?

2 Angelo – as in scene 2 line 48 – insists Claudio must die (lines 33 and 36). What is different about his insistence now? When Isabella asks for time for Claudio to be '*fitted*' for death (lines 39–41), why does Angelo not say that he has arranged a confessor for him (Act 2 scene 1 lines 35–36)?

3 From lines 30 to 147, Angelo and Isabella argue brilliantly. Yet each has a different mind set. Only the audience knows both sides. Read this section carefully. How does Angelo become more 'gross'? Why doesn't Isabella understand him until line 148? On what matter do they seem to agree? What opening does she give him so that he catches her out in lines 114–116? How does her way of asking pardon (lines 117–120) lead directly to his declaration of '*love*' (line 140)? What is the implication of 'love'? (Note how Isabella picks up on the word.) Relate '*Plainly conceive*' to lines 6–7.

4 From lines 150 to 169 each resorts to blackmail. Who has the greater power? What aspects of Angelo's speech (lines 153–169) show that he has succumbed to the full flow of his passions? Contrast this with his earlier soliloquies. Why is he so confident now? What is the impact of his last line in this scene?

5 Isabella (lines 170–176) attacks the corruptions of power. What are they? Compare her use of '*will*' (line 174) with Angelo's (line 163).

6 Between line 176 and the end of the scene Isabella makes a decision. From the evidence of these lines, with how much ease or difficulty does she do so?

## Imagery

Look for images of:
- clothing, uniforms (scene 2)
- farming (scenes 1, 2)
- the natural world (scene 2)
- money, coinage, precious metals (scene 2)
- sickness, medicine (scenes 2, 3)
- physical control and punishment of those who transgress (scene 4).

## Key scenes

### Scenes 2 and 4

These are separate scenes and it is necessary that they are, yet they are also a self-contained drama.

1  They develop a debate about power, justice, law, judgement, punishment and mercy.
   - Consider the characters and situation at the start and finish. What has happened to the debate?
   - There is much biblical and Christian reference. How much can you find? What is its effect on the debate?
2  The scenes take place as a result of Claudio's request to Lucio in Act 1 scene 2 lines 167–176.
   - Are Claudio's hopes in Isabella borne out in the two scenes?
3  The scenes reveal Angelo in action as judge. Remember his debate with Escalus in Act 2 scene 1 lines 1–31.
   - How does Angelo compare with Escalus as a judge?
4  They develop a dramatic conflict between Angelo and Isabella.
   - In what ways are they similar characters? How does this make for effective drama?
   - Do the following in pairs: one play Angelo's accuser and take the line that he is an evil, arrogant hypocrite; the other defend Angelo as a man deserving some sympathy. Draw your evidence from these two scenes.
5  They dramatise a process on which Claudio's life depends.
   - At this point in the play, Shakespeare removes Angelo, the judge, from the play not to reappear until the end. Why do you think he might have decided to do this?
6  They set up the dramatic focus for the rest of the play.
   - How will the events of these scenes affect Claudio; Isabella; the Duke?

## Writing

1 What serious and comic perspectives on judgement and law
enforcement are offered in Act 2? Think about these examples:
   • Angelo, Escalus and Elbow in scene 1
   • Angelo and the Provost in scene 2
   • Angelo in scene 4.
2 In what way do scenes 2 and 4 form a drama in their own right?
Imagine that you have been asked to produce a television programme
about *Measure for Measure*, in which you are to present these two
scenes as a short self-contained play. Describe how you might do this.
You should include answers to some or all of these questions:
   • How would you introduce the play to your audience?
   • How would you edit each scene to make it suitable for television?
   • Would you need to add any additional material:
     – during each scene?
     – between the two scenes?
     – after the second scene?
   If so, what?
3 Does Angelo know himself any better by the end of Act 2?
4 How do these scenes provide a crux for what has come before and
what is to follow? ('Crux: the chief problem; the central or decisive
point' *Oxford English Dictionary*)

The Duke, disguised as a friar, sets about persuading Claudio that he should not hope for pardon from Angelo: he should assume he is going to die, and see this as better than life with all its suffering and disappointment.

2 **medicine**: comfort
5 **Be absolute for death**: accept that you are certainly going to die
6 **Reason**: argue
8 **would**: would wish to
9 **Servile to all the skyey influences**: obedient to and at the mercy of all the powers of the universe
10 **habitation**: place
  **keep'st**: live
11 **Merely...fool**: one whose only role is to entertain and obey Death
12 **thou labour'st...shun**: you toil to escape by running away
13 **still**: always
14–15 **For all...baseness**: because everything that makes your life comfortable and enjoyable is born from degradation
16–17 **soft and tender...worm**: the gentle tongue of a lowly snake, i.e. a snake which is not dangerous at all
17 **Thy best...sleep**: your best experience of resting is to sleep
18 **And that**: i.e. sleep
19 **no more**: no different from sleep
  **Thou art not thyself**: you have no one single identity
20–21 **For thou...dust**: you are made up of thousands of atoms that come from dust
23 **certain**: emotionally secure
24 **complexion**: mood
25 **After the moon**: according to the position of the moon
26 **ingots**: lumps of precious metal

> • *The scene begins as if in mid-conversation. What do you think Claudio has been saying and what was his mood?*

# Act three

## Scene  1

*The prison*
*Enter* DUKE *disguised and* PROVOST *with* CLAUDIO

DUKE     So then you hope of pardon from Lord Angelo?

CLAUDIO   The miserable have no other medicine
But only hope:
I have hope to live, and am prepared to die.

DUKE     Be absolute for death: either death or life     5
Shall thereby be a sweeter. Reason thus with life:
If I do lose thee, I do lose a thing
That none but fools would keep. A breath thou art,
Servile to all the skyey influences
That dost this habitation where thou keep'st     10
Hourly afflict. Merely, thou art Death's fool;
For him thou labour'st by the flight to shun,
And yet run'st toward him still. Thou art not noble;
For all th'accommodations that thou bear'st
Are nursed by baseness. Thou'rt by no means
    valiant;     15
For thou dost fear the soft and tender fork
Of a poor worm. Thy best of rest is sleep;
And that thou oft provok'st, yet grossly fear'st
Thy death, which is no more. Thou art not thyself;
For thou exists on many a thousand grains     20
That issue out of dust. Happy thou art not;
For what thou hast not, still thou striv'st to get,
For what thou hast, forget'st. Thou art not certain;
For thy complexion shifts to strange effects
After the moon. If thou art rich, thou'rt poor;     25
For, like an ass whose back with ingots bows,

The Duke/friar concludes that life contains thousands of little deaths; death itself levels all. Claudio appears to accept his advice. Isabella arrives, and the Duke arranges with the Provost to overhear their conversation. Claudio asks Isabella if there is any comfort: is he really reconciled to death?

**29 bowels**: children
**30 mere effusion...loins**: the only offspring of your own body
**31 serpigo**: a spreading skin disease
    **rheum**: a cold
**33 after-dinner's**: afternoon (after the main meal of the day which was then taken in the middle of the day)
**35 Becomes as aged**: grows too old
    **beg the alms**: requires support from
**36 palsied eld**: diseased old people
**37 heat, affection, limb**: passion, love, fit body
**38–39 What's yet...life?**: What is there in this experience which deserves the name of life?
**40 moe thousand**: a thousand more
**40–41 yet death...even**: yet we fear death which actually evens out all these problems
**42 sue**: beg
**44 Peace.....company**: Isabella (outside the prison door) is assuring the Provost (within) that she has peaceful and friendly intentions
**45 the wish deserves a welcome**: the Provost replies that Isabella's wish means that she deserves a welcome

- *What is the dramatic impact of Isabella calling from 'within' just as Claudio has said 'Let it come on? (line 43)?*
- *How does the Provost affect the mood of these moments?*

Thou bear'st thy heavy riches but a journey,
And Death unloads thee. Friends hast thou none;
For thine own bowels which do call thee sire,
The mere effusion of thy proper loins,                    30
Do curse the gout, serpigo, and the rheum
For ending thee no sooner. Thou hast nor youth,
        nor age,
But as it were an after-dinner's sleep
Dreaming on both; for all thy blessed youth
Becomes as aged, and doth beg the alms          35
Of palsied eld: and when thou art old and rich,
Thou hast neither heat, affection, limb, nor beauty
To make thy riches pleasant. What's yet in this
That bears the name of life? Yet in this life
Lie hid moe thousand deaths; yet death we fear    40
That makes these odds all even.

CLAUDIO                                    I humbly thank
        you.
To sue to live, I find I seek to die,
And seeking death, find life. Let it come on.

ISABELLA    [*Within*] What hoa! Peace here; grace and good
        company!

PROVOST    Who's there? Come in; the wish deserves a
        welcome.                                      45

DUKE    Dear sir, ere long I'll visit you again.

CLAUDIO    Most holy sir, I thank you.

*Enter* ISABELLA

ISABELLA    My business is a word or two with Claudio.

PROVOST    And very welcome. Look, signior, here's your sister.

DUKE    Provost, a word with you.                     50

PROVOST    As many as you please.

DUKE    Bring me to hear them speak, where I may be
        concealed.                    [DUKE *and* PROVOST *retire*

CLAUDIO    Now, sister, what's the comfort?

Isabella says that Angelo still intends Claudio to die, then reveals his impossible offer. Without explaining, she says accepting would bring utter damnation. She begins to play down the terror of death.

**56 having affairs to heaven**: since he communicates with heaven
**58 leiger**: ambassador
**59 your best appointment make**: make yourself ready
**60 set on**: go
**66 fetter you till death**: bind you in everlasting imprisonment
**Perpetual durance**: everlasting imprisonment
**68 world's vastidity**: the whole wide world
**69 To a determined scope**: to a defined limit in your soul
**71 Would bark...bear**: would strip the bark of honour from your family tree
**74 a feverous...entertain**: enjoy a corrupted life
**75–76 And six...honour**: and value six or seven years of life more than eternal honour
**77 The sense...apprehension**: the feeling of death is most painful in anticipating it
**79 corporal sufferance**: bodily pain
**pang**: spasm of pain
**80 Why give...shame?**: Why do you have this dishonourable suspicion about me?

- *Note that all Claudio's speeches on this page are the second halves of verse lines begun by Isabella. What do you think Shakepeare is telling the actors about how to play the characters at this point? (The device continues on the next page.)*

| | |
|---|---|
| ISABELLA | Why, |
| | As all comforts are: most good, most good |
| |     indeed.      55 |
| | Lord Angelo, having affairs to heaven, |
| | Intends you for his swift ambassador, |
| | Where you shall be an everlasting leiger. |
| | Therefore your best appointment make with speed; |
| | Tomorrow you set on. |
| CLAUDIO | Is there no remedy?    60 |
| ISABELLA | None, but such remedy as, to save a head, |
| | To cleave a heart in twain. |
| CLAUDIO | But is there any? |
| ISABELLA | Yes, brother, you may live; |
| | There is a devilish mercy in the judge, |
| | If you'll implore it, that will free your life,    65 |
| | But fetter you till death. |
| CLAUDIO | Perpetual durance? |
| ISABELLA | Ay, just, perpetual durance; a restraint, |
| | Though all the world's vastidity you had, |
| | To a determined scope. |
| CLAUDIO | But in what nature? |
| ISABELLA | In such a one as, you consenting to't,    70 |
| | Would bark your honour from that trunk you bear, |
| | And leave you naked. |
| CLAUDIO | Let me know the point. |
| ISABELLA | O, I do fear thee, Claudio, and I quake |
| | Lest thou a feverous life shouldst entertain, |
| | And six or seven winters more respect    75 |
| | Than a perpetual honour. Dar'st thou die? |
| | The sense of death is most in apprehension; |
| | And the poor beetle that we tread upon |
| | In corporal sufferance finds a pang as great |
| | As when a giant dies. |
| CLAUDIO | Why give you me this |
| |     shame?    80 |

Claudio says he's not afraid to die. Isabella praises his courage and reveals Angelo's demand. Claudio rejects it instantly, horrified. He wonders what sort of person Angelo can be.

**81 resolution**: determination and courage

**83 encounter darkness**: meet death

**88 base appliances**: dishonourable strategies
**outward-sainted**: seeming like a saint

**89 settled visage**: unwavering expression

**90–91 Nips...fowl**: bites the heads off young people and drives their follies into the water as a falcon does a fowl

**90 enew**: what a bird of prey does when it drives a fowl into water

**92 His filth within being cast**: if his inner corruption were diagnosed

**93 precise**: strict, scrupulous (*OED*)

**94 livery of hell**: devil's uniform

**95 invest**: dress

**96 guards**: trimmings

**99 rank offence**: foul sin (of mine)

**100 So to offend him still**: you could carry on sinning as before

**105 frankly**: freely

**107 affections**: passions

**108 bite...nose**: treat the law with ridicule

**109 force**: enforce

- *Look at the patterns of Claudio's speeches on this page. What does it tell us about his state of mind?*
- *What does Claudio's image of biting the law by the nose (line 108) echo earlier in the play?*

|          | Think you I can a resolution fetch |
|          | From flowery tenderness? If I must die, |
|          | I will encounter darkness as a bride |
|          | And hug it in mine arms. |
| ISABELLA | There spake my brother: there my father's grave    85 |
|          | Did utter forth a voice. Yes, thou must die. |
|          | Thou art too noble to conserve a life |
|          | In base appliances. This outward-sainted deputy, |
|          | Whose settled visage and deliberate word |
|          | Nips youth i'th'head and follies doth enew    90 |
|          | As falcon doth the fowl, is yet a devil: |
|          | His filth within being cast, he would appear |
|          | A pond as deep as hell. |
| CLAUDIO  |                                   The precise Angelo! |
| ISABELLA | O, 'tis the cunning livery of hell |
|          | The damnedst body to invest and cover    95 |
|          | In precise guards! Dost thou think, Claudio, |
|          | If I would yield him my virginity |
|          | Thou mightst be freed? |
| CLAUDIO  |                                   O heavens, it cannot be! |
| ISABELLA | Yes, he would give't thee, from this rank offence, |
|          | So to offend him still. This night's the time    100 |
|          | That I should do what I abhor to name; |
|          | Or else thou diest tomorrow. |
| CLAUDIO  |                                   Thou shalt not do't. |
| ISABELLA | O, were it but my life, |
|          | I'd throw it down for your deliverance |
|          | As frankly as a pin. |
| CLAUDIO  |                                   Thanks, dear Isabel.    105 |
| ISABELLA | Be ready, Claudio, for your death tomorrow. |
| CLAUDIO  | Yes. – Has he affections in him, |
|          | That thus can make him bite the law by th'nose |
|          | When he would force it? – Sure, it is no sin; |
|          | Or of the deadly seven it is the least.    110 |
| ISABELLA | Which is the least? |

Claudio wonders why fornication is so deadly a sin. He fears death; Isabella compares it with living a shamed life. Claudio describes a vision of hell, and pleads to Isabella to let him live. She rejects him as a beast and accuses him of suggesting a kind of incest.

**112 damnable**: a sin that brings damnation

**113 momentary trick**: pleasure of the moment

**114 perdurably fined**: condemned for ever

**118 cold obstruction**: frozen rigidity of death

**119–120 This sensible...clod**: the warmth, feeling and movement of life turned into a lump of clay

**120–122 and the delighted...ice**: and to plunge a joyful spirit in floods of fire, or to exist in a piercingly cold region of thickly ridged ice (a powerful vision of the pains of hell and purgatory)

**123 viewless**: invisible

**125 pendent**: that hangs in space

**126–127 that lawless...howling**: that fantasists and poets imagine crying in anguish

**129 penury**: poverty

**130 Can...nature**: can impose on life

**134 Nature dispenses...far**: nature allows the deed to be excused so far

**137 made a man**: made a man again

**140 Heaven...fair**: I pray that my mother was not unfaithful to my father

**141 such a warped slip of wilderness**: a slip is a cutting taken from a plant in order to grow a new plant. Normally this reproduces exactly the qualities of the original plant, but here Isabella sees her brother as so wildly different from their parents that she asks herself whether the only explanation can be that her mother was unfaithful to her father

> • *What do you think of Isabella's idea that Claudio would be committing a kind of incest if he lives through her lost of chastity (lines 138–139)? What does this suggest about Isabella's state of mind?*

| | |
|---|---|
| CLAUDIO | If it were damnable, he being so wise, |
| | Why would he for the momentary trick |
| | Be perdurably fined? – O Isabel! |
| ISABELLA | What says my brother? |
| CLAUDIO | Death is a fearful thing. 115 |
| ISABELLA | And shamed life a hateful. |
| CLAUDIO | Ay, but to die, and go we know not where; |
| | To lie in cold obstruction, and to rot; |
| | This sensible warm motion to become |
| | A kneaded clod; and the delighted spirit 120 |
| | To bath in fiery floods, or to reside |
| | In thrilling region of thick-ribbed ice; |
| | To be imprisoned in the viewless winds |
| | And blown with restless violence round about |
| | The pendent world: or to be worse than worst 125 |
| | Of those that lawless and incertain thought |
| | Imagine howling, – 'tis too horrible. |
| | The weariest and most loathed worldly life |
| | That age, ache, penury and imprisonment |
| | Can lay on nature, is a paradise 130 |
| | To what we fear of death. |
| ISABELLA | Alas, alas! |
| CLAUDIO | Sweet sister, let me live. |
| | What sin you do to save a brother's life, |
| | Nature dispenses with the deed so far |
| | That it becomes a virtue. |
| ISABELLA | O, you beast! 135 |
| | O faithless coward! O dishonest wretch! |
| | Wilt thou be made a man out of my vice? |
| | Is't not a kind of incest, to take life |
| | From thine own sister's shame? What should I |
| | think? |
| | Heaven shield my mother played my father fair: 140 |
| | For such a warped slip of wilderness |
| | Ne'er issued from his blood. Take my defiance, |

Isabella tells Claudio she will pray for him, but he must die; she makes to leave. The Duke/friar tells her to wait while he tells Claudio that Angelo was only testing Isabella and that she did not yield. He repeats that Claudio should prepare for death. Claudio retires.

**143 bending down**: kneeling to pray

**144 it should proceed**: I would do it

**148 not accidental, but a trade**: is not a chance occurrence, but a regular business

**149 Mercy...bawd**: being merciful to you would simply give you the chance to carry on fornicating

**151 Vouchsafe**: allow

**153 Might...leisure**: if you would give me some of your time

**154–155 the satisfaction...benefit**: what I want from you is to your advantage

**156 no superfluous leisure**: no time to spare

**161–162 made an assay of her virtue**: has tested her moral strength

**162–163 to practise...natures**: to put into practice his law which aims at controlling people's behaviour

**167–168 Do not satisfy...fallible**: do not allow your determination to be softened by false hopes

> • *Compare Isabella's speech (lines 156–158) with Claudio's (lines 170–171). They have both been involved in a highly charged scene. How are they reacting?*

Die, perish! Might but my bending down
Reprieve thee from thy fate, it should proceed.
I'll pray a thousand prayers for thy death;     145
No word to save thee.

CLAUDIO                                    Nay hear me, Isabel.

ISABELLA    O fie, fie, fie!
Thy sin's not accidental, but a trade;
Mercy to thee would prove itself a bawd;
'Tis best that thou diest quickly.           [*Going*

CLAUDIO                              O hear me,
            Isabella.                                  150

DUKE        [*Advancing*] Vouchsafe a word, young sister, but
            one word.

ISABELLA    What is your will?

DUKE        Might you dispense with your leisure, I would by
            and by have some speech with you: the satisfaction
            I would require is likewise your own benefit.     155

ISABELLA    I have no superfluous leisure; my stay must be
            stolen out of other affairs: but I will attend you a
            while.                          [*Waits behind*

DUKE        Son, I have overheard what hath passed between
            you and your sister. Angelo had never the      160
            purpose to corrupt her; only he hath made an assay
            of her virtue, to practise his judgement with the
            disposition of natures. She, having the truth of
            honour in her, hath made him that gracious denial
            which he is most glad to receive. I am confessor  165
            to Angelo, and I know this to be true; therefore
            prepare yourself to death. Do not satisfy your
            resolution with hopes that are fallible; tomorrow
            you must die; go to your knees, and make ready.

CLAUDIO    Let me ask my sister pardon; I am so out of    170
            love with life that I will sue to be rid of it.

DUKE        Hold you there: farewell. – [CLAUDIO *retires*]
            Provost, a word with you.

The Duke/friar tells Isabella that he knows all. She repeats that Claudio must die, reflects on the absent Duke's judgement of Angelo, and promises to tell him all on his return. The Duke says he has a plan which will benefit all. Isabella is keen to hear it.

**176–177  with my habit**: along with my friar's clothing

**180–181  The goodness...goodness**: the goodness that is only as superficial as good looks means that beauty lacks real moral quality

**181–183  but grace...fair**: but God-given goodness which is the 'soul' of your looks ensures that your body will always remain good and beautiful

**184 fortune**: chance

**185 frailty**: human weakness

**188 resolve**: give my answer

**192  I will open my lips in vain, or**: either I will open my lips in vain, or

**193 discover his government**: reveal how he has acted in power

**194 much amiss**: very wide of the mark

**203 peradventure**: by chance

- *Are lines 179–183 the first hint of the Duke's attraction to Isabella? If so, is she aware of this? What are the implications?*
- *What is the effect of the irony in lines 190–191?*

PROVOST  [*Advancing*] What's your will, father?

DUKE  That, now you are come, you will be gone. Leave 175
me a while with the maid; my mind promises with
my habit no loss shall touch her by my company.

PROVOST  In good time.    [*Exit with* CLAUDIO. ISABELLA *comes*
*forward*

DUKE  The hand that hath made you fair hath made you
good. The goodness that is cheap in beauty        180
makes beauty brief in goodness; but grace, being the
soul of your complexion, shall keep the body of it
ever fair. The assault that Angelo hath made to you,
fortune hath conveyed to my understanding; and,
but that frailty hath examples for his falling, I      185
should wonder at Angelo. How will you do to
content this substitute, and to save your brother?

ISABELLA  I am now going to resolve him. I had rather my
brother die by the law, than my son should be
unlawfully born. But O, how much is the good    190
Duke deceived in Angelo! If ever he return, and I
can speak to him, I will open my lips in vain, or
discover his government.

DUKE  That shall not be much amiss. Yet, as the matter
now stands, he will avoid your accusation – he      195
made trial of you only. Therefore fasten your ear on
my advisings, to the love I have in doing good; a
remedy presents itself. I do make myself believe
that you may most uprighteously do a poor
wronged lady a merited benefit; redeem your      200
brother from the angry law; do no stain to your
own gracious person; and much please the absent
Duke, if peradventure he shall ever return to have
hearing of this business.

ISABELLA  Let me hear you speak farther. I have spirit to    205
do anything that appears not foul in the truth of my
spirit.

The Duke/friar tells Isabella about Angelo's past engagement to Mariana and his rejection of her because of her loss of dowry – she still pines for him. Having aroused Isabella's anger against Angelo further, and her sympathy for Mariana, the Duke says he can help them both.

**210 miscarried**: was wrecked and drowned

**213–214 was affianced...appointed**: engaged and the wedding arranged

**215–216 limit of the solemnity**: end of the time leading up to the ceremony

**221 portion and sinew**: the sinewy portion, i.e. the strongest part – an example of *hendiadys* (see GLOSSARY page 272)

**223 combinate**: bound, committed

**226 swallowed**: took back his vows unspoken

**227 pretending...dishonour**: pretending to reveal she was dishonourable

 **in few**: in short

**228–229 bestowed...his sake**: left her to her tears which she still sheds for him

**229 a marble to**: hardened against

**231–232 What a merit...world!**: it would be good if death were to relieve this lady of the cares of this world

**233–234 But...avail?**: how can she gain any advantage from this situation

**235 rupture**: broken promise

**239–240 hath yet in her...affection**: still feels the love she originally felt

**242 like...current**: like a blockage in a stream

> • *The Duke explains Mariana's current situation at some length. Why is this necessary from a dramatic point of view?*

| | |
|---|---|
| DUKE | Virtue is bold, and goodness never fearful. Have you not heard speak of Mariana, the sister of Frederick, the great soldier who miscarried at sea?    210 |
| ISABELLA | I have heard of the lady, and good words went with her name. |
| DUKE | She should this Angelo have married: was affianced to her oath, and the nuptial appointed. Between which time of the contract and limit    215 of the solemnity, her brother Frederick was wracked at sea, having in that perished vessel the dowry of his sister. But mark how heavily this befell to the poor gentlewoman. There she lost a noble and renowned brother, in his love toward her ever most kind    220 and natural; with him, the portion and sinew of her fortune, her marriage dowry; with both, her combinate husband, this well-seeming Angelo. |
| ISABELLA | Can this be so? Did Angelo so leave her? |
| DUKE | Left her in her tears, and dried not one of them    225 with his comfort: swallowed his vows whole, pretending in her discoveries of dishonour: in few, bestowed her on her own lamentation, which she yet wears for his sake; and he, a marble to her tears, is washed with them, but relents not.    230 |
| ISABELLA | What a merit were it in death to take this poor maid from the world! What corruption in this life, that it will let this man live! But how out of this can she avail? |
| DUKE | It is a rupture that you may easily heal: and the    235 cure of it not only saves your brother, but keeps you from dishonour in doing it. |
| ISABELLA | Show me how, good father. |
| DUKE | This forenamed maid hath yet in her the continuance of her first affection. His unjust    240 unkindness, that in all reason should have quenched her love, hath, like an impediment in the current, |

The Duke/friar tells Isabella to agree to Angelo's plan, but to specify a brief assignation in a dark place. The Duke will arrange for Mariana to go in her place; when all is revealed, Angelo will be exposed. Isabella is pleased with the plan and agrees to meet the Duke at Mariana's house.

**246 Only…advantage**: only make this one condition for yourself

**249 answer to convenience**: be suitable for you

**249–250 in course**: as a matter of course

**251 stead…appointment**: take your place in this assignation

**252–253 If the encounter…recompense**: if this affair becomes known in the future, it may force him to take her back

**256 scaled**: weighed in the balance of justice and condemned
   **The maid will I frame**: I will explain everything to this woman

**258–259 the doubleness…reproof**: the fact that both parties benefit means that the trickery cannot be condemned as a sin

**261 The image of it**: imagining it

**263 your holding up**: you playing your part strongly

**266–267 moated grange**: country house surrounded by a moat

**268 dispatch**: deal quickly with

> • *Mariana is to be asked to have sex with Angelo to save Isabella from having to do the same. Look at Isabella's words in lines 261–262 and consider what her choice of words tells us.*

made it more violent and unruly. Go you to
Angelo; answer his requiring with a plausible
obedience; agree with his demands to the point. 245
Only refer yourself to this advantage: first, that your
stay with him may not be long; that the place may
have all shadow and silence in it; and the time
answer to convenience. This being granted in
course, and now follows all. We shall advise this   250
wronged maid to stead up your appointment, go in
your place. If the encounter acknowledge itself
hereafter, it may compel him to her recompense;
and hear, by this is your brother saved, your honour
untainted, the poor Mariana advantaged, and      255
the corrupt deputy scaled. The maid will I frame,
and make fit for his attempt. If you think well to
carry this as you may, the doubleness of the benefit
defends the deceit from reproof. What think you of
it?                                                 260

ISABELLA    The image of it gives me content already, and I
trust it will grow to a most prosperous perfection.

DUKE    It lies much in your holding up. Haste you speedily
to Angelo; if for this night he entreat you to his
bed, give him promise of satisfaction. I will        265
presently to Saint Luke's; there at the moated
grange resides this dejected Mariana; at that place
call upon me; and dispatch with Angelo, that it may
be quickly.

ISABELLA    I thank you for this comfort. Fare you well,       270
good father.                                   [*Exit*

Elbow, the constable, arrives at the prison with Pompey who is under arrest, apparently suspected of being a thief. The Duke/friar preaches to Pompey that he lives off corruption and should mend his ways. He encourages Elbow to take Pompey into the prison.

1–2 **if there be...needs**: if there is no way of stopping you

3–4 **drink...bastard**: turning into mixed-race bastards (with a pun on 'bastard' meaning a kind of sweet wine)

6 **two usuries**: making money on interest from pimping and loans

8 **him**: the usurer

9–10 **furred...facing**: the fur is fox on top of lambskin as well, to show that cunning is more profitable than innocence

11 **Come your way**: follow

16 **pick-lock**: skeleton key or tool designed to open many different locks – for example to a chastity belt

20–21 **Do thou...back**: Just think what it is to fill a mouth or clothe a body

23 **abominable...touches**: foul sexual acts

24 **array**: clothe

25 **thy living...life**: your life is worth living

28–29 **prove...proofs**: justify...justifications

30 **prove his**: turn out to be his, i.e. the devil's

---

- *Though Elbow is only a minor comic character, his opening lines carry great significance. What is it?*
- *Pompey's first words are significant, too. In what way?*
- *How successful has Escalus been in dealing with Elbow and Froth in Act 2 scene 1?*

# Scene  2

*Enter* ELBOW *and* OFFICERS *with* POMPEY

ELBOW  Nay, if there be no remedy for it, but that you will needs buy and sell men and women like beasts, we shall have all the world drink brown and white bastard.

DUKE  O heavens, what stuff is here!   5

POMPEY  'Twas never merry world since, of two usuries, the merriest was put down, and the worser allowed by order of law; a furred gown to keep him warm; and furred with fox on lambskins too, to signify that craft, being richer than innocency, stands for the facing.   10

ELBOW  Come your way, sir. – Bless you, good father friar.

DUKE  And you, good brother father. What offence hath this man made you, sir?

ELBOW  Marry, sir, he hath offended the law; and, sir, we take him to be a thief too, sir: for we have found   15 upon him, sir, a strange pick-lock, which we have sent to the deputy.

DUKE  Fie, sirrah, a bawd, a wicked bawd;
The evil that thou causest to be done,
That is thy means to live. Do thou but think   20
What 'tis to cram a maw or clothe a back
From such a filthy vice. Say to thyself,
From their abominable and beastly touches
I drink, I eat, array myself, and live.
Canst thou believe thy living is a life,   25
So stinkingly depending? Go mend, go mend.

POMPEY  Indeed it does stink in some sort, sir. But yet, sir, I would prove –

DUKE  Nay, if the devil have given thee proofs for sin,
Thou wilt prove his. Take him to prison, officer:   30

The Duke/friar emphasises the need for punishment and reformation. Elbow explains that Pompey has to go before Angelo, and will certainly be hanged for pimping. Lucio arrives and mocks Pompey, though Pompey asks him to stand bail for him as a friend.

**36 he were...errand**: he'd be better off doing anything else

**37–38 That...free**: I wish that we were all free from our faults, as some seem to be, and faults were free from deceitful outward appearances of innocence

**39 His neck...sir**: he will be hanged by the neck with a rope just like the one round your waist

**42–43 at the wheels of Caesar**: a prisoner behind Caesar's chariot

**43 in triumph**: in Caesar's triumph

**43–46 What, is there...clutched**: What! Aren't there any prostitutes available now if we put our hands in our pockets and take out money

**44 Pygmalion's images**: implies prostitutes because of the Classical myth of the sculptor, Pygmalion, whose statues come to life and because, in Shakespeare's time, statues were often painted garishly

**47 tune, matter and method**: this old idea

**48 drowned...rain**: out of fashion

**49 trot**: old hag

**50 trick**: current fashion

**52 morsel**: 'bit of skirt' – attractive woman

**54 Troth**: in fact

**54–57 eaten up all her beef...powdered bawd**: this is a pun on pro-*cures*. Beef was put in a tub with salt to cure it (like bacon). Mistress Overdone, like others who thought they might be suffering from venereal disease, would probably sit in a steaming tub of hot water to attempt to 'sweat it off' and then powder herself to beautify her skin

**58 unshunned**: inevitable

> • *What is the effect of the Duke's rhyming couplet (lines 37–38)?*

|          |                                                                                                                 |
|----------|-----------------------------------------------------------------------------------------------------------------|
|          | Correction and instruction must both work<br>Ere this rude beast will profit.                                    |
| ELBOW    | He must before the deputy, sir; he has given him warning. The deputy cannot abide a whoremaster. If he be a whoremonger and comes before him, 35 he were as good go a mile on his errand. |
| DUKE     | That we were all, as some would seem to be, From our faults, as faults from seeming, free!                        |
| ELBOW    | His neck will come to your waist – a cord, sir.                                                                   |
|          | *Enter* LUCIO                                                                                                    |
| POMPEY   | I spy comfort, I cry bail! Here's a gentleman,        40<br>and a friend of mine.                                 |
| LUCIO    | How now, noble Pompey! What, at the wheels of Caesar? Art thou led in triumph? What, is there none of Pygmalion's images newly made woman to be had now, for putting the hand in the pocket 45 and extracting clutched? What reply, ha? What say'st thou to this tune, matter and method? Is't not drowned i'th'last rain? Ha? What say'st thou, trot? Is the world as it was, man? Which is the way? Is it sad, and few words? Or how? The trick of it? 50 |
| DUKE     | Still thus, and thus: still worse!                                                                                |
| LUCIO    | How doth my dear morsel, thy mistress? Procures she still, ha?                                                    |
| POMPEY   | Troth, sir, she hath eaten up all her beef, and she is herself in the tub.                                  55   |
| LUCIO    | Why, 'tis good: it is the right of it: it must be so. Ever your fresh whore, and your powdered bawd; an unshunned consequence; it must be so. Art going to prison, Pompey? |
| POMPEY   | Yes, faith, sir.                                                                              60                  |
| LUCIO    | Why, 'tis not amiss, Pompey. Farewell: go, say I sent thee thither. – For debt, Pompey, or how?                  |
| POMPEY   | For being a bawd, for being a bawd.                                                                              |

Lucio refuses bail and Pompey is taken away. Lucio turns to the Duke/friar and asks where the Duke is, his absence being a foolish error in the light of Angelo's strictness. The Duke is non-committal.

**66 of antiquity**: from a long time ago
**69 keep the house**: look after the prison (with a pun on 'house', meaning brothel)
**71 wear**: the fashion, i.e. I will not be seen bailing a bawd out of prison
**72–73 if you...more**: pun on mettle/metal – if you don't put up with prison quietly:
   (**a**) it will show you still have spirit (mettle)
   (**b**) you will end up with leg–irons (metal)
**76 paint**: put on a whore's make–up
**82 kennel**: prison
**90 usurp the beggary**: take on the role of beggar
**91 dukes it**: plays the role of duke
**92 puts...to't**: gives sinners a hard time
**94 lenity to lechery**: leniency to fornication
**95 crabbed**: hard-hearted and narrow-minded

> • *Lucio judges Pompey to be a pimp not worth bail and the Duke mad to have gone away. What seems to be Lucio's role here?*
> • *Would there be any dramatic advantage in playing Lucio as knowing who the friar is?*

| | |
|---|---|
| LUCIO | Well, then, imprison him. If imprisonment be the due of a bawd, why, 'tis his right. Bawd is he   65 doubtless, and of antiquity, too: bawd born. Farewell, good Pompey. Commend me to the prison, Pompey; you will turn good husband now, Pompey; you will keep the house. |
| POMPEY | I hope, sir, your good worship will be my bail?   70 |
| LUCIO | No, indeed will I not, Pompey; it is not the wear. I will pray, Pompey, to increase your bondage; if you take it not patiently, why, your mettle is the more! Adieu, trusty Pompey. – Bless you, friar. |
| DUKE | And you.   75 |
| LUCIO | Does Bridget paint still, Pompey? Ha? |
| ELBOW | [*To* POMPEY] Come your ways, sir, come. |
| POMPEY | You will not bail me then, sir? |
| LUCIO | Then, Pompey, nor now. – What news abroad, friar? What news?   80 |
| ELBOW | [*To* POMPEY] Come your ways, sir, come. |
| LUCIO | Go to kennel, Pompey, go.<br>          [*Exeunt* ELBOW *and* OFFICERS *with* POMPEY<br>What news, friar, of the Duke? |
| DUKE | I know none: can you tell me of any? |
| LUCIO | Some say he is with the Emperor of Russia; other   85 some, he is in Rome: but where is he, think you? |
| DUKE | I know not where: but wheresoever, I wish him well. |
| LUCIO | It was a mad, fantastical trick of him to steal from the state and usurp the beggary he was never   90 born to. Lord Angelo dukes it well in his absence: he puts transgression to't. |
| DUKE | He does well in't. |
| LUCIO | A little more lenity to lechery would do no harm in him. Something too crabbed that way, friar.   95 |

Lucio says that Angelo must be odd not to see lust as normal, and points out that the Duke saw sex as sport. When the Duke/friar objects, Lucio adds that he was a close companion of the Duke and knew him also as a drinker. He hints that he knows why the Duke has gone away.

**96 general**: widespread
**97 is of a great kindred**: has a lot of people involved in it
**98 extirp it quite**: root it out, destroy it completely
**101 after...creation**: by normal human means
**105 stockfishes**: cod or haddock that have been slit open, gutted, and dried to preserve them
**107–108 a motion ungenerative**: moves like a puppet – in other words he can't have sex. (Some editions have 'generative' and argue that what Lucio means is that even though he has sexual organs he still behaves like a puppet)
**108 infallible**: absolutely certain
**109 pleasant**: amusing
**110–111 for the rebellion of a codpiece**: as punishment for promiscuity
**115–116 He had...service**: he knew about fornication; he knew the reality of prostitution
**122 your...fifty**: an old woman begging
**123 use**: habit
**clack-dish**: collection plate
**124 crotchets**: human failings
**127 inward**: intimate friend

---

- *Look at lines 118–119, then back at the start of Act 1 scene 3. Is the Duke lying here?*
- *Generally, what are the effects if the ironies of this scenario?*
- *Why does Lucio claim to be an 'inward' of the Duke (line 127)?*

| | |
|---|---|
| DUKE | It is too general a vice, and severity must cure it. |
| LUCIO | Yes, in good sooth, the vice is of a great kindred; it is well allied; but it is impossible to extirp it quite, friar, till eating and drinking be put down. – They say this Angelo was not made by man and     100 woman, after this downright way of creation: is it true, think you? |
| DUKE | How should he be made, then? |
| LUCIO | Some report, a sea-maid spawned him. Some, that he was begot between two stockfishes. But it is   105 certain that when he makes water, his urine is congealed ice; that I know to be true. And he is a motion ungenerative; that's infallible. |
| DUKE | You are pleasant, sir, and speak apace. |
| LUCIO | Why, what a ruthless thing is this in him, for the  110 rebellion of a codpiece to take away the life of a man! Would the Duke that is absent have done this? Ere he would have hanged a man for the getting a hundred bastards, he would have paid for the nursing a thousand. He had some     115 feeling of the sport; he knew the service; and that instructed him to mercy. |
| DUKE | I have never heard the absent Duke much detected for women; he was not inclined that way. |
| LUCIO | O sir, you are deceived.     120 |
| DUKE | 'Tis not possible. |
| LUCIO | Who, not the Duke? Yes, your beggar of fifty; and his use was to put a ducat in her clack-dish; the Duke had crotchets in him. He would be drunk too, that let me inform you.     125 |
| DUKE | You do him wrong, surely. |
| LUCIO | Sir, I was an inward of his. A shy fellow was the Duke; and I believe I know the cause of his withdrawing. |
| DUKE | What, I prithee, might be the cause?     130 |

Lucio reveals no more, but claims that people are mistaken to think the Duke wise. The Duke/friar argues that the Duke should be judged by his actions, not rumour, and that Lucio does not sound like a friend. He challenges Lucio to prove himself if the Duke returns.

**133 the greater file...subject**: the majority of the people
**136 unweighing**: lacking judgement
**138 helmed**: directed
**139 upon a warranted need**: in a situation of need
**140 proclamation**: reputation
    **testimonied**: called to judgement
**141 bringings-forth**: actions
**160 unhurtful an opposite**: harmless opponent
**161 forswear this**: swear you did not say this

> • *'Thou art deceived in me' says Lucio in line 163.*
> *Does he know that the friar is the Duke?*

| | |
|---|---|
| LUCIO | No, pardon: 'tis a secret must be locked within the teeth and the lips. But this I can let you understand: the greater file of the subject held the Duke to be wise. |
| DUKE | Wise? Why, no question but he was.                                    135 |
| LUCIO | A very superficial, ignorant, unweighing fellow – |
| DUKE | Either this is envy in you, folly, or mistaking. The very stream of his life, and the business he hath helmed, must upon a warranted need give him a better proclamation. Let him be but testimonied in          140 his own bringings-forth, and he shall appear to the envious a scholar, a statesman, and a soldier. Therefore you speak unskilfully: or, if your knowledge be more, it is much darkened in your malice. |
| LUCIO | Sir, I know him and I love him.                                    145 |
| DUKE | Love talks with better knowledge, and knowledge with dearer love. |
| LUCIO | Come, sir, I know what I know. |
| DUKE | I can hardly believe that, since you know not what you speak. But if ever the Duke return –          150 as our prayers are he may – let me desire you to make your answer before him. If it be honest you have spoke, you have courage to maintain it; I am bound to call upon you, and I pray you your name. |
| LUCIO | Sir, my name is Lucio, well known to the Duke. 155 |
| DUKE | He shall know you better, sir, if I may live to report you. |
| LUCIO | I fear you not. |
| DUKE | O, you hope the Duke will return no more; or you imagine me too unhurtful an opposite. But          160 indeed, I can do you little harm. You'll forswear this again? |
| LUCIO | I'll be hanged first. Thou art deceived in me, friar. But no more of this. – Canst thou tell if Claudio die tomorrow, or no?                                    165 |

Lucio tells the Duke/friar about Claudio's situation, repeating his views of Angelo and the Duke. He goes, and the Duke ponders the destructive power of rumour. Mistress Overdone is brought before Escalus and condemned, despite protesting that Lucio has framed her.

167 **For filling...tun-dish**: having a poke (tun-dish: funnel)
169 **ungenitured**: sterile, sexless
170 **continency**: sexual inhibition
171–172 **The Duke...answered**: the duke would ensure that furtive acts would be paid for in secret
175 **untrussing**: stripping (for sex)
177 **eat mutton on Fridays**: i.e. disobey the church's law
178 **mouth with**: kiss
182 **censure 'scape**: escape criticism or gossip
**Back-wounding calumny**: salacious stories told behind one's back
184 **tie the gall up**: dam up the poison
189 **admonition**: warning, caution
**forfeit**: guilty
194–195 **one...me**: Lucio has informed on me
197–198 **Philip and Jacob**: religious festival on May 1st

- *Is Escalus being consistent (lines 189–191) with his earlier judgement in Act 2 scene 1?*
- *What reasons are there for bringing Mistress Overdone into the scene at this point?*

DUKE          Why should he die, sir?

LUCIO         Why? For filling a bottle with a tun-dish. I would
              the Duke we talk of were returned again: this
              ungenitured agent will unpeople the province with
              continency. Sparrows must not build in his         170
              house-eaves, because they are lecherous. – The
              Duke yet would have dark deeds darkly answered:
              he would never bring them to light: would he were
              returned! Marry, this Claudio is condemned for
              untrussing. – Farewell, good friar, I prithee       175
              pray for me. The Duke, I say to thee again, would
              eat mutton on Fridays. He's not past it; yet, and I
              say to thee, he would mouth with a beggar though
              she smelt brown bread and garlic, say that I said so.
              Farewell.                                           180

                                                          [*Exit*

DUKE          No might nor greatness in mortality
              Can censure 'scape. Back-wounding calumny
              The whitest virtue strikes. What king so strong
              Can tie the gall up in the slanderous tongue?
              But who comes here?                                185

              *Enter severally* ESCALUS, PROVOST, *and* OFFICERS
              *with* MISTRESS OVERDONE

ESCALUS       Go, away with her to prison.

M. OVERDONE   Good my lord, be good to me. Your honour is
              accounted a merciful man. Good my lord.

ESCALUS       Double and treble admonition, and still forfeit in
              the same kind! This would make mercy swear        190
              and play the tyrant.

PROVOST       A bawd of eleven years' continuance, may it please
              your honour.

M. OVERDONE   My lord, this is one Lucio's information against
              me, Mistress Kate Keep-down was with child by     195
              him in the Duke's time, he promised her marriage.
              His child is a year and a quarter old come Philip

Escalus sends for Lucio and confirms Claudio's sentence.
The Provost tells Escalus that the Duke/friar has advised
Claudio on facing death. The Duke says he is not Viennese
and is unimpressed by the state of Vienna. He asks Escalus
for his opinion of the Duke. Escalus replies that he strove for
self-knowledge and the happiness of others.

**199 goes about to abuse me**: sets about abusing me
**200 of much license**: of very loose behaviour
**204–205 Let him...preparation**: let him have priests in
   attendance and all the other preparation that should be
   provided by charity
**206 wrought by my pity**: judged with my mercy
**209 entertainment**: readiness
**213 my chance**: it happens that; it's my present fate that
**215 the See**: the pope's Holy See in Rome
**219 the dissolution of it**: only the death of the sufferer will
   remedy it
**219–220 Novelty...request**: people only want novelty
**220–222 and it is...undertaking**: the text here is unclear.
   Possibly what is meant is 'and it is as dangerous to be
   experienced in any activity as it is virtuous to be trustworthy
   in any position of responsibility'
**223 societies secure**: businesses reliable
**223–224 but...accurst**: but sufficient carelessness to make
   businesses liable to ruin
**225 riddle**: i.e. the opposite meanings of 'secure' and 'security'
**225–226 This news...news**: this is an old story, yet it's retold
   afresh every day
**227 disposition**: character
**228 strifes**: efforts
**231–233 than merry...rejoice**: than joyful for anything which
   might be likely to bring pleasure to himself

> • *Is Escalus' question in line 217 merely polite
> conversation or more significant? What comments does
> the Duke make on 'the world' in his reply (lines
> 218–227)? Are they 'polite' or more significant?*

|           | and Jacob. I have kept it myself; and see how he goes about to abuse me. |
|-----------|------|
| ESCALUS   | That fellow is a fellow of much license. Let him 200 be called before us. Away with her to prison. – Go to, no more words.<br><br>[*Exeunt* OFFICERS *with* MISTRESS OVERDONE<br>Provost, my brother Angelo will not be altered; Claudio must die tomorrow. Let him be furnished with divines, and have all charitable preparation. 205 If my brother wrought by my pity, it should not be so with him. |
| PROVOST   | So please you, this friar hath been with him, and advised him for th'entertainment of death. |
| ESCALUS   | Good even, good father.                              210 |
| DUKE      | Bliss and goodness on you! |
| ESCALUS   | Of whence are you? |
| DUKE      | Not of this country, though my chance is now To use it for my time. I am a brother Of gracious order, late come from the See 215 In special business from his Holiness. |
| ESCALUS   | What news abroad i'th'world? |
| DUKE      | None, but that there is so great a fever on goodness that the dissolution of it must cure it. Novelty is only in request, and it is as dangerous to be 220 aged in any kind of course as it is virtuous to be constant in any undertaking. There is scarce truth enough  alive to make societies secure; but security enough to make fellowships accurst. Much upon this riddle runs the wisdom of the world. This 225 news is old enough, yet it is every day's news. I pray you, sir, of what disposition was the Duke? |
| ESCALUS   | One that, above all other strifes, contended especially to know himself. |
| DUKE      | What pleasure was he given to?                       230 |
| ESCALUS   | Rather rejoicing to see another merry, than merry |

Escalus declares that he has tried to speak on Claudio's
behalf but Angelo has been adamant. The Duke/friar
comments that this is only acceptable if Angelo's own life
is above reproach. Alone, the Duke reflects on the need for
those in authority to be as holy as they are severe, and is
shocked at the revelations about Angelo.

**233 temperance**: moderation
**234 to his events**: to whatever fate brings him
**237 lent him visitation**: visited him as a friar
**238 no sinister measure**: no unjust treatment
**240 to the determination of justice**: to whatever justice decides
**240–242 Yet had he...of life**: because of his weak position, he
   had deceived himself into imagining many reasons for
   hoping that he would live
**242–243 by my good leisure**: giving my time to his situation
**243 have...him**: have freed him of the delusion
**245–246 You have paid...calling**: you have paid the heavens
   back what you owed them for having given you the role
   of friar, and the prisoner has paid back his debt to you,
   for giving him your time, by resolving to die
**247–248 to the...modesty**: as far as I possibly can within the
   limits of the justice which I have to put into effect
**250 indeed Justice**: justice itself
**251–252 answer...well**: accords with or runs parallel with
   the strictness of his dealing with the others, it will be to
   his credit
**256 He who...bear**: whoever undertakes to deal out holy justice
**258–259 Pattern...go**: he should be an example by having
   self-knowledge and showing grace and virtue
**260–261 More...weighing**: punishing others no more nor less
   than he would judge fitting for his own sins

• *What are the ironies in lines 266–267?*

to anything which professed to make him
rejoice. A gentleman of all temperance. But leave
we him to his events, with a prayer they may prove
prosperous, and let me desire to know how          235
you find Claudio prepared. I am made to
understand that you have lent him visitation.

DUKE        He professes to have received no sinister measure
            from his judge, but most willingly humbles himself
            to the determination of justice. Yet had he          240
            framed to himself, by the instruction of his frailty,
            many deceiving promises of life, which I, by my
            good leisure, have discredited to him; and now is
            he resolved to die.

ESCALUS     You have paid the heavens your function, and     245
            the prisoner the very debt of your calling. I have
            laboured for the poor gentleman to the
            extremest shore of my modesty, but my brother-
            justice have I found so severe that he hath forced
            me to tell him he is indeed Justice.          250

DUKE        If his own life answer the straitness of his
            proceeding, it shall become him well: wherein if
            he chance to fail, he hath sentenced himself.

ESCALUS     I am going to visit the prisoner; fare you well.

DUKE        Peace be with you. [ *Exeunt* ESCALUS *and* PROVOST  255
                He who the sword of heaven will bear
                Should be as holy as severe:
                Pattern in himself to know,
                Grace to stand, and virtue, go:
                More nor less to others paying          260
                Than by self-offences weighing.
                Shame to him whose cruel striking
                Kills for faults of his own liking!
                Twice treble shame on Angelo,
                To weed my vice, and let his grow!          265
                O, what may man within him hide,
                Though angel on the outward side!

**The Duke concludes that cunning is necessary to defeat vice.**

**268–271  How may...things**: this section of the scene is
obscure, because two lines seem to be missing. The meaning
seems to be: how can a criminal deception, using deceitful
tricks on the world ... achieve great effects by such trivial
(idle) and flimsy means
**275–276  So disguise...exacting**: Mariana's disguise as Isabella
will pay the deceitful Angelo's false demands with deception
**277  perform an old contracting**: carry out the originally
promised consummation

> • *Do lines 275–277 have the ring of justice? If so, what
> kind of justice? Look back at Angelo's last words in Act
> 2 scene 4 – his last appearance.*

How may likeness made in crimes,
Making practice on the times
[
                                                ]
To draw with idle spiders' strings                    270
Most ponderous and substantial things!
Craft against vice I must apply.
With Angelo tonight shall lie
His old betrothed, but despised:
So disguise shall by th'disguised                     275
Pay with falsehood false exacting,
And perform an old contracting.

[*Exit*

## Keeping track

### Scene 1

1 How does Claudio react to the advice of the Duke (disguised as a friar)?
2 What problems face Isabella on meeting Claudio?
3 In what ways does Claudio react to her news?
4 On what terms do they part?
5 How does the Duke deal first with Claudio and then Isabella?
6 What problems face:
   • the Duke
   • Claudio
   • Isabella
   by the end of the scene?

### Scene 2

1 Before leaving the prison, the Duke/friar witnesses a sequence of events involving Elbow, Lucio, Pompey, Mistress Overdone and Escalus. What does he see and hear? In what ways does he participate in these events?
2 What contrasting views of himself does he hear from Lucio and Escalus?
3 How does he sum up the situation at the end of the scene?

## Discussion

The Duke/friar is on stage throughout this act.
1 In what ways – and how well – does he play the friar?
2 What are his motives:
   • in his 'sermon' to Claudio?
   • in secretly overhearing Claudio and Isabella?
   • in his treatment of Claudio and Isabella after they part?
   • in his plan to exchange Mariana for Isabella in Angelo's bed?
3 At the end of the play the Duke proposes to Isabella. Is there any sign of such feelings for her in this act?

## Drama

### *The relationship between Claudio and the Duke*

**1  Scene 1 lines 1–43**

In pairs, explore the relationship between the Duke/friar and Claudio.
- One of you plays the Duke/friar in several different ways, e.g. fatherly, mocking, cynical, kind, as a teacher, as a priest, cold, cheerful.
- The other responds appropriately.

Which interpretations seem more suitable and convincing?

### *Who has the moral advantage, Claudio or Isabella?*

**2  Scene 1 lines 53–116**

In small groups, work on these lines. Think about these points:
- how do they move in relation to each other?
- what is each thinking?
- what are they **not** saying?

Use FORUM THEATRE techniques to analyse the tension of the moment when Claudio says, '*The precise Angelo!*' (line 93). What thoughts are running through his head? What are Isabella's intentions? How do we want the audience to respond to her at this point?

**3  Scene 1 lines 117–131**

In pairs, explore Claudio's intentions in this speech. Is it directed at:
- Isabella?
- into thin air?
- a mixture of the two?

What are her reactions?

**4  Hotseating**

In groups, hotseat Isabella on these lines:
-                '*O, you beast!*
  *O faithless coward! O dishonest wretch!*' (scene 1 lines 135–136)
- '*The image of it gives me content already, and I trust it will grow to a most prosperous perfection.*' (scene 1 lines 261–262)

Why is she so easily persuaded?

# Close study

## Scene 1

**1 Lines 1–52**
- For Claudio, life is to be hoped for but death is to be prepared for. How does the Duke/friar contrast life and death? Does his advice seem to be like that of a friar? What seem to be his motives?
- How does Claudio respond? Compare his words before and after the Duke's advice.
- What is the irony of Isabella's call from within?
- What is the significance of the Provost's reply?
- Why does the Duke's request to the Provost (line 52) require no explanation?

**2 Lines 53–150**
- Between lines 53 and 84, Claudio asks six direct questions and makes one other direct request for information (line 73). He finishes with a promise (lines 82–84). Look at Isabella's answers.

  What can you tell about her motives and intentions? What is her attitude to Claudio? How does she delay the truth and with what kind of language?
- Between lines 54 and 93, Isabella gives descriptions of, and expresses her attitudes to, Angelo. What are they? What do they add up to? How is Claudio affected by them?
- Between lines 94 and 107, Claudio comes to accept that he must die.

  How has this frame of mind come about?
- Between lines 107 and 134, Claudio exhibits great distress and confusion. What feelings can you detect running through him? What effects do they seem to have on Isabella?
- What do you make of Isabella's response (lines 135–149)? How rational is she?

**3 Lines 151–271**
- The Duke has heard all. How does he treat first Isabella, then Claudio? (lines 151–172) Does he show any understanding of their emotional state? Is his treatment appropriate for a friar? What seem to be his motives?
- How do you understand the Duke's words to the Provost (lines 175–177)? What might his motives be?

- From line 179 onwards, the Duke, as friar, puts forward his plan to Isabella. What qualities in it appeal to her and why does she agree to it? Look especially at lines 261–262. What demands does the Duke make of Isabella?
- In lines 150–151, the form of language changes from verse to prose. In what way(s) does this change the tone or style of the scene (and play) hereafter?

## Scene 2

4  **Lines 1–39**
Look at the Duke's/friar's speeches at lines 18, 29 and 37.
What tone of voice and attitude is he adopting? Why? How far do you think he is saying these things to keep up the role of the friar?

5  **Lines 40–82**
- What do we learn about Lucio from his refusal of bail for Pompey and the way he does it?
- Why does the Duke not intervene?

6  **Lines 83–180**
- What images of Angelo does Lucio offer?
- What images of the absent Duke does Lucio offer?
- How does the Duke (as friar) defend the absent Duke?
- What is the comic focus of this passage?
- Why is this passage a vital aspect of the plot and of Shakespeare's development of the Duke's character? You should look ahead to the Duke's questioning of Escalus after Lucio has gone at lines 226–233. Further references are Act 4 scene 3 lines 158–177, Act 5 scene 1 lines 72–90, 129–151, 178–214, 281–358 and 498–521.

7  **Lines 181–184**
What is the impact of this mini-soliloquy? Consider it as:
- a device to 'cover' the previous exit and the new arrivals
- a way of revealing the Duke's character and/or response to Lucio
- a philosophical thought 'from the author'.

8  **Lines 186–207**
- Compare and contrast Escalus' language and judgements here with those in Act 2 scene 2.
- Why is it important that the Duke should hear Escalus' words in lines 203–7?

9 **Lines 210–254**
- What is the significance of the Duke's comments on the '*news abroad i'th'world*' (line 217)?
- What is the importance of Escalus' words about the absent Duke?
- What is the importance of Escalus' words to the Duke as Friar?

10 **Lines 256–277**
- What frame of mind is the Duke in?
- What is the effect of his ending the scene in rhyming verse?

## Imagery

1 In scene 1, look for images of mortality, wealth and poverty (especially in lines 5–41, 76–80, 117–131).
2 In scene 2 look for images of honesty, dishonesty, wealth and usury, sexuality.

## Key scene

### Scene 1

1 The scene contains two major speeches about death:
- The Duke (lines 5–41) tries to persuade Claudio to accept death as preferable to all the tribulation and suffering of life.
- Claudio (lines 117–131) expresses a horrifying vision of dying and what follows.

Why do you think this central scene contains two such powerful but different speeches when Claudio's life has reached such a crisis?

2 At the start of the play, the Duke withdraws from responsibility and becomes an 'invisible' observer. After Claudio's terrified view of death and Isabella's reaction to it, the Duke (still 'invisible') takes charge of the situation at line 151. What seem to be the Duke's concerns at this point? How does he treat Claudio and Isabella throughout the rest of the scene? How do they react to him? Why doesn't he reveal who he is? What are we interested to know by the end of the scene? Compare this with our concerns at line 151.

# Writing

1 What dramatic interest has Shakespeare created through his portrayal of the Duke/friar in Act 3?
2 How has Shakespeare directed our sympathies towards Claudio and Isabella during Act 3?
3 How is scene 2 a development of the dramatic interest created at the end of scene 1?

A boy sings for Mariana of love promised and withdrawn, still hoped for in vain. The Duke/friar arrives and Mariana is embarrassed at her musical indulgence. The Duke asks if anyone, i.e. Isabella, has asked for him, but no-one has.

**2 were forsworn**: gave false promises

**3–4 the break...morn**: which brought the light of love and hope to the day, but turned out to be deceivers (a reference to the so-called 'false dawn' – a lightening in the sky that precedes the real dawn)

**5 bring again**: bring back

**6 seals of...vain**: kisses which confirmed love, though ultimately meant nothing

**9 brawling discontent**: the turmoil of my unhappiness

**10 I...mercy**: I beg your mercy

**13 My...woe**: the music didn't feed a happy mood but a sad one

**14 charm**: magic power

- *What new mood does this scene opening set? How?*
- *How do you respond to the implication that Mariana has often been counselled by this 'friar' before?*

# Act four

## Scene 1

*A grange*

*Enter* MARIANA, *and a* BOY *singing*

[*Song*]
 Take, o take those lips away
  that so sweetly were forsworn,
 And those eyes, the break of day
  lights that do mislead the morn:
 But my kisses bring again,
       bring again;    5
 Seals of love, but sealed in vain,
        sealed in vain.

*Enter* DUKE *[disguised]*

MARIANA Break off thy song, and haste thee quick away;
Here comes a man of comfort, whose advice
Hath often stilled my brawling discontent.
          [*Exit* BOY
I cry you mercy, sir, and well could wish  10
You had not found me here so musical.
Let me excuse me, and believe me so;
My mirth it much displeased, but pleased my woe.

DUKE 'Tis good; thou music oft hath such a charm
To make bad good, and good provoke to harm. 15
I pray you tell me, hath anybody enquired for me
here-to-day? Much upon this time have I promised
here to meet.

MARIANA You have not been enquired after: I have sat
here all day.         20

Isabella enters and the Duke/friar asks Mariana to
withdraw, hinting at future advantage for her. Isabella
reports Angelo's compliance and describes the location. The
Duke calls Mariana back and introduces the women.

**21 constantly**: certainly
**22 crave...little**: ask you to withdraw and give me a few
moments
**23 anon**: straightaway
**28 circummured**: walled around
**30 planched**: made of wooden boards
**31 makes his opening**: is opened
**32 doth command**: unlocks
**37 on your knowledge**: with the knowledge you have
**38 due and wary**: suitable and careful
**39 guilty diligence**: guilty care
**40 In...precept**: he showed me how to do it by explanation
**42 her observance**: how she should behave
**43 a repair i'th'dark**: she must make her way there in the dark
**44–45 I...brief**: I have made him understand that the longest I
can stay is a short time
**47–48 whose...brother**: whom I have persuaded I am visiting
on my brother's behalf
**48 borne up**: planned

> • *How does Shakespeare lead us to believe in the
> possibility of this highly improbable liaison between
> Angelo and Isabella (lines 28–48)?*

*Enter* ISABELLA

DUKE      I do constantly believe you: the time is come even
          now. I shall crave your forbearance a little; may be
          I will call upon you anon for some advantage to
          yourself.

MARIANA   I am always bound to you.                          25
                                                          [*Exit*

DUKE      [*To* ISABELLA] Very well met, and well come.
          What is the news from his good deputy?

ISABELLA  He hath a garden circummured with brick,
          Whose western side is with a vineyard backed;
          And to that vineyard is a planched gate,           30
          That makes his opening with his bigger key.
          This other doth command a little door
          Which from the vineyard to the garden leads;
          There have I made my promise
          Upon the heavy middle of the night                 35
          To call upon him.

DUKE      But shall you on your knowledge find this way?

ISABELLA  I have ta'en a due and wary note upon't;
          With whispering and most guilty diligence,
          In action all of precept, he did show me            40
          The way twice o'er.

DUKE                           Are there no other tokens
          Between you 'greed, concerning her observance?

ISABELLA  No; none, but only a repair i'th'dark;
          And that I have possessed him my most stay
          Can be but brief: for I have made him know          45
          I have a servant comes with me along,
          That stays upon me; whose persuasion is
          I come about my brother.

DUKE                                'Tis well borne up.
          I have not yet made known to Mariana
          A word of this. – What hoa, within! Come forth.  50
          [*To* MARIANA] I pray you be acquainted with this
              maid;

The Duke/friar asks Isabella to explain the plan to Mariana, assuring them of mutual advantage. In their absence, he reflects on the power of false rumour. Having agreed, the women return, and Isabella reminds Mariana to insist on Angelo's mercy for Claudio.

**52 the like**: the same thing, i.e. good

**53 Do...yourself**: are you convinced

**57 attend your leisure**: wait until you are ready

**58 vaporous**: misty

**60 O...greatness**: Oh, what a burden are high position and power

**61 stuck**: focused

**61–63 volumes...doings**: masses of bad rumours spread by these false eye-witnesses and enemies prey upon all one's actions

**63–65 thousand...fancies**: thousands of malicious jokes which make you their butt and create torturing fantasies about you, are spread about

**66 take the enterprise upon her**: she'll go along with the plan

**67–68 It...too**: I don't simply agree to it, I beg you to do it

**71 fear...all**: don't fear for your soul

**72 pre-contract**: by an earlier promise; by a promise yet to be fulfilled

**75 flourish**: give a fine gloss

**76 Our...sow**: if we're going to reap the harvest, we need to sow the corn. 'Tithe' literally means the one-tenth of their produce given by parishioners to support the priest; here it is used to refer to seed corn

- *Why does the Duke say what he does in the brief period he is alone?*
- *Isabella reports that Mariana has agreed to the plan. Mariana scarcely speaks. Why?*
- *What are the friar-like qualities in the Duke's last speech (lines 71–76)?*

She comes to do you good.

ISABELLA                                  I do desire the like.

DUKE        Do you persuade yourself that I respect you?

MARIANA     Good friar, I know you do, and so have found it.

DUKE        Take, then, this your companion by the hand,      55
            Who hath a story ready for your ear.
            I shall attend your leisure; but make haste,
            The vaporous night approaches.

MARIANA     [*To* ISABELLA] Will't please you walk aside?
                        [MARIANA *and* ISABELLA *withdraw*

DUKE        O place and greatness! Millions of false eyes      60
            Are stuck upon thee: volumes of report
            Run with these false, and most contrarious quest
            Upon thy doings: thousand escapes of wit
            Make thee the father of their idle dream
            And rack thee in their fancies.
                        [MARIANA *and* ISABELLA *return*
                                    Welcome; how
            agreed?                                             65

ISABELLA    She'll take the enterprise upon her, father,
            If you advise it

DUKE                        It is not my consent,
            But my entreaty too.

ISABELLA                        Little have you to say
            When you depart from him, but, soft and low,
            'Remember now my brother'.

MARIANA                             Fear me not.      70

DUKE        Nor, gentle daughter, fear you not at all.
            He is your husband on a pre-contract:
            To bring you thus together 'tis no sin,
            Sith that the justice of your title to him
            Doth flourish the deceit. – Come, let us go;       75
            Our corn's to reap, for yet our tithe's to sow.
                                            [*Exeunt*

The Provost offers Pompey the job of assistant executioner in return for leniency. Pompey agrees but when Abhorson hears this he says that Pompey, being a pimp, will bring the executioner's art into disrepute.

1 **sirrah**: man, fellow – an appropriate address to someone of lower status
3–4 **head**: pun on 'head' as head of the family and as part of the anatomy
5 **snatches**: jokes
8 **office**: job, duty
10 **gyves**: ankle irons
12 **deliverance**: freedom
14–15 **time...mind**: since I don't know when
21 **meet**: all right, suitable
21–22 **compound...year**: work out together what he should be paid per year
24 **plead his estimation**: quibble over his worth
27 **mystery**: the 'special art' of the executioner

- *The Provost tells Pompey that if he helps the executioner he will be redeemed from his full sentence and 'an unpitied whipping'. What new perspective does this offer on the main plot?*
- *What is the effect of presenting Claudio's executioners in comic style?*

# Scene  2

*The prison*

*Enter* PROVOST *and* POMPEY

PROVOST    Come hither, sirrah. Can you cut off a man's head?

POMPEY    If the man be a bachelor, sir, I can; but if he be a
married man, he's his wife's head; and I can never
cut off a woman's head.

PROVOST    Come, sir, leave me your snatches, and yield me a   5
direct answer. Tomorrow morning are to die
Claudio and Barnardine. Here is in our prison a
common executioner, who in his office lacks a
helper; if you will take it on you to assist him, it
shall redeem you from your gyves: if not, you        10
shall have your full time of imprisonment, and your
deliverance with an unpitied whipping; for you have
been a notorious bawd.

POMPEY    Sir, I have been an unlawful bawd time out of
mind, but yet I will be content to be a lawful        15
hangman. I would be glad to receive some
instruction from my fellow-partner.

PROVOST    What hoa, Abhorson! Where's Abhorson there?

*Enter* ABHORSON

ABHORSON    Do you call, sir?

PROVOST    Sirrah, here's a fellow will help you tomorrow in  20
your execution. If you think it meet, compound
with him by the year, and let him abide here with
you; if not, use him for the present, and dismiss
him. He cannot plead his estimation with you: he
hath been a bawd.                                      25

ABHORSON    A bawd, sir? Fie upon him, he will discredit our
mystery.

The Provost sees no distinction between hangman and pimp.
Pompey wittily demonstrates that whoring is an art and asks
what art there is in hanging. Abhorson replies mysteriously!
The Provost orders them to prepare for Claudio's execution
the next morning and sends for Barnardine and Claudio.

**28–29 Go...scale**: don't waste time, you're of equal value –
there's scarcely any difference between you. 'Feather' is a
reference to the idea that the scales of justice are so finely
balanced that a feather would tip the balance

**30–31 favour**: a pun as in doing a favour and as in a person's
face; Pompey is punning ironically, indicating that a face as
good as Abhorson's will do any one the favour of hanging
them

**31–32 hanging look**: a pun as in a hangdog expression and as in
the look of a hangman

**34 mystery**: this word had many different meanings and several
are played on by Abhorson (lines 41–45):
(a) a job or profession
(b) a special skill
(c) something hidden or secret
(d) a religious truth that could only be known to those who
had been initiated

**36 using painting**: by putting on cosmetics
**do...mystery**: prove that my job (prostitution) is an art as well

**41–45 Every true man's apparel...thief**: the 'thief' is the
hangman who received as part of his payment the clothes of
the executed man; 'big' and 'little' refer to either the size or
the value of the clothing – if the clothes are too little in size or
value, the owner still thinks them big enough in value; if they
are too big in size, the hangman doesn't think a lot of the
value ('*little enough*'), but the hangman can then sell them

**48–49 he doth...forgiveness**: every time the executioner
executes he asks the victim's forgiveness first

**54–55 if you have...turn**: if it happens that you have to ask me
to execute you

**56 yare**: deft, skilful

> • *Is Pompey being sincere in lines 47–49 and 54–57?*

| | |
|---|---|
| PROVOST | Go to, sir, you weigh equally: a feather will turn the scale.                                  [*Exit* |
| POMPEY | Pray, sir, by your good favour – for surely, sir, a   30 good favour you have, but that you have a hanging look – do you call, sir, your occupation a mystery? |
| ABHORSON | Ay, sir, a mystery. |
| POMPEY | Painting, sir, I have heard say, is a mystery; and your whores, sir, being members of my occupation,   35 using painting, do prove my occupation a mystery. But what mystery there should be in hanging, if I should be hanged, I cannot imagine. |
| ABHORSON | Sir, it is a mystery. |
| POMPEY | Proof?                                        40 |
| ABHORSON | Every true man's apparel fits your thief. If it be too little for your thief, your true man thinks it big enough. If it be too big for your thief, your thief thinks it little enough. So every true man's apparel fits your thief.                            45 |

*Enter* PROVOST

| | |
|---|---|
| PROVOST | Are you agreed? |
| POMPEY | Sir, I will serve him; for I do find your hangman is a more penitent trade than your bawd; he doth oftener ask forgiveness. |
| PROVOST | You, sirrah, provide your block and your axe   50 tomorrow four o'clock. |
| ABHORSON | Come on, bawd, I will instruct thee in my trade. Follow. |
| POMPEY | I do desire to learn, sir; and I hope, if you have occasion to use me for your own turn, you shall   55 find me yare. For truly, sir, for your kindness I owe you a good turn. |
| PROVOST | Call hither Barnardine and Claudio.                    [*Exeunt* ABHORSON *and* POMPEY |

Claudio is informed of his imminent execution and reports that Barnardine cannot be woken from drunken sleep. The Provost hopes a knock heralds a reprieve for Claudio, but it is the Duke/friar expecting to see Isabella. The Duke begins to reject the Provost's reservations about Angelo.

**60 though**: even if; i.e. Barnardine, a murderer, would have no pity from me, even if he were my brother

**64–65 As fast...bones**: he is as sound asleep as someone whose bones are stiff and exhausted after the innocent toil of travel

**66 do good on**: help

**68 By and by**: I'll be with you in a moment

**73 curfew**: the bell which was rung to tell everyone to return to their homes

**75 There's...hope**: there's some cause for hope

**77–78 his life...justice**: he lives his life in strict accordance with the demands of all-powerful justice

> • *What is the effect of the Duke/friar insisting that Angelo is abstemious and just (lines 77–81)?*

The'one has my pity; not a jot the other,
Being a murderer, though he were my brother.    60

*Enter* CLAUDIO

Look, here's the warrant, Claudio, for thy death;
'Tis now dead midnight, and by eight tomorrow
Thou must be made immortal. Where's Barnardine?

CLAUDIO  As fast locked up in sleep as guiltless labour
When it lies starkly in the traveller's bones.    65
He will not wake.

PROVOST                            Who can do good on him?
Well, go; prepare yourself.        [*Knocking within*
                        But hark, what noise?
Heaven give your spirits comfort!    [*Exit* CLAUDIO
[*Knocking*]                        – By and by. –
I hope it is some pardon or reprieve
For the most gentle Claudio.

*Enter* DUKE [*disguised*]

                            Welcome, father.    70

DUKE  The best and wholesom'st spirits of the night
Envelop you, good Provost! Who called here of
        late?

PROVOST  None since the curfew rung.

DUKE  Not Isabel?

PROVOST              No.

DUKE                            They will then, ere't be long.

PROVOST  What comfort is for Claudio?

DUKE                                There's some in
        hope.    75

PROVOST  It is a bitter deputy.

DUKE  Not so, not so; his life is paralleled
Even with the stroke and line of his great justice.
He doth with holy abstinence subdue

A further knock takes the Provost away, and the Duke/friar reflects on his humane character. There is no countermand of the execution from Angelo and the Provost believes there won't be. A letter arrives which the Duke expects will be the pardon.

**80–81 That...others**: that lust in himself which he uses all his strength to moderate in others
**81 mealed with**: mixed up in
**84 seldom when**: it's rare that
**85 steeled**: hard
**87 unsisting postern**: immovable (unresisting) gate
**90 countermand**: order cancelling a previous order
**93–94 Happily...know**: I hope you know something good
**95 example**: precedent
**96 siege**: throne
**102 article**: detail

- *The messenger arrives with a note. What is the dramatic effect of the messenger having to add oral instructions from Angelo at this point (lines 100–104)?*

That in himself which he spurs on his power        80
To qualify in others: were he mealed with that
Which he corrects, then were he tyrannous;
But this being so, he's just.
                    [*Knocking within*. PROVOST *goes to the door*
                                        – Now are they come.
This is a gentle provost; seldom when
The steeled gaoler is the friend of men.                85
                                        [*Knocking*
How now? What noise? That spirit's possessed with
    haste
That wounds th'unsisting postern with these strokes
                                        [PROVOST *returns*

PROVOST   There must he stay until the officer
          Arise to let him in. He is called up.

DUKE      Have you no countermand for Claudio yet,       90
          But he must die tomorrow?

PROVOST                                 None, sir, none.

DUKE      As near the dawning, Provost, as it is,
          You shall hear more ere morning.

PROVOST                                 Happily
          You something know: yet I believe there comes
          No countermand. No such example have we.        95
          Besides, upon the very siege of justice
          Lord Angelo hath to the public ear
          Professed the contrary.

          *Enter a* MESSENGER

                                 This is his lordship's man.

DUKE      And here comes Claudio's pardon.

MESSENGER My lord hath sent you this note, and by me      100
          this further charge: that you swerve not from the
          smallest article of it, neither in time, matter, or
          other circumstance. Good-morrow; for, as I take it,
          it is almost day.

A boy sings for Mariana of love promised and withdrawn, still hoped for in vain. The Duke/friar arrives and Mariana is embarrassed at her musical indulgence. The Duke asks if anyone, i.e. Isabella, has asked for him, but no-one has.

**2 were forsworn**: gave false promises
**3–4 the break...morn**: which brought the light of love and hope to the day, but turned out to be deceivers (a reference to the so-called 'false dawn' – a lightening in the sky that precedes the real dawn)
**5 bring again**: bring back
**6 seals of...vain**: kisses which confirmed love, though ultimately meant nothing
**9 brawling discontent**: the turmoil of my unhappiness
**10 I...mercy**: I beg your mercy
**13 My...woe**: the music didn't feed a happy mood but a sad one
**14 charm**: magic power

- *What new mood does this scene opening set? How?*
- *How do you respond to the implication that Mariana has often been counselled by this 'friar' before?*

| PROVOST | I shall obey him. | [*Exit* MESSENGER | 105 |

DUKE   [*Aside*] This is his pardon, purchased by such sin
For which the pardoner himself is in.
Hence hath offence his quick celerity,
When it is borne in high authority.
When vice makes mercy, mercy's so extended      110
That for the fault's love is th'offender friended.
Nor, sir, what news?

PROVOST   I told you: Lord Angelo, belike thinking me
remiss in mine office, awakens me with this
unwonted putting-on; methinks strangely, for      115
he hath not used it before.

DUKE   Pray you, let's hear.

PROVOST   [*Reads*] 'Whatsoever you may hear to the contrary,
let Claudio be executed by four of the clock, and in
the afternoon, Barnardine. For my better      120
satisfaction, let me have Claudio's head sent me by
five. Let this be duly performed, with a thought that
more depends on it than we must yet deliver. Thus
fail not to do your office, as you will answer it at
your peril.' What say you to this, sir?      125

DUKE   What is that Barnardine, who is to be executed in
th'afternoon?

PROVOST   A Bohemian born, but here nursed up and bred;
one that is a prisoner nine years old.

DUKE   How came it that the absent Duke had not      130
either delivered him to his liberty, or executed him?
I have heard it was ever his manner to do so.

PROVOST   His friends still wrought reprieves for him; and
indeed, his fact till now in the government of Lord
Angelo came not to an undoubtful proof.      135

DUKE   It is now apparent?

PROVOST   Most manifest, and not denied by himself.

DUKE   Hath he borne himself penitently in prison? How

The Provost explains that Barnardine is too drunk to care
and is institutionalised. The Duke/friar praises the Provost's
humanity and asks him to delay Claudio's death and to send
Barnardine's head instead.

**139 touched**: affected

**140 apprehends**: thinks of

**143 insensible of mortality...mortal**: unconcerned about death
   and hopelessly in love with life and unaware that he is
   doomed

**144 wants advice**: lacks the guidance (that I as friar can give
   him)

**150 a seeming warrant for it**: an imitation of a death warrant

**154 beguiles**: deceives

**155–156 lay...hazard**: place myself at risk by talking to you

**157 no greater forfeit to the law**: no more guilty

**159 in a manifested effect**: in a way that shows you the
   evidence

**160–161 a present and a dangerous courtesy**: an immediate
   and risky favour

**164 limited**: laid down, defined

**165 express**: precise, specific

**167 cross**: ignore, go against

**172–173 discover the favour**: see and recognise the face

---

- *Look at the Provost's description of Barnardine and
  his attitude (lines 140–143 and 145–151). What is the
  significance of these characteristics in relation to the
  play as a whole?*

seems he to be touched?

PROVOST   A man that apprehends death no more                    140
dreadfully but as a drunken sleep; careless, reckless,
and fearless of what's past, present, or to come:
insensible of mortality, and desperately mortal.

DUKE   He wants advice.

PROVOST   He will hear none. He hath evermore had the          145
liberty of the prison: give him leave to escape
hence, he would not. Drunk many times a day, if
not many days entirely drunk. We have very oft
awaked him, as if to carry him to execution, and
showed him a seeming warrant for it; hath not     150
moved him at all.

DUKE   More of him anon. There is written in your brow,
Provost, honesty and constancy; if I read it not
truly, my ancient skill beguiles me. But in the
boldness of my cunning, I will lay myself in       155
hazard. Claudio, whom here you have warrant to
execute, is no greater forfeit to the law than Angelo
who hath sentenced him. To make you understand
this in a manifested effect, I crave but four days'
respite: for the which, you are to do me both a   160
present and a dangerous courtesy.

PROVOST   Pray sir, in what?

DUKE   In the delaying death.

PROVOST   Alack, how may I do it? Having the hour limited,
and an express command under penalty to          165
deliver his head in the view of Angelo? I may make
my case as Claudio's to cross this in the smallest.

DUKE   By the vow of mine order, I warrant you, if my
instructions may be your guide: let this Barnardine
be this morning executed, and his head borne     170
to Angelo.

PROVOST   Angelo hath seen them both, and will discover the
favour.

The Duke/friar promises to give his life in defence of the
Provost if his deceit is discovered. The Provost protests that
he will be breaking his oath of office, but the Duke points
out that he swore to the Duke, and he can guarantee his
immediate return and support. He shows the proof, ordering
preparations for Barnardine's execution.

**177–178 If anything...this**: if you get into any trouble for this
**185 avouch**: vouches for
**187 resemblance**: likelihood
**189 attempt you**: bring you round
**191 hand**: hand writing
**192 character**: style
**193 signet**: seal
**199 of strange tenour**: with mysterious information
**201–202 nothing...writ**: nothing written down about what has
actually happened
**202 unfolding star...shepherd**: star of dawn that calls the
shepherd to work
**207 present shift**: immediate absolution and forgiveness for his
sins
**208–209 absolutely resolve you**: make everything completely
clear to you

> • *The Duke's order to execute Barnardine after
> confession is perfunctory (lines 205–206). How does
> this correspond with the role of friar?*

| | |
|---|---|
| DUKE | O, death's a great disguiser; and you may add to it. Shave the head, and tie the beard, and say it     175 was the desire of the penitent to be so bared before his death: you know the course is common. If anything fall to you upon this, more than thanks and good fortune, by the saint whom I profess, I will plead against it with my life.     180 |
| PROVOST | Pardon me, good father; it is against my oath. |
| DUKE | Were you sworn to the Duke, or to the Deputy? |
| PROVOST | To him, and to his substitutes. |
| DUKE | You will think you have made no offence if the Duke avouch the justice of your dealing?     185 |
| PROVOST | But what likelihood is in that? |
| DUKE | Not a resemblance, but a certainty. Yet, since I see you fearful, that neither my coat, integrity, nor persuasion can with ease attempt you, I will go further than I meant, to pluck all fears out of     190 you. Look you, sir, here is the hand and seal of the Duke: you know the character, I doubt not, and the signet is not strange to you? |
| PROVOST | I know them both. |
| DUKE | The contents of this is the return of the Duke:     195 you shall anon over-read it at your pleasure, where you shall find within these two days he will be here. This is a thing that Angelo knows not; for he this very day receives letters of strange tenour, perchance of the Duke's death, perchance entering into     200 some monastery; but, by chance, nothing of what is writ. Look, th'unfolding star calls up the shepherd. Put not yourself into amazement how these things should be; all difficulties are but easy when they are known. Call your executioner,     205 and off with Barnardine's head. I will give him a present shrift, and advise him for a better place. Yet you are amazed; but this shall absolutely resolve you. Come away; it is almost clear dawn.     [*Exeunt* |

Pompey comically reflects that his whole world of
acquaintance and business is now in prison with him.
Abhorson arrives and they call Barnardine to his execution.
He does not seem keen.

1–2 **house of profession**: brothel

4 **Rash**: wild and careless; with a pun on a kind of smooth silk

5 **commodity**: business deal which involved making a loan, part
of which was a commodity that was useless, and deliberately
overvaluing it
**ginger**: chewed by old women to make their breath sweeter

8 **not much in request**: not much in demand

9 **Caper**: athletic leaping in dance; with a pun on trick or fiddle

9–10 **at the suit of**: at the request of, with a pun on a suit of
clothes

10 **Three-pile**: fabric of triple thickness, i.e. expensive
**mercer**: fabric merchant

12 **peaches him**: accuses him of being

13 **Dizie**: in a daze, stupid
**Deep-vow**: one who swears a lot

14 **Copperspur**: fake gold
**Starve-Lackey**: man who starves his servants

15 **Drop-heir**: one who leaches off the well-to-do with a pun on
drop-hair, i.e. diseased

16 **killed lusty Pudding**: ate red-blooded pudding, with a pun
and obvious sexual innuendo on sausage

16–17 **Forthright the tilter**: one who thrusts straight when
tilting (jousting) – further sexual innuendo

17 **Shoe-tie the great traveller**: one who has picked up the
latest shoe fashion on his travels

18 **wild...pots**: crazy 'Half-pint' who cheated on measures by
mis-marking the ale-pots

19 **doers in our trade**: users of whores

20 **'for...sake'**: people who appeal for help from prison

- *Pompey's opening speech is a piece of topical theatre,
  but it is also a comic perspective on the play's themes.
  What perspective does it offer?*

# Scene 3

*The same*

*Enter* POMPEY

POMPEY    I am as well acquainted here as I was in our house
of profession: one would think it were Mistress
Overdone's own house, for here be many of her old
customers. First, here's young Master Rash; he's in
for a commodity of brown paper and old ginger,    5
nine score and seventeen pounds; of which he
made five marks ready money: marry, then, ginger
was not much in request, for the old women were
all dead. Then is there here one Master Caper, at
the suit of Master Three-pile the mercer, for    10
some four suits of peach-coloured satin, which now
peaches him a beggar. Then have we here young
Dizie, and young Master Deep-vow, and Master
Copperspur, and Master Starve-Lackey the rapier
and dagger man, and young Drop-heir that    15
killed lusty Pudding, and Master Forthright the
tilter, and brave Master Shoe-tie the great traveller,
and wild Half-can that stabbed pots, and I think
forty more, all great doers in our trade, and are
now 'for the Lord's sake'.    20

*Enter* ABHORSON

ABHORSON    Sirrah, bring Barnardine hither.

POMPEY    Master Barnardine! You must rise and be hanged,
Master Barnardine.

ABHORSON    What hoa, Barnardine!

BARNARDINE    [*Within*] A pox o' your throats! Who makes    25
that noise there? What are you?

POMPEY    Your friends, sir, the hangman. You must be so

Barnardine finally appears, but refuses to be hanged, saying he is not ready because he hasn't been absolved of his sins. The Duke/friar offers, but Barnardine says he can't be absolved yet because he's drunk.

**40 clap into**: get started on
**41 look you**: you know
**43 fitted**: ready
**45 betimes in**: in the early hours of
**47 ghostly**: spiritual
**49 induced**: led on
   **charity**: desire to give help
**53 will**: wish for, need, want
**54 billets**: sticks
**54–55 I will not consent...certain**: to a modern audience this argument seems not only comic (which, in part, it was intended to be), but also strange. It would not have been so to Shakespeare's audience, to whom the prospect of heaven or hell after death was very real. A man condemned to death might have forfeited the right to live, but he still had rights as a Christian soul, and the chief of these was to confess his sins properly, i.e. when sober, and thus prepare himself for the possibility of heaven rather than hell

> • *What is the effect of Pompey's repeated jokes about how Barnardine can get on with doing what he wants after his execution?*

good, sir, to rise and be put to death.

BARNARDINE  [*Within*] Away, you rogue, away; I am sleepy.

ABHORSON  Tell him he must awake, and that quickly too.   30

POMPEY  Pray, Master Barnardine, awake till you are
executed, and sleep afterwards.

ABHORSON  Go in to him and fetch him out.

POMPEY  He is coming, sir, he is coming. I hear his straw
rustle.   35

*Enter* BARNARDINE

ABHORSON  Is the axe upon the block, sirrah?

POMPEY  Very ready, sir.

BARNARDINE  How now, Abhorson? What's the news with
you?

ABHORSON  Truly, sir, I would desire you to clap into your   40
prayers; for look you, the warrant's come.

BARNARDINE  You rogue, I have been drinking all night; I
am not fitted for't.

POMPEY  O, the better, sir; for he that drinks all night, and
is hanged betimes in the morning, may sleep the  45
sounder all the next day.

*Enter* DUKE [*disguised*]

ABHORSON  Look you, sir, here comes your ghostly father. Do
we jest now, think you?

DUKE  Sir, induced by my charity, and hearing now hastily
you are to depart, I am come to advise you,   50
comfort you, and pray with you.

BARNARDINE  Friar, not I. I have been drinking hard all
night, and I will have more time to prepare me, or
they shall beat out my brains with billets. I will not
consent to die this day, that's certain.   55

DUKE  O sir, you must; and therefore I beseech you
Look forward on the journey you shall go.

No-one can force or persuade Barnardine to be hanged and the Duke/friar insists that he cannot be hanged unabsolved. The Provost announces the death of another prisoner, Ragozine, who looks like Claudio. The Duke sees this as a gift from heaven: a substitute head.

**62 ward**: cell

**63 gravel**: of stone

**66 unmeet**: unfit

**67–68 transport...damnable**: to send him to the next world in his present mental state will ensure he's condemned to hell

**72 Just**: exactly

**72–73 omit this reprobate**: let this villain off

**73 well inclined**: in a positive frame of mind about dying

**74 visage**: face

**77 Dispatch it**: get on with it, deal with it
**presently**: straightaway

**78 Prefixed**: decided in advance

**83 continue Claudio**: keep Claudio alive but hidden

**86 holds**: cells

**88 Ere...greeting**: before two dawns have passed

> • *What kind of scenario is this: 'a most notorious pirate', whom we have never seen but who looks like the man who is unfairly condemned to die, conveniently dies and can be substituted for the doomed man? The Duke explains that it is good fortune 'that heaven provides'. Are you convinced?*

| | |
|---|---|
| BARNARDINE | I swear I will not die today for any man's persuasion. |
| DUKE | But hear you –                                          60 |
| BARNARDINE | Not a word. If you have anything to say to me, come to my ward: for thence will not I today. |

[*Exit*

*Enter* PROVOST

| | |
|---|---|
| DUKE | Unfit to live or die! O gravel heart. |
| PROVOST | After him, fellows, bring him to the block! |

[*Exeunt* ABHORSON *and* POMPEY

| | |
|---|---|
| | Now, sir, how do you find the prisoner?                65 |
| DUKE | A creature unprepared, unmeet for death; And to transport him in the mind he is Were damnable. |
| PROVOST | Here in the prison, father, There died this morning of a cruel fever One Ragozine, a most notorious pirate,       70 A man of Claudio's years; his beard and head Just of his colour. What if we do omit This reprobate till he were well inclined, And satisfy the deputy with the visage Of Ragozine, more like to Claudio?       75 |
| DUKE | O, 'tis an accident that heaven provides. Dispatch it presently; the hour draws on Prefixed by Angelo. See this be done, And sent according to command, whiles I Persuade this rude wretch willingly to die.       80 |
| PROVOST | This shall be done, good father, presently. But Barnardine must die this afternoon; And how shall we continue Claudio, To save me from the danger that might come If he were known alive?       85 |
| DUKE | Let this be done: put them in secret holds, Both Barnardine and Claudio. Ere twice the sun hath made his journal greeting |

The Provost is to arrange everything while the Duke/friar writes to Angelo informing him that he is about to return with public ceremony. The Provost crosses the stage on his way to Angelo with Ragozine's head. Isabella arrives expecting Claudio's pardon, but the Duke decides not to tell her the truth, believing her comfort will in the end be more heavenly for believing the worst first.

**89 yonder generation**: the rest of the human race
**90 manifested**: given evidence
   **your free dependant**: the servant who readily does your will
**94 near at home**: nearly home
**95–96 by great...publicly**: I give strict instructions that I must enter the city with public ceremony
**97 consecrated fount**: sacred spring
**99 By cold...form**: by a cool rational process, with moderation and attention to proper formality
**100 proceed**: deal with
**103 commune**: discuss
**108 good**: the good news
**109 heavenly...despair**: that out of despair she may learn the comforting power of heaven

> • *What is the dramatic effect of the Duke telling the audience his plans?*
> • *Do you think the return of the Provost with Ragozine's head is grim or comic?*

To yonder generation, you shall find
Your safety manifested.

PROVOST                              I am your free
            dependant.                                    90

DUKE        Quick, dispatch, and send the head to Angelo.
                                        [*Exit* PROVOST
            Now will I write letters to Angelo,
            The Provost, he shall bear them, whose contents
            Shall witness to him I am near at home;
            And that by great injunctions I am bound        95
            To enter publicly. Him I'll desire
            To meet me at the consecrated fount
            A league below the city; and from thence,
            By cold gradation and well-balanced form,
            We shall proceed with Angelo.                   100

            *Enter* PROVOST

PROVOST     Here is the head; I'll carry it myself.

DUKE        Convenient is it. Make a swift return;
            For I would commune with you of such things
            That want no ear but yours.

PROVOST                              I'll make all speed.
                                                [*Exit*

ISABELLA    [*Within*] Peace, hoa, be here!                 105

DUKE        The tongue of Isabel. She's come to know
            If yet her brother's pardon be come hither;
            But I will keep her ignorant of her good,
            To make her heavenly comforts of despair
            When it is least expected.

            *Enter* ISABELLA

ISABELLA                             Hoa, by your leave!  110

DUKE        Good morning to you, fair and gracious daughter.

ISABELLA    The better, given me by so holy a man.
            Hath yet the deputy sent my brother's pardon?

The Duke/friar tells Isabella that Claudio is dead. She curses Angelo but the Duke promises her just revenge and honour when the absent Duke returns the next day. She puts herself in his hands, and he plans for her to meet Mariana and Friar Peter (Friar Thomas) and go before the Duke to accuse Angelo.

**118 close patience**: private suffering
**123 a jot**: in the slightest
**124 Forbear it**: give it up
    **give...heaven**: put your case entirely in God's hands
**126 verity**: truth
**128 covent**: monastery
**129 instance**: information
**132–133 pace your wisdom...go**: be wise enough to follow the path along which I want to lead you
**134 have your bosom...wretch**: have your heart's desire at this villain's expense
**139 by this token**: using this letter as evidence of good faith
**141 I'll perfect him**: I'll give him full knowledge of
**142 to the head of**: face to face with
**143 home and home**: in every detail
**144 combined**: confined

> • *First the Duke lies to Isabella, then he tells her that grief for her brother is unprofitable, then he promises revenge, then he uses her as a messenger and finally, he tells her to have 'a light heart' (line 147). What is your reaction to this?*

| | |
|---|---|
| DUKE | He hath released him, Isabel, – from the world. |
| | His head is off, and sent to Angelo. 115 |
| ISABELLA | Nay, but it is not so! |
| DUKE | It is no other. Show your wisdom, daughter, |
| | In your close patience. |
| ISABELLA | O, I will to him and pluck out his eyes! |
| DUKE | You shall not be admitted to his sight. 120 |
| ISABELLA | Unhappy Claudio! wretched Isabel! |
| | Injurious world! most damnèd Angelo! |
| DUKE | This nor hurts him, nor profits you a jot. |
| | Forbear it therefore; give your cause to heaven. |
| | Mark what I say, which you shall find 125 |
| | By every syllable a faithful verity. |
| | The Duke comes home tomorrow; – nay, dry your |
| | eyes – |
| | One of our covent, and his confessor |
| | Gives me this instance. Already he hath carried |
| | Notice to Escalus and Angelo, 130 |
| | Who do prepare to meet him at the gates |
| | There to give up their power. If you can pace your |
| | wisdom |
| | In that good path that I would wish it go, |
| | And you shall have your bosom on this wretch, |
| | Grace of the Duke, revenges to your heart, 135 |
| | And general honour. |
| ISABELLA |                      I am directed by you. |
| DUKE | This letter then to Friar Peter give; |
| | 'Tis that he sent me of the Duke's return. |
| | Say, by this token I desire his company |
| | At Mariana's house tonight. Her cause and |
| | yours 140 |
| | I'll perfect him withal, and he shall bring you |
| | Before the Duke; and to the head of Angelo |
| | Accuse him home and home. For my poor self, |
| | I am combined by a sacred vow, |

The Duke/friar explains that he will have to be absent. Lucio
arrives, condoles with Isabella and says nothing would have
happened if the Duke hadn't gone away. Isabella goes, and
Lucio continues to irritate the Duke.

**145 Wend**: go

**148 pervert your course**: do not follow your cause truly

**150 pale to mine heart**: weak at heart

**151–152 I am fain to**: I feel the need to

**152–153 I dare...belly**: I dare not give my stomach rich food if
I'm to keep my head cool

**153–154 one fruitful...to't**: one tasty meal would arouse my
desires

**156 old...corners**: the extraordinary old Duke who liked secret
carryings on

**157 he had lived**: Claudio would still be alive

**158–159 marvellous...reports**: remarkably unimpressed by
your reports of him

**159 he lives not in them**: they are not true to his character

**161 woodman**: womaniser; literally, a hunter

**164 pretty**: intriguing

**170 was fain to forswear**: had to deny

**171–172 rotten medlar**: overripe fruit, i.e. prostitute

> • *What is the effect of Lucio's words (lines 160–161)?
> Is he right in any way?*
> • *What is the significance of Lucio's confession
> (lines 167–168 and 170–172)?*

And shall be absent. Wend you with this letter.    145
Command these fretting waters from your eyes
With a light heart; trust not my holy order,
If I pervert your course. – Who's here?

*Enter* LUCIO

LUCIO                                                 Good even.
Friar, where's the Provost?

DUKE                                          Not within, sir.

LUCIO    O pretty Isabella, I am pale to mine heart to    150
see thine eyes so red: thou must be patient. – I am
fain to dine and sup with water and bran: I dare not
for my head fill my belly: one fruitful meal would set
me to't. – But they say the Duke will be here
tomorrow. By my troth, Isabel, I loved thy    155
brother; if the old fantastical duke of dark corners
had been at home, he had lived.    [*Exit* ISABELLA

DUKE    Sir, the Duke is marvellous little beholding to
your reports; but the best is, he lives not in them.

LUCIO    Friar, thou knowest not the Duke so well as I    160
do. He's a better woodman than thou tak'st him for.

DUKE    Well! You'll answer this one day. Fare ye well.
[*going*

LUCIO    Nay tarry, I'll go along with thee: I can tell thee
pretty tales of the Duke.

DUKE    You have told me too many of him already, sir,    165
if they be true: if not true, none were enough.

LUCIO    I was once before him for getting a wench with
child.

DUKE    Did you such a thing?

LUCIO    Yes, marry, did I; but I was fain to forswear it;    170
they would else have married me to the rotten
medlar.

Lucio will not leave the Duke/friar.

**173 fairer**: more pleasant
**177 a kind of burr**: seed with hooks on it so that it clings to clothing or animals

Angelo is disturbed by the Duke's return with his demands for public ceremony and the opportunity for complaints of injustice. Escalus sees this as a good policy against future complaints. Escalus goes, and Angelo's conscience starts to plague him.

**1 disvouched other**: contradicted the previous one
**2 In...manner**: yes, and in a very inconsistent and deranged manner
**4 tainted**: damaged
**5 redeliver**: give back
**9 exhibit their petitions**: reveal their requests openly
**10 a dispatch**: an immediate sorting out, resolution
**11 to...hereafter**: to free us from any malicious complaints in the future
**14 Betimes**: early
**15 such...suit**: all the people of appropriate status
**18 This deed**: either:
  (a) everything I've done with regard to Isabella and Claudio
  (b) the Duke's return
  **unshapes me quite**: disconcerts me completely
**18–19 makes...proceedings**: makes me unable to plan, and unresponsive to everything that happens
**20 an eminent body**: a person of high position and virtue
**21 it**: fornication
  **tender shame**: gentle sense of shame

> • *Angelo is reintroduced to the play after a long absence. Why here?*

| | |
|---|---|
| DUKE | Sir, your company is fairer than honest; rest you well. *[going* |
| LUCIO | By my troth, I'll go with thee to the lane's end. 175 <br> If bawdy talk offend you, we'll have very little of it. <br> Nay, friar, I am a kind of burr, I shall stick. [*Exeunt* |

# Scene 4

*In Vienna*

*Enter* ANGELO *and* ESCALUS

| | |
|---|---|
| ESCALUS | Every letter he hath writ hath disvouched other. |
| ANGELO | In most uneven and distracted manner. His actions <br> show much like to madness; pray heaven his <br> wisdom be not tainted. And why meet him at <br> the gates and redeliver our authorities there?   5 |
| ESCALUS | I guess not. |
| ANGELO | And why should we proclaim it in an hour before <br> his entering, that if any crave redress of injustice, <br> they should exhibit their petitions in the street? |
| ESCALUS | He shows his reason for that: to have a dispatch   10 <br> of complaints, and to deliver us from devices hereafte <br> which shall then have no power to stand against us. |
| ANGELO | Well, I beseech you, let it be proclaimed <br> Betimes i'th'morn: I'll call you at your house. <br> Give notice to such men of sort and suit   15 <br> As are to meet him. |
| ESCALUS |             I shall, sir; fare you well. |
| ANGELO | Good night              [*Exit* ESCALUS <br> This deed unshapes me quite; makes me unpregnant <br> And dull to all proceedings. A deflowered maid; <br> And by an eminent body, that enforced   20 <br> The law against it! But that her tender shame |

Angelo worries about what Isabella may say, but tries to build his confidence by remembering the power of his reputation. Nevertheless, he wishes Claudio were still alive; he feels helpless.

22 **proclaim...loss**: make a public outcry against her loss of virginity
23 **tongue me**: spell out my crime
   **reason...no**: good sense prevents her from doing so
24 **bears so credent bulk**: is held in such firm trust
25 **particular**: one
26 **it...breather**: it discredits the person who uttered it
27–30 **Save that...shame**: except that his high-spirited youth with its impulsive feelings might have led him in time to take revenge because he was living a life dishonoured by the shameful way it was ransomed
31 **our grace**: the favour god gives us
32 **we...not**: we both wish and don't wish things to have happened

The Duke employs Friar Peter as his messenger for his final plans. He tells him that the Provost has full knowledge of it.

   *in his own habit*: dressed as the Duke
3 **The matter being afoot**: once the plan is in action
   **keep**: follow
4 **special drift**: particular purpose
5 **blench**: waver
6 **As...minister**: as the occasion demands

> • *Would you cut scene 5 from the play? What problems would arise if you did?*

Will not proclaim against her maiden loss,
How might she tongue me! Yet reason dares her
    no,
For my authority bears so credent bulk
That no particular scandal once can touch,        25
But it confounds the breather. He should have
    lived;
Save that his riotous youth, with dangerous sense,
Might in the times to come have ta'en revenge
By so receiving a dishonoured life
With ransom of such shame. Would yet he had
    lived.                                        30
Alack, when once our grace we have forgot,
Nothing goes right; we would, and we would not.

                                        [ *Exit*

## Scene  5

*A FRIAR'S cell*

*Enter* DUKE *in his own habit and* FRIAR PETER

DUKE            These letters at fit time deliver me.
                The Provost knows our purpose and our plot;
                The matter being afoot, keep your instruction,
                And hold you ever to our special drift,
                Though sometimes you do blench from this to
                    that                          5
                As cause doth minister. Go call at Flavius' house,
                And tell him where I stay. Give the like notice
                To Valencius, Rowland, and to Crassus,
                And bid them bring the trumpets to the gate:
                But send me Flavius first.

FRIAR PETER                          It shall be speeded
                well.                             10

                                        [ *Exit* FRIAR

The Duke greets Varrius, the first, presumably, of many friends to join him.

Isabella chafes at not being allowed to accuse Angelo herself. The Duke has warned that he may have to appear hostile to her pleas. Mariana advises trusting him. Friar Peter shows them a vantage point for intercepting the Duke.

1 **To...loth**: I am reluctant to have to speak so indirectly
4 **to veil full purpose**: to conceal the full significance (or intention)
5 **peradventure**: by chance
6 **speak against me...side**: takes sides against me
7 **physic**: treatment, medicine
8 **to sweet end**: for a good purpose
10 **a stand**: a vantage point
13 **generous and gravest citizens**: citizens of highest birth and greatest importance
14 **hent**: taken up their position at

> • *Why does Friar Peter specify that 'the generous and gravest citizens' are at the gate?*

*Enter* VARRIUS

DUKE        I thank thee, Varrius, thou hast made good haste.
            Come, we will walk. There's other of our friends
            Will greet us here anon. My gentle Varrius!

                                                    [*Exeunt*

# Scene 6

*In Vienna*

*Enter* ISABELLA *and* MARIANA

ISABELLA    To speak so indirectly I am loth;
            I would say the truth, but to accuse him so
            That is your part; yet I am advised to do it,
            He says, to veil full purpose.

MARIANA                                     Be ruled by him.

ISABELLA    Besides, he tells me that, if peradventure        5
            He speak against me on the adverse side,
            I should not think it strange, for 'tis a physic
            That's bitter to sweet end.

*Enter* FRIAR PETER

MARIANA                            I would Friar Peter –

ISABELLA    O peace, the friar is come.

FRIAR PETER Come, I have found you out a stand most fit,      10
            Where you may have such vantage on the Duke
            He shall not pass you. Twice have the trumpets
                sounded.
            The generous and gravest citizens
            Have hent the gates, and very near upon
            The Duke is ent'ring: therefore hence, away.       15

                                                    [*Exeunt*

## Keeping track

### Scene 1

1 What is the relationship between Mariana and the Duke/friar?
2 What details of the planned assignation between Isabella/Mariana and Angelo are revealed?
3 How does the Duke/friar react to Mariana's agreement?

### Scene 2

4 For what reasons is Pompey glad to be an executioner's assistant? What is Abhorson's attitude to this?
5 What happens to show that the Duke/friar is not in control of events?
6 What new plan does the Duke invent?

### Scene 3

7 What does Pompey's opening speech tell us abut Angelo's régime and the 'brothel' strand of the plot?
8 How is the Duke's plan thwarted again?
9 How does the Provost save the plan?
10 In what ways does the Duke manipulate Isabella and why?
11 What contrasting aspects of Lucio's character are shown at the end of the scene? Is he becoming more, or less, likeable?

### Scene 4

12 What differences are there between Escalus' and Angelo's reactions to the news of the Duke's return?

### Scene 5

13 What does this scene tell us about the Duke and the state of his plan?

### Scene 6

14 What situations and events does this scene prepare us for?
15 In what ways is the Duke significant in this scene even though he is not present?

# Discussion

## Scene 1

Mariana says to the boy that the '*man of comfort*', i.e. the Duke, has 'often' helped her in her unhappiness. Has Shakespeare made a mistake, or has the Duke disguised himself as a friar on several previous occasions to visit her? If so, why?

## Scenes 2 and 3

Consider the melodramatic and black comic aspects of these scenes:
- an executioner who relishes his work
- furtive knockings, comings-and-goings at '*dead midnight*'
- a condemned '*innocent*'
- a drunkard on death row who jokes about his hanging
- a life-saving severed head, the absolute image of the condemned man, carried across the stage.

How might they affect the audience? How do they affect the 'serious' content of the play?

## Scenes 4 and 5

What are the effects of re-introducing Angelo at this point, and juxtaposing this scene with the next, in which the Duke first appears out of disguise?

# Drama

## Scene 1

Work in pairs. How hard does Isabella have to work (if at all) to persuade Mariana to go along with the Duke's plan? Improvise possible versions of the scene, using your understanding of each character at this point. (You might like to discuss why Shakespeare did not put this on stage, or have the Duke explain his plan directly to Mariana.)

## Scenes 2 and 3

- How melodramatic and/or funny are these scenes? In groups:
  - take one of the ideas listed under DISCUSSION, SCENES 2 AND 3, above
  - choose relevant sections of the scenes and interpret them in this way, going 'over the top' to achieve comedy/melodrama
  - what do you discover?
- Now imagine you are script editors working for a director who

wants to cut Act 4 as much as possible, without losing the story. Argue for or against savage cuts to the two scenes.

- If you are in favour of cuts, where would you make them and how would you convey the necessary plot information in good dramatic style? Re-write the scenes to deal with the cuts.
- If you are not in favour of cuts, work out where else in Act 4 cuts could be made and do the necessary re-writes.

### Scene 4

1 Use FORUM THEATRE techniques on this scene.
   Two of you play Escalus and Angelo. Explore:
   - possible attitudes of Escalus to Angelo
   - how effectively (or not) Angelo suppresses his anxiety in Escalus' company
   - what is released in Angelo when Escalus leaves.
2 In groups, hotseat the Duke. Consider:
   - what his intentions are
   - whether he is a competent planner
   - what he is hoping to achieve
   - whether he cares about anyone else.

## Close study

### Scene 1

1 What mood does the song (lines 1–6) establish? How does it prepare us for Mariana's appearance? In the ensuing scene, what is there which echoes this mood?
2 Isabella's speech (lines 28–48) is the only impression we are to have of this part of the plot. What do we learn of Angelo and his plan from Isabella's description?
3 The Duke describes Angelo as '*good*' in line 27, and speaks to Mariana of doing her some '*good*' in line 52. In what ways is the Duke using this word? What do you think of him?
4 What has prompted the Duke's thoughts (lines 60–65) at this moment? What is there about their expression which tells you his feelings are strong?
5 How do the women talk to and about the Duke/friar in this scene? What impression of him and his relationship to them emerges?

## Scene 2

6 In line 28, the Provost tells Abhorson that he and Pompey '*weigh equally*'. What does he mean, and how do we know from the dialogue so far that Abhorson will not agree?

7 How do Pompey and Abhorson each prove their respective trades (pimping and hanging) a '*mystery*' (lines 30–45)? What is the significance of this witty exchange?

8 How does Shakespeare use the lines between the Duke and the Provost (lines 71–105) to build up the tension over Claudio's execution?

9 Look at the Duke's lines in the scene.
   • What signs are there of his positive attempts to speak like a friar?
   • What else does he have to think about?
   • What do you make of lines 106–112 which are spoken aside and, therefore, do not need to be part of the friar 'act'?
   • What do you learn of the Provost's character and attitude to his job in this scene?

## Scene 3

10 How does Pompey's speech (lines 1–20) affect our view of the prison world? What is the effect of its being a direct communication with the audience?

11 What is the effect of the passage (lines 21–62) – a condemned man refusing to be hanged and the Duke/friar's failure to prepare him for death – in the context of this scene and the play as a whole?

12 **Lines 63–80**
   • What problems does the Duke as friar have at this point? What are the ironies of his situation?
   • How do you react to the Provost's instant solution? How does the Duke react and explain this good fortune?

13 What is the dramatic purpose and effect of the Provost entering with Ragozine's head (line 101)?

14 The Duke is alone with the audience again (lines 106–110). How do you react to his decision and the motives he expresses?

15 **Lines 119–136**
   Isabella is stricken with grief, anger and a desire for revenge. By line 136, she has agreed to be directed by the Duke and not to follow her impulses. Study the Duke's speech and consider how he has achieved this effect. Are there signs of concern for Isabella, or is he focused on his own plot and her role in it?

16 What insights into the Duke's character emerge from this passage (lines 158–177)?

## Scene 4

**17 Lines 1–16**
Who seems more disturbed – Escalus or Angelo?
**18 Lines 18–32**
Angelo describes himself as '*unshaped*'. What different and contrasting thoughts does he have in this speech? There is much vivid language here. What qualities does each expression give to its particular thought?
**19** What does the language in lines 18–32 reveal about Angelo's state of mind?

## Scene 5

**20** What evidence is there in lines 1–10 that the Duke is out of disguise and speaking as Duke?

## Scene 6

**21** What do Isabella's first lines tell us of her character and state of mind as the climax approaches?
**22** What is the significance and irony of her experience '*to veil full purpose*' (line 4)? Does she know its full implications?

# Imagery

In this act, look for images of:
* appearance and reality
* clothing and uniform.

# Key scene

### Scene 4
1 How does this scene return us to the central issue of the play? What does it prepare us for?
2 Has Angelo changed from when we last saw him in Act 2? Compare his speech here with:
  • his speech at the end of Act 2 scene 2
  • his speech at the start of Act 2 scene 4
  • his words at the end of Act 2 scene 4.
  Why does Shakespeare reveal him now, before Act 5? Do we have any sympathy for him?
3 How does this scene represent issues of authority and law? Are they seen in a new light?

# Writing

1 How comic are scenes 2 and 3 and what is their dramatic function?
2 What is the dramatic impact of returning Angelo to the stage in scene 4? Think not about only the scene itself, but its positioning after the events of scenes 2 and 3, and before scene 5.
3 On the evidence of Act 4, assess Lucio's description of the Duke as '*fantastical*' (Act 3 scene 2 line 89).

The Duke greets Angelo and Escalus, having heard much praise of their justice. He singles out Angelo for special commendation. As they process through the crowd, Friar Peter cues Isabella to speak.

1 **cousin**: i.e. Angelo. Shakespeare uses the word in a number of different ways. Here he is using it as the formal mode of address from a sovereign to a nobleman
2 **friend**: i.e. Escalus
6 **justice**: approach to law enforcement
7 **Cannot...thanks**: can do nothing but offer you up for gratitude from the people
8 **Forerunning more requital**: before giving you more deserved rewards
9 **bonds**: obligations
10 **desert**: merit, deserving
11 **lock...bosom**: to keep it locked up in secret in my heart
12 **characters**: letters, writing
13–14 **A forted residence...oblivion**: a permanent place protected against the eroding power of time and the destruction wrought by loss of memory
15 **the subject**: the people
16–17 **That...within**: the appearances of courtesy would gladly show that we offer favours from deep within our hearts

---

- *What tone do you think the actor playing Angelo should adopt for line 9?*

# Act five

## Scene 1

*A public place near the city gate*

*Enter at several doors* DUKE *in his own habit,* VARRIUS,
LORDS *and* ATTENDANTS; ANGELO, ESCALUS, LUCIO,
*and* CITIZENS

| | |
|---|---|
| DUKE | My very worthy cousin, fairly met. |
| | Our old and faithful friend, we are glad to see you. |
| ANGELO and | |
| ESCALUS | Happy return be to your royal grace! |
| DUKE | Many and hearty thankings to you both. |
| | We have made enquiry of you, and we hear 5 |
| | Such goodness of your justice that our soul |
| | Cannot but yield you forth to public thanks, |
| | Forerunning more requital. |
| ANGELO | You make my bonds still greater. |
| DUKE | O, but your desert speaks loud, and I should |
| | wrong it 10 |
| | To lock it in the wards of covert bosom, |
| | When it deserves with characters of brass |
| | A forted residence 'gainst the tooth of time |
| | And razure of oblivion. Give we our hand, |
| | And let the subject see, to make them know 15 |
| | That outward courtesies would fain proclaim |
| | Favours that keep within. Come, Escalus, |
| | You must walk by us on our other hand; |
| | And good supporters are you. |

*Enter* FRIAR PETER *and* ISABELLA

| | |
|---|---|
| FRIAR PETER | Now is your time: speak loud, and kneel before |

Isabella makes her plea, but when the Duke says she should complain to Angelo she says he's a devil and only the Duke can give redress. Angelo says she's mad, but she lists his crimes. The Duke says she should be taken away.

**21 Vail your regard**: cast your eyes down
**32 not being believed**: if I am not believed
**33 wring redress**: bring just recompense
**37 course**: process
**40 forsworn**: broken his oath
**49 To th'...reck'ning**: to the end of time
**50 in...sense**: in madness, from weak senses

- *Notice the amount of repetition here. What is its impact and significance?*

|           |                                                          |    |
|-----------|----------------------------------------------------------|----|
|           | him.                                                     | 20 |
| ISABELLA  | Justice, O royal Duke! Vail your regard                  |    |
|           | Upon a wronged – I would fain have said, a maid.         |    |
|           | O worthy prince, dishonour not your eye                  |    |
|           | By throwing it on any other object,                      |    |
|           | Till you have heard me in my true complaint,             | 25 |
|           | And given me justice! Justice! Justice! Justice!         |    |
| DUKE      | Relate your wrongs. In what? By whom? Be brief.          |    |
|           | Here is Lord Angelo shall give you justice,              |    |
|           | Reveal yourself to him.                                  |    |
| ISABELLA  |         O worthy Duke, |    |
|           | You bid me seek redemption of the devil.                 | 30 |
|           | Hear me yourself: for that which I must speak            |    |
|           | Must either punish me, not being believed,               |    |
|           | Or wring redress from you.                               |    |
|           | Hear me! O hear me, hear!                                |    |
| ANGELO    | My lord, her wits I fear me are not firm.                | 35 |
|           | She hath been a suitor to me for her brother,            |    |
|           | Cut off by course of justice.                            |    |
| ISABELLA  |       By course of justice! |    |
| ANGELO    | And she will speak most bitterly and strange.            |    |
| ISABELLA  | Most strange: but yet most truly will I speak.           |    |
|           | That Angelo's forsworn, is it not strange?               | 40 |
|           | That Angelo's a murderer, is't not strange?              |    |
|           | That Angelo is an adulterous thief,                      |    |
|           | An hypocrite, a virgin-violator,                         |    |
|           | Is it not strange, and strange?                          |    |
| DUKE      | Nay, it is ten times strange!                            | 45 |
| ISABELLA  | It is not truer he is Angelo,                            |    |
|           | Than this is all as true as it is strange;               |    |
|           | Nay, it is ten times true, for truth is truth            |    |
|           | To th'end of reck'ning.                                  |    |
| DUKE      |       Away with her. Poor soul, |    |
|           | She speaks this in th'infirmity of sense.                | 50 |

Isabella protests that she is not mad and that Angelo's virtue may be a deception. The Duke notes that her speech seems rational, and she begins to describe her visit to Angelo and the circumstances surrounding the visit. Lucio supports her story.

**51 conjure thee**: beg you with all my power. The word also means to call upon, constrain (a devil or spirit) to appear or do one's bidding, by the invocation of some sacred name or the use of some spell (*OED*). It may be coincidence that Isabella uses this word and another word from magic ('caracts', line 59), or it may show her inner feelings – that she needs to cast a spell to free herself from the danger she is in

**52 another comfort**: another place of peace

**53 neglect**: choose to ignore me

**55 but seems unlike**: only seems improbable

**56 the wicked'st...ground**: the most evil scoundrel on earth

**57 absolute**: omnipotent in a perfect way

**59 caracts**: signs of office. The word also means a magical character or symbol, a charm (*OED*) – (see note on 'conjure', line 51

   **forms**: rituals of office

**64 frame**: logic, structure

**65 Such...thing**: such a logical relationship of one thing to another

**67 Harp not on that**: do not keep playing on that idea of madness

**67–68 nor...inequality**: and do not abandon the idea that I am rational just because I am not of equal rank

**68 serve**: help

**70 the...true**: the false which seems true

**75 in...sisterhood**: seeking approval to become a nun, as a postulant

**77 As then**: was then

> • *Angelo has implied that Isabella is mad. Notice the debate about reason and madness, falseness and truth on this page.*

| ISABELLA | O Prince, I conjure thee, as thou believ'st |
| | There is another comfort than this world, |
| | That thou neglect me not with that opinion |
| | That I am touched with madness. Make not |
| | impossible |
| | That which but seems unlike. 'Tis not impossible 55 |
| | But one, the wicked'st caitiff on the ground, |
| | May seem as shy, as grave, as just, as absolute, |
| | As Angelo; even so may Angelo, |
| | In all his dressings, caracts, titles, forms, |
| | Be an arch-villain. Believe it, royal Prince, 60 |
| | If he be less, he's nothing; but he's more, |
| | Had I more name for badness. |
| DUKE | By mine honesty, |
| | If she be mad, as I believe no other, |
| | Her madness hath the oddest frame of sense, |
| | Such a dependency of thing on thing, 65 |
| | As e'er I heard in madness. |
| ISABELLA | O gracious Duke, |
| | Harp not on that; nor do not banish reason |
| | For inequality; but let your reason serve |
| | To make the truth appear where it seems hid, |
| | And hide the false seems true. |
| DUKE | Many that are not |
| | mad 70 |
| | Have, sure, more lack of reason. What would you |
| | say? |
| ISABELLA | I am the sister of one Claudio, |
| | Condemned upon the act of fornication |
| | To lose his head; condemned by Angelo. |
| | I – in probation of a sisterhood – 75 |
| | Was sent to by my brother; one Lucio |
| | As then the messenger. |
| LUCIO | That's I, and't like your |
| | Grace. |
| | I came to her from Claudio, and desired her |

Lucio persists until the Duke silences him. Isabella continues her impassioned account of her meeting with Angelo despite the Duke pointing out her intemperance.

79 **To...with**: to see if her heavenly gifts might work on
84 **you...yourself**: you have some business of your own
85 **be perfect**: state your case perfectly
   **warrant**: promise it, guarantee it
91 **pernicious caitiff**: deadly, corrupt villain
94 **Mended again**: she seems sane again
95 **to...by**: to cut a long story short
97 **refelled**: denied, rejected
101 **concupiscible intemperate lust**: uncontrolled and violent sexual desire

> • *Lucio, cued by Isabella (lines 77–79), seems to be trying to help. Why does the Duke order him to be silent?*
> • *What is the impact of Isabella's choice of language in line 101?*

To try her gracious fortune with Lord Angelo
For her poor brother's pardon.

ISABELLA                                    That's he
indeed.                                                          80

DUKE            [*To* LUCIO] You were not bid to speak.

LUCIO                                                No, my
good lord,
Nor wished to hold my peace.

DUKE                                        I wish you now,
then;
Pray you take note of it;
And when you have a business for yourself,
Pray heaven you then be perfect.

LUCIO                                        I warrant your
honour.                                                        85

DUKE            The warrant's for yourself: take heed to't.

ISABELLA        This gentleman told somewhat of my tale.

LUCIO            Right.

DUKE            It may be right, but you are i'the wrong
To speak before your time. – Proceed.

ISABELLA                                    I went    90
To this pernicious caitiff Deputy.

DUKE            That's somewhat madly spoken.

ISABELLA                                        Pardon it;
The phrase is to the matter.

DUKE            Mended again. The matter: proceed.

ISABELLA        In brief, to set the needless process by –        95
How I persuaded, how I prayed and kneeled,
How he refelled me, and how I replied
(For this was of much length) – the vile conclusion
I now begin with grief and shame to utter.
He would not, but by gift of my chaste body        100
To his concupiscible intemperate lust,
Release my brother; and after much debatement,

Isabella says Angelo betrayed his side of the bargain. The Duke refuses to believe her and says she was put up to it. Isabella, with a deep sense of wrong, decides to give up and go. The Duke arrests her for plotting malicious accusations. She reveals that a 'Friar Lodowick' knew of her plan. She is taken away.

103 **remorse**: pity
   **confutes**: defeats, confounds
105 **His...surfeiting**: having satisfied his desires to excess
108 **fond**: foolish, slightly mad
109 **suborned against**: tricked into attacking
110 **In hateful practice**: in some hostile conspiracy
111 **it...reason**: there can be no sense
112 **vehemency**: passionate vigour
113 **Faults...himself**: faults of his own
114 **He...himself**: he would have judged your brother with an awareness of his own failings
115 **set you on**: put you up to this
118 **ministers above**: angels
119 **with ripened time**: when the time of fulfilment comes
120 **Unfold**: reveal
120–121 **wrapt...countenance**: covered up by an outward show of dignity
125 **blasting...breath**: a perverted and libellous utterance
126 **him so near us**: he who is so close to us in power and authority
   **practice**: conspiracy
129 **ghostly**: literally 'spiritual', but here ironically also 'invisible' or 'non-existent'

> • *Notice that following accusations of madness, the next way of dismissing Isabella's claims is to suggest that she has been put up to it by some mischieveous party. These are classic ploys.*

My sisterly remorse confutes mine honour,
And I did yield to him. But the next morn
   betimes,
His purpose surfeiting, he sends a warrant     105
For my poor brother's head.

DUKE                              This is most likely!

ISABELLA   O, that it were as like as it is true.

DUKE       By heaven, fond wretch, thou know'st not what
   thou speak'st,
Or else thou art suborned against his honour
In hateful practice. First, his integrity     110
Stands without blemish; next, it imports no reason
That with such vehemency he should pursue
Faults proper to himself. If he had so offended,
He would have weighed thy brother by himself,
And not have cut him off. Someone hath set you
   on:                                 115
Confess the truth, and say by whose advice
Thou cam'st here to complain.

ISABELLA                   And is this all?
Then, O you blessed ministers above,
Keep me in patience, and with ripened time
Unfold the evil which is here wrapt up     120
In countenance! Heaven shield your Grace from
   woe,
As I, thus wronged, hence unbelieved go.

DUKE       I know you'd fain be gone. An officer!
To prison with her! [ISABELLA *is placed under guard*
                Shall we thus permit
A blasting and a scandalous breath to fall     125
On him so near us? This needs must be a practice.
Who knew of your intent and coming hither?

ISABELLA   One that I would were here, Friar Lodowick.
                         [*Exit guarded*

DUKE       A ghostly father, belike. – Who knows that

Lucio says that Lodowick is devious and has spread malicious rumours about the Duke. The Duke affects shock and the suspicion of a conspiracy. Friar Peter steps in to support Angelo and Lodowick as good men. He claims to speak for Lodowick, whom illness has detained.

**131 lay**: not an ordained priest

**133 swinged**: whipped (pronounced to rhyme with 'hinged')

**134 This' a good friar belike**: this is certainly a good friar (irony)

**136 substitute**: deputy

**138 saucy**: impertinent

**139 scurvy**: foul

**143–144 as free...ungot**: as innocent from the taint of guilt of sleeping with her as she is untouched by one not yet conceived

**147 temporary meddler**: one who meddles in worldly affairs

**150 as he vouches**: as he (Lucio) insists or proclaims

**151 most villainously**: he (Friar Lodowick) did most villainously

**154 mere**: personal

**159–160 with his oath...probation**: with his sworn testimony

> • *Notice the ways in which the identity of Friar Lodowick is disputed here. Why is this significant?*

Lodowick?

LUCIO       My lord, I know him. 'Tis a meddling friar;       130
            I do not like the man; had he been lay, my lord,
            For certain words he spake against your Grace
            In your retirement, I had swinged him soundly.

DUKE        Words against me! This' a good friar belike.
            And to set on this wretched woman here       135
            Against our substitute! Let this friar be found.

LUCIO       But yesternight, my lord, she and that friar,
            I saw them at the prison: a saucy friar,
            A very scurvy fellow.

FRIAR PETER                      Blessed be your royal Grace!
            I have stood by, my lord, and I have heard       140
            Your royal ear abused. First hath this woman
            Most wrongfully accused your substitute,
            Who is as free from touch or soil with her
            As she from one ungot.

DUKE                            We did believe no less.
            Know you that Friar Lodowick that she speaks
                of?       145

FRIAR PETER  I know him for a man divine and holy,
            Nor scurvy, not a temporary meddler,
            As he's reported by this gentleman;
            And, on my trust, a man that never yet
            Did, as he vouches, misreport your Grace.       150

LUCIO       My lord, most villainously; believe it.

FRIAR PETER  Well, he in time may come to clear himself;
            But at this instant he is sick, my lord:
            Of a strange fever. Upon his mere request,
            Being come to knowledge that there was
                complaint       155
            Intended 'gainst Lord Angelo, came I hither,
            To speak, as from his mouth, what he doth know
            Is true and false; and what he with his oath
            And all probation will make up full clear

Friar Peter says Isabella will be proved false and the Duke reassuringly turns the conduct of the affair over to Angelo. Mariana is brought in veiled and refuses to reveal her face until her husband tells her. Her identitity is unknown, though Lucio, ironically, says she's a prostitute.

**160 convented**: called to these proceedings
**161 justify**: give justice to
**162 vulgarly**: publicly
**166 vanity**: presumptuous pride
**168–169 I'll be impartial...cause**: the irony here is that judges should be impartial; the audience will understand that the Duke is implying that Angelo cannot be impartial in judging his own case. He further implies that he is, in fact, still the impartial judge of Angelo's case
**180 punk**: prostitute
**182 I...himself**: I wish I could find a reason for him to have to talk on his own behalf
**187 known**: had sexual intercourse with

> • *Since the Duke knows the answer to everything that he asks Mariana, and so does the audience, what is the dramatic purpose and effect of this questioning?*

Whensoever he's convented. First, for this
    woman,                        160
To justify this worthy nobleman
So vulgarly and personally accused,
Her shall you hear disproved to her eyes,
Till she herself confess it.

DUKE                             Good friar, let's hear it.
Do you not smile as this, Lord Angelo?    165
O heaven, the vanity of wretched fools!
Give us some seats. – Come, cousin Angelo,
In this I'll be impartial: be you judge
Of your own cause.

*Enter* MARIANA *veiled*

                       Is this the witness, friar?
First, let her show her face, and after, speak.   170

MARIANA    Pardon, my lord; I will not show my face
Until my husband bid me.

DUKE                       What, are you married?

MARIANA    No, my lord.

DUKE    Are you a maid?

MARIANA    No, my lord.                           175

DUKE    A widow, then?

MARIANA    Neither, my lord.

DUKE    Why, you are nothing then: neither maid,
widow, nor wife!

LUCIO    My lord, she may be a punk; for many of them   180
are neither maid, widow nor wife.

DUKE    Silence that fellow! I would he had some cause
to prattle for himself.

LUCIO    Well, my lord.

MARIANA    My lord, I do confess I ne'er was married;   185
And I confess besides, I am no maid.
I have known my husband; yet my husband

Despite Lucio's crude interjections and the Duke's doubts about her veracity, Mariana leads Angelo to ask to see her face. She reveals who she is, and says that it was she with whom Angelo made love. Angelo admits knowing her.

**196–198  And charges...of love**: and accuses him of the crime committed at the precise moment when I'll swear I had him in my arms and was making love with him

**199  moe**: more (men)

**201  just**: exactly, precisely

**204  abuse**: complication, confusion

**208  with a vowed contract**: with a solemn promise

**210  match**: secret lover's tryst, assignation

**211  supply**: deliver what was agreed

**213  Carnally**: sexually

> • *Notice the repetition of the word 'know'. In what ways is it being used and to what effect?*

Knows not that ever he knew me.

LUCIO      He was drunk then, my lord; it can be no better.

DUKE       For the benefit of silence, would thou wert so
           too.                                                        190

LUCIO      Well, my lord.

DUKE       This is no witness for Lord Angelo.

MARIANA    Now I come to't, my lord.
           She that accuses him of fornication
           In self-same manner doth accuse my husband,      195
           And charges him, my lord, with such a time
           When I'll depose I had him in mine arms
           With all th'effect of love.

ANGELO     Charges she moe than me?

MARIANA                                Not that I know.

DUKE       No? You say your husband.                                  200

MARIANA    Why just, my lord, and that is Angelo,
           Who thinks he knows that he ne'er knew my body,
           But knows, he thinks, that he knows Isabel's.

ANGELO     This is a strange abuse. Let's see thy face.

MARIANA    [*Unveiling*] My husband bids me; now I will
               unmask.                                                 205
           This is that face, thou cruel Angelo,
           Which once thou swor'st was worth the looking on:
           This is the hand which, with a vowed contract,
           Was fast belocked in thine: this is the body
           That took away the match from Isabel            210
           And did supply thee at thy garden-house,
           In her imagined person.

DUKE                                Know you this woman?

LUCIO      Carnally, she says.

DUKE                                Sirrah, no more!

LUCIO      Enough, my lord.

ANGELO     My lord, I must confess I know this woman;      215

Angelo says he broke off their engagement because of
Mariana's looseness. Mariana swears she is in every sense his
wife. Angelo wants full power to investigate what he calls a
mad conspiracy. The Duke agrees, asking Escalus to join
him, and gives them full powers of punishment.

**216 since**: ago

**218–219 Partly for that…composition**: partly because the
dowry she offered fell short of what was agreed

**219–221 but in chief…levity**: but mainly because her
reputation was damaged by her immoral/frivolous
behaviour

**225 sense in truth**: signficant meaning in true speech

**226 affianced**: engaged to be

**230 in safety**: without fear of punishment

**231 confixed**: fixed for ever

**233 the scope of justice**: the full range of power and
opportunity given by the law

**234 touched**: affected

**235 informal**: deranged

**236 mightier member**: more powerful figure

**241 Compact with**: in conspiracy with her that's gone:
i.e. Isabella

**242 swear down**: call to their aid, invoke
**particular**: individual

**243 testimonies**: witnesses
**credit**: credibility

**244 That's…approbation**: who is proved beyond doubt

> • *At the end of Act 2 scene 2, Angelo says he used to*
> *smile at men who were infatuated by women. Now, in*
> *line 232, he again speaks of stopping smiling. Why?*
> *What does smiling seem to mean to Angelo?*

And five years since, there was some speech of
   marriage
Betwixt myself and her; which was broke off,
Partly for that her promised proportions
Came short of composition; but in chief
For that her reputation was disvalued         220
In levity: since which time of five years
I never spake with her, saw her, nor heard from her,
Upon my faith and honour.

MARIANA                          Noble Prince,
As there comes light from heaven, and words from
   breath,
As there is sense in truth, and truth in virtue,   225
I am affianced this man's wife, as strongly
As words could make up vows. And, my good lord,
But Tuesday night last gone, in's garden house,
He knew me as a wife. As this is true
Let me in safety raise me from my knees,       230
Or else for ever be confixed here,
A marble monument.

ANGELO                I did but smile till now:
Now, good my lord, give me the scope of justice.
My patience here is touched: I do perceive
These poor informal woman are no more     235
But instruments of some more mightier member
That sets them on. Let me have way, my lord,
To find this practice out.

DUKE                   Ay, with my heart;
And punish them to your height of pleasure.
Thou foolish friar, and thou pernicious woman, 240
Compact with her that's gone: think'st thou thy
   oaths,
Though they would swear down each particular
   saint,
Were testimonies against his worth and credit,
That's sealed in approbation? You, Lord Escalus,

The Duke wants to see Lodowick. Friar Peter confirms him as the instigator of the women's plot. The Provost is sent to find Lodowick. The Duke makes an excuse to leave. Lucio tells Escalus of Lodowick's malice; Escalus tells him to repeat his story when Lodowick arrives and then sends for Isabella.

**245 Sit with my cousin**: hold court with Angelo
**253 well-warranted**: well-trusted
**254 forth**: out in the open, to its conclusion
**255 Do with your injuries**: deal with the wrongs done to you
**256 chastisement**: punishment
**261 *Cucullus...monachum***: a hood doesn't make a friar
**265 enforce...him**: bring the full force of his speeches against him
**266 a notable fellow**: an obvious scoundrel
**272 Not...report**: you won't handle her better than she alleges he (Angelo) did
**273 Say you**: what do you mean

- *What is the impact of Lucio's innuendo about handling Isabella (lines 271–275)?*

|  | Sit with my cousin; lend him your kind pains | 245 |

Sit with my cousin; lend him your kind pains 245
To find out this abuse, whence 'tis derived.
There is another friar that set them on;
Let him be sent for.

FRIAR PETER Would he were here, my lord; for he indeed
Hath set the women on to this complaint.        250
Your Provost knows the place where he abides,
And he may fetch him.

DUKE                                    Go, do it instantly.
                                    [*Exit an* ATTENDANT
And you, my noble and well-warranted cousin,
Whom it concerns to hear this matter forth,
Do with your injuries as seems you best        255
In any chastisement. I for a while will leave you;
But stir not you till you have well determined
Upon these slanderers.

ESCALUS                                    My lord, we'll do it
        throughly.                                [*Exit* DUKE
Signior Lucio, did not you say you knew that Friar
Lodowick to be a dishonest person?        260

LUCIO *Cucullus non facit monachum:* honest in nothing
but in his clothes, and one that hath spoke most
villainous speeches of the Duke.

ESCALUS We shall entreat you to abide here till he come, and
enforce them against him. We shall find this        265
friar a notable fellow.

LUCIO As any in Vienna, on my word!

ESCALUS Call that same Isabel here once again; I would
speak with her.                        [*Exit an* ATTENDANT
Pray you, my lord, give me leave to question;        270
you shall see how I'll handle her.

LUCIO Not better than he, by her own report.

ESCALUS Say you?

LUCIO Marry, sir, I think if you handled her privately
she would sooner confess; perchance publicly        275

The Provost brings in the Duke, disguised as the friar, and
Isabella returns, guarded. Questioned by Escalus, 'Lodowick'
says the case is a mockery in the Duke's unjust absence,
because the responsibility has been given to the villain,
i.e. Angelo. Escalus loses control and accuses Lodowick of
stirring the women up to subvert justice.

**277 darkly**: in private
**278 light**: loose, easy
**285 Mum**: I'll keep quiet
**290 great place**: high status
**290–291 let...throne**: let even the devil sometimes be respected
for his hellfire throne
**293 The Duke's in us**: we have the Duke's authority
**295 poor souls**: i.e. Isabella and Mariana
**296 Come...fox**: do you come to try to rescue the innocent
from the killer
**297 redress**: hope of just treatment
**299 retort**: reject
**manifest appeal**: obvious claim
**300–311 And...accuse**: and put responsibility for the trial into
the pronouncements of the villain whom you've come to
accuse
**304 suborned**: put (these women) up to
**305 in foul mouth**: with lying words
**306 in the...ear**: for his own ear to hear

> • *What are the implications of the Duke's words*
> *'Respect...burning throne' (lines 290–292)?*

she'll be ashamed.

*Enter at several doors* PROVOST *with* DUKE *in disguise and hooded, and* ISABELLA *under guard*

| | |
|---|---|
| ESCALUS | I will go darkly to work with her. |
| LUCIO | That's the way; for women are light at midnight. |
| ESCALUS | Come on, mistress, here's a gentlewoman denies all that you have said. 280 |
| LUCIO | My lord, here comes the rascal I spoke of, here with the Provost. |
| ESCALUS | In very good time. Speak not you to him till we call upon you. |
| LUCIO | Mum. 285 |
| ESCALUS | Come, sir: did you set these women on to slander Lord Angelo? They have confessed you did. |
| DUKE | 'Tis false. |
| ESCALUS | How! Know you where you are? |
| DUKE | Respect to your great place; and let the devil 290 <br> Be sometime honoured for his burning throne. <br> Where is the Duke? 'Tis he should hear me speak. |
| ESCALUS | The Duke's in us; and we will hear you speak; <br> Look you speak justly. |
| DUKE | Boldly, at least. But O, poor souls, 295 <br> Come you to seek the lamb here of the fox? <br> Good-night to your redress! Is the Duke gone? <br> Then is your cause gone too. The Duke's unjust <br> Thus to retort your manifest appeal, <br> And put your trial in the villain's mouth 300 <br> Which here you come to accuse. |
| LUCIO | This is the rascal: this is he I spoke of. |
| ESCALUS | Why, thou unreverend and unhallowed friar! <br> Is't not enough thou hast suborned these women <br> To accuse this worthy man, but in foul mouth, 305 <br> And in the witness of his proper ear, |

Escalus erupts at the idea that the Duke/friar is
irresponsible. Lodowick claims immunity as a foreigner and
comments on the corruption he has seen in high places in
Vienna. Escalus is furious and Angelo tells Lucio to produce
his evidence against Lodowick. Lucio offers a string of
falsehoods which the Duke/friar denies.

307 **glance**: move on
309 **rack**: torture wheel
    **touse**: stretch violently, rack
313–314 **His subject...provincial**: I am not a Viennese subject
    of his, nor do I come under his law
315 **looker–on**: observer, witness
317 **stew**: as in food (metaphor), but also brothel
317–320 **laws...mark**: there is a law to deal with all crimes, but
    the crimes are so overlooked that the strong laws look like
    the comic threats in barbers' shop windows, and are as
    much to be mocked as paid attention to. (Barbers, who
    were also surgeons, as a joke, put in their windows, lists of
    gruesome penalties for bad manners towards them)
324–325 **goodman Baldpate**: old baldie
331 **fleshmonger**: pimp, procurer of prostitutes
334 **change...me**: pretend to me

- *What is the impact of the Duke's images for corruption
  and the law (lines 316–320)?*
- *Why does Lucio lie so blatantly (lines 331–333)?*
- *Why is 'plucking by the nose' such a significant
  expression for Lucio to use (lines 337–338)?*

To call him villain? And then to glance from him
To th'Duke himself, to tax him with injustice?
Take him hence! To th'rack with him! – We'll
    touse you
Joint by joint, but we will know his purpose.    310
What! Unjust!

DUKE                        Be not so hot: the Duke
Dare no more stretch this finger of mine than he
Dare rack his own. His subject am I not,
Nor here provincial. My business in this state
Made me a looker-on here in Vienna,    315
Where I have seen corruption boil and bubble
Till it o'errun the stew: laws for all faults,
But faults so countenanced that the strong statutes
Stand like the forfeits in a barber's shop,
As much in mock as mark.

ESCALUS                Slander to th'state!  320
Away with him to prison!

ANGELO    What can you vouch against him, Signior Lucio?
Is this the man that you did tell us of?

LUCIO    'Tis he, my lord. – Come hither, goodman
Baldpate, do you know me?    325

DUKE    I remember you, sir, by the sound of your voice;
I met you at the prison, in the absence of the Duke.

LUCIO    O, did you so? And do you remember what you
said of the Duke?

DUKE    Most notedly, sir.    330

LUCIO    Do you so, sir? And was the Duke a fleshmonger,
a fool, and a coward, as you then reported him to
be?

DUKE    You must, sir, change persons with me, ere you
make that my report. You indeed spoke so of    335
him, and much more, much worse.

LUCIO    O, thou damnable fellow! Did not I pluck thee by
the nose for thy speeches?

Lodowick protests he loves the Duke, and Escalus, completely out of patience, orders Lodowick and the women to gaol. The Duke/friar resists, Angelo orders Lucio to help and, in a scuffle, Lucio reveals the Duke under the hood. The Duke orders Lucio to await judgement, forgives Escalus and offers Angelo a chance to explain himself. Angelo feels deep guilt, like a sinner before God.

**340 close**: make a deal
**341 treasonable abuses**: treacherous lies
**342 withal**: with
**345 giglets**: mad women, loose women
**346 confederate companion**: fellow conspirator
**351 knave's visage**: crook's face
**352 a pox to you**: curse you
  **sheep-biting face**: the face of a dog that worries sheep (expression for a criminal)
**353 hanged an hour**: sheep-worrying dogs and women criminals were hanged for an hour
**354 mad'st**: made, created someone a duke
**355 bail these gentle three**: free these innocents on my security, i.e. Isabella, Mariana, Friar Peter
**356 the friar**: he wishes to talk about the things Lucio said to him earlier as 'friar'
**357 anon**: as soon as possible
**360 We'll...him**: I'll take his (Angelo's) place
**361–362 Hast...office?**: have you any words, cleverness or sheer cheek by which you can do your self any good
**366 be undiscernible**: go undetected
**368 passes**: actions

- *Why does the Provost disobey Escalus and not remove the Duke?*
- *Why does Shakespeare choose Lucio to be the character who reveals the Duke?*
- *What is the significance of the Duke not being in control of his own revelation?*

| | |
|---|---|
| DUKE | I protest, I love the Duke as I love myself. |
| ANGELO | Hark how the villain would close now, after his   340<br>treasonable abuses! |
| ESCALUS | Such a fellow is not to be talked withal. Away with<br>him to prison! Where is the Provost? Away with<br>him to prison! Lay bolts enough upon him: let him<br>speak no more. Away with those giglets too,   345<br>and with the other confederate companion!<br>*[The* PROVOST *lays hands on the* DUKE |
| DUKE | Stay, sir, stay a while. |
| ANGELO | What, resists he? Help him, Lucio. |
| LUCIO | Come, sir! Come, sir! Come, sir! Foh, sir! Why,<br>you bald-pated, lying rascal! – You must be   350<br>hooded, must you? Show your knave's visage, with<br>a pox to you! Show your sheep-biting face, and be<br>hanged an hour! Will't not off?    *[Pulls off the*<br>FRIAR'S *hood and discovers the* DUKE |
| DUKE | Thou art the first knave that e'er mad'st a duke.<br>First, Provost, let me bail these gentle three.   355<br>*[To* LUCIO*]* Sneak not away, sir, for the friar and you<br>Must have a word anon. – Lay hold on him. |
| LUCIO | *[Aside]* This may prove worse than hanging. |
| DUKE | *[To* ESCALUS*]* What you have spoke, I pardon: sit<br>   you down.<br>We'll borrow place of him *[To* ANGELO*]* Sir, by<br>   your leave.   360<br>Hast thou or word, or wit, or impudence,<br>That yet can do thee office? If thou hast,<br>Rely upon it till my tale be heard,<br>And hold no longer out. |
| ANGELO |                O my dread lord,<br>I should be guiltier than my guiltiness   365<br>To think I can be undiscernible,<br>When I perceive your Grace, like power divine,<br>Hath looked upon my passes. Then, good prince, |

The Duke orders Angelo to marry Mariana. The Duke declares himself Isabella's 'prince' and at her service. She begs his pardon, which he gives, asking her to pardon him for remaining in disguise and not using his powers to save Claudio. He says events ran too quickly for him.

**369 session:** session of the court

**370 let...confession:** let my trial contain my confession

**371 sequent:** following

**372 thou:** i.e. Angelo

**376 Do you the office:** you carry out the ceremony
　　**consummate:** completed

**378–379 I am...of it:** I am more amazed that he has dishonoured himself than by the way he has done it – it is competely out of character

**381 Advertising...business:** paying reverend attention to your needs

**382 Not...habit:** not changing my attitude now that I've changed my clothes

**383 Attorneyed at your service:** committed to act on your behalf

**384 vassal:** subject
　　**pained:** troubled

**385 unknown:** that I did not know about

**386 free:** generous

**387 sits at:** is a constant trouble to

**390 rash remonstrance:** instant revelation

**392 celerity:** speed

**393 came on:** would have come on

**394 brained:** killed

> • *What is the distinction Escalus is making in lines 378–379? What does it tell us?*

No longer session hold upon my shame,
But let my trial be mine own confession.                    370
Immediate sentence, then, and sequent death
Is all the grace I beg.

DUKE                                    Come hither, Mariana. –
Say: wast thou e'er contracted to this woman?

ANGELO      I was, my lord.

DUKE        Go, take her hence, and marry her instantly.      375
Do you the office, friar; which consummate,
Return him here again. Go with him, Provost.
            [*Exeunt* ANGELO, MARIANA, FRIAR PETER
                                    *and* PROVOST

ESCALUS     My lord, I am more amazed at his dishonour
Than at the strangeness of it.

DUKE                              Come hither, Isabel.
Your friar is now your prince. As I was then,            380
Advertising and holy to your business,
Not changing heart with habit, I am still
Attorneyed at your service.

ISABELLA                          O, give me pardon,
That I, your vassal, have employed and pained
Your unknown sovereignty.

DUKE                              You are pardoned,
      Isabel.                                              385
And now, dear maid, be you as free to us.
Your brother's death, I know, sits at your heart:
And you may marvel why I obscured myself,
Labouring to save his life, and would not rather
Make rash remonstrance of my hidden power              390
Than let him so be lost. O most kind maid,
It was the swift celerity of his death,
Which I did think with slower foot came on,
That brained my purpose. But peace be with him.
That life is better life, past fearing death,            395
Than that which lives to fear. Make it your comfort,

Angelo and Mariana return married and the Duke tells
Isabella she must pardon Angelo for Mariana's sake. He
points out vehemently that justice demands Angelo's death
for Claudio's, and condemns him to death. Despite
Mariana's protest, the Duke insists and says all Angelo's
wealth will come to her and make her worth a husband with
more wealth and status. Mariana says she wants no-one
better.

**399 salt imagination**: sexual fantasy

**401 adjudged**: condemned

**402–404 Being...life**: as he (Angelo) is guilty of two crimes:
violating sacred chastity and breach of the promise to restore
your brother's life (which followed from the violation)

**406 even...tongue**: as though he were saying it himself

**410 manifested**: fully revealed

**411 denies thee vantage**: denies you any right to advantageous
treatment

**415 mock...husband**: mock me by giving me a husband and
then executing him

**417 Consenting...honour**: agreeing to protect your honourable
reputation

**418–419 else...life**: otherwise rumours that he had made love
to you might condemn your future reputation

**424 crave**: wish for

---

• *The Duke orders Angelo away to be executed (line
414). Mariana's intervention stops this. Why does the
Duke allow it to? What methods is the Duke adopting?*

ISABELLA                         I do, my lord.

*Enter* ANGELO, MARIANA, FRIAR PETER, *and* PROVOST

DUKE        For this new-married man approaching here,
            Whose salt imagination yet hath wronged
            Your well defended honour, you must pardon     400
            For Mariana's sake: but as he adjudged your
                brother,
            Being criminal in double violation
            Of sacred chastity and of promise-breach
            Thereon dependent, of your brother's life,
            The very mercy of the law cries out            405
            Most audible, even from his proper tongue:
            'An Angelo for Claudio; death for death.
            Haste still pays haste, and leisure answers leisure;
            Like doth quit like, and Measure still for Measure.'
            Then, Angelo, thy fault's thus manifested,      410
            Which, though thou would'st deny, denies thee
                vantage.
            We do condemn thee to the very block
            Where Claudio stopped to death, and with like
                haste.
            Away with him.

MARIANA                          O my most gracious lord,
            I hope you will not mock me with a husband.     415

DUKE        It is your husband mocked you with a husband.
            Consenting to the safeguard of your honour,
            I thought your marriage fit: else imputation,
            For that he knew you, might reproach your life,
            And choke your good to come. For his
                possessions,                                 420
            Although by confiscation they are ours,
            We do instate and widow you with all,
            To buy you a better husband.

MARIANA                          O my dear lord,
            I crave no other, nor no better man.

Desperately, Mariana pleads with Isabella to support her request, but the Duke points out that she's unlikely to because of her brother's death. As the Duke pronounces Angelo's death in payment for Claudio's, Isabella kneels and pleads for Angelo saying he was, in a way, sincere, and did not, unlike Claudio, actually commit the crime.

**425 we are definitive**: I am adamant
**426 lose your labour**: waste your effort
**431 importune**: beg desperately
**432 in mercy of this fact**: praying for mercy for Angelo
**433 paved bed**: tomb
**436 Hold up your hands**: hold your hands in prayer
**438 for the most**: in most cases; for the most part
**441 bounteous**: generous
**446 but**: only, i.e. no more, no less than
**449 His act...intent**: what he did was not as bad as he intended
**451–452 Thoughts...thoughts**: we cannot expect to have completely obedient thoughts, and intentions are only thoughts

> • *What do you think Mariana and the Duke say to make Isabella forgive Angelo? What seem to be her feelings as she does so? Is her reasoning convincing?*

| | |
|---|---|
| DUKE | Never crave him; we are definitive. 425 |
| MARIANA | Gentle my liege – |
| DUKE | You do but lose your labour.<br>Away with him to death. [*To* LUCIO] Now, sir, to<br>you. |
| MARIANA | [*Kneeling*] O my good lord – sweet Isabel, take my<br>part;<br>Lend me your knees, and all my life to come<br>I'll lend you all my life to do you service. 430 |
| DUKE | Against all sense you do importune her.<br>Should she kneel down in mercy of this fact,<br>Her brother's ghost his paved bed would break,<br>And take her hence in horror. |
| MARIANA | Isabel!<br>Sweet Isabel, do yet but kneel by me; 435<br>Hold up your hands, say nothing: I'll speak all.<br>They say best men are moulded out of faults,<br>And, for the most, become much more the better<br>For being a little bad. So may my husband.<br>O Isabel! Will you not lend a knee? 440 |
| DUKE | He dies for Claudio's death. |
| ISABELLA | [*Kneeling*] Most bounteous sir:<br>Look, if it please you, on this man condemned<br>As if my brother lived. I partly think<br>A due sincerity governed his deeds<br>Till he did look on me. Since it is so, 445<br>Let him not die. My brother had but justice,<br>In that he did the thing for which he died:<br>For Angelo,<br>His act did not o'ertake his bad intent,<br>And must be buried but as an intent 450<br>That perished by the way. Thoughts are no<br>subjects;<br>Intents, but merely thoughts. |
| MARIANA | Merely, my lord. |

The Duke ignores the plea and turns on the Provost,
stripping him of office for disobedience over Claudio's
execution. The Provost pretends that, feeling guilty, he saved
Barnardine. The Duke orders Barnardine to be brought.
Escalus expresses his sorrow to Angelo who prays for death.
The Provost returns with Barnardine, Claudio and Juliet.
Claudio's face is hidden.

**453 suit's:** your begging is
**458 private:** personal
**459 discharge:** sack/relieve
**461 I thought it...not:** I thought it might be wrong to execute
   him on the strength of a private message, but was not
   certain
**462 advice:** contemplation
**463 testimony:** evidence
**469 still:** always
**470 in the heat of blood:** in the grip of passion
**471 tempered:** balanced
**472 procure:** produce, arouse

> • *Why does the Duke discharge the Provost of his office
> (lines 459–460)? What does the Provost say between
> here and the end of the scene to make the Duke change
> from ordering discharge to conferring promotion?*

DUKE        Your suit's unprofitable. Stand up, I say.
            I have bethought me of another fault.
            Provost, how came it Claudio was beheaded        455
            At an unusual hour?

PROVOST                             It was commanded so.

DUKE        Had you a special warrant for the deed?

PROVOST     No, my good lord: it was by private message.

DUKE        For which I do discharge you of your office.
            Give up your keys.

PROVOST                         Pardon me, noble lord;        460
            I thought it was a fault, but knew it not;
            Yet did repent me after more advice.
            For testimony whereof, one in the prison
            That should by private order else have died,
            I have reserved alive.

DUKE                              What's he?

PROVOST                                      His name is
            Barnardine.                                       465

DUKE        I would thou hadst done so by Claudio.
            Go, fetch him hither, let me look upon him.
                                          [*Exit* PROVOST

ESCALUS     I am sorry one so learned and so wise
            As you, Lord Angelo, have still appeared,
            Should slip so grossly, both in the heat of blood 470
            And lack of tempered judgement afterward.

ANGELO      I am sorry that such sorrow I procure,
            And so deep sticks it in my penitent heart
            That I crave death more willingly than mercy;
            'Tis my deserving, and I do entreat it.           475

            *Enter* PROVOST *with* BARNARDINE, CLAUDIO,
            *muffled, and* JULIET

DUKE        Which is that Barnardine?

PROVOST                                This, my lord.

DUKE        There was a friar told me of this man.

In an act of mercy, the Duke releases Barnardine. The
Provost reveals a man exactly like Claudio, and the Duke
pardons him for Isabella's brother's sake. The Duke asks for
Isabella's hand, but does not wait for an answer. He pardons
Angelo, then turns to Lucio and, despite all his merciful
feelings, sentences him to a whipping and then hanging. A
proclamation is to be made for any woman wronged by him
to come forward.

**479 apprehends**: knows
**480 squar'st thy life**: live your life
**481 quit**: release from
**488 his**: i.e. Claudio's
**493 quickening**: coming to life
**494 quits**: leaves
**496 an apt remission**: a readiness to forgive
**499 luxury**: indulgence, licentiousness
**501 extol**: praise (sarcasm)
**503 trick**: standing joke

- *What is the significance of the Duke's merciful*
  *forgiveness of Barnardine's 'earthly faults'*
  *(lines 481–483)?*
- *What does Lucio mean when he says that he ran down*
  *the Duke's character 'according to the trick'*
  *(lines 502–503)? What does this tell us about his*
  *character and role?*

Sirrah, thou art said to have a stubborn soul
That apprehends no further than this world,
And squar'st thy life according. Thou'rt
    condemned;          480
But, for those earthly faults, I quit them all,
And pray thee take this mercy to provide
For better times to come. Friar, advise him;
I leave him to your hand. – What muffled fellow's
    that?

PROVOST    This is another prisoner that I saved,    485
Who should have died when Claudio lost his head;
As like almost to Claudio as himself.    [ *Unmuffles*
                                    CLAUDIO

DUKE    [ *To* ISABELLA] If he be like your brother, for his
    sake
Is he pardoned; and for your lovely sake
Give me your hand and say you will be mine.    490
He is my brother too: but fitter time for that.
By this Lord Angelo perceives he's safe;
Methinks I see a quickening in his eye.
Well, Angelo, your evil quits you well.
Look that you love your wife: her worth, worth
    yours.    495
I find an apt remission in myself.
And yet here's one in place I cannot pardon.
[ *To* LUCIO] You, sirrah, that knew me for a fool, a
    coward,
One all of luxury, an ass, a madman:
Wherein have I so deserved of you    500
That you extol me thus?

LUCIO    Faith, my lord, I spoke it but according to the
trick: if you will hang me for it, you may: but I had
rather it would please you I might be whipped.

DUKE    Whipped first, sir, and hanged after.    505
Proclaim it, Provost, round about the city,
If any woman wronged by this lewd fellow,

The Duke orders that Lucio marry a woman whom he has made pregnant, then suffer the other punishments. Although Lucio protests against having to marry a whore, the Duke insists, but releases him from the other punishments. Lucio says that to marry a whore is the same as death. The Duke ends the play with expressions of joy, love and thanks and repeats his proposal to Isabella. She does not answer.

**510 nuptial**: wedding
**513 even now**: just now
**514 recompense**: pay back
**515 cuckold**: husband of an unfaithful wife
**518 Remit...forfeits**: let you off your other punishments
**520 pressing to death**: execution by having heavy stones piled upon you
**522 restore**: give rightful treatment to, i.e. marry
**524 confessed her**: heard her confession
**526 behind**: to come
   **gratulate**: to be thanked
**532 motion...good**: a desire that brings you much good
**536 yet behind**: yet to be told
   **meet**: fitting

> • *'Slandering a prince deserves it.' (line 521) Do you
>   think the Duke is serious, or is he speaking ironically?*

– As I have heard him swear himself there's one
Whom he begot with child – let her appear,
And he shall marry her. The nuptial finished,                510
Let him be whipped and hanged.

LUCIO    I beseech your Highness, do not marry me to a
whore. Your Highness said even now, I made you
a duke; good my lord, do not recompense me in
making me a cuckold.                                         515

DUKE     Upon mine honour, thou shalt marry her.
Thy slanders I forgive, and therewithal
Remit thy other forfeits. – Take him to prison,
And see our pleasure herein executed.

LUCIO    Marrying a punk, my lord, is pressing to death,     520
Whipping, and hanging.

DUKE                             Slandering a prince
        deserves it.
She, Claudio, that you wronged, look you restore.
Joy to you, Mariana; love her, Angelo:
I have confessed her, and I know her virtue.
Thanks, good friend Escalus, for thy much
        goodness;                                            525
There's more behind that is more gratulate.
Thanks, Provost, for thy care and secrecy;
We shall employ thee in a worthier place.
Forgive him, Angelo, that brought you home
The head of Ragozine for Claudio's:                          530
Th'offence pardons itself. Dear Isabel,
I have a motion much imports your good;
Whereto if you'll a willing ear incline,
What's mine is yours, and what is yours is mine.
So bring us to our palace, where we'll show               535
What's yet behind that's meet you all should know.
                                        [*Exeunt* OMNES

# ACTIVITIES

## Keeping track

### Lines 1–169

1 In what style does the Duke greet Angelo and Escalus?
2 How does he respond to Isabella's accusation – in tone of voice, in action?
3 How does Friar Peter move the plot forward? What view of Friar Lodowick does he offer?
4 How does Lucio set himself up for judgement during this passage?
5 How far might Angelo be given confidence by the words and events in this passage?

### Lines 169–258

6 What are the major revelations that spring from Mariana's unveiling?
7 How does Angelo explain the matter? How does he explain the actions of Isabella and Mariana?
8 How does the Duke seem to respond to all this?

### Lines 258–353

9 How successful are Escalus' attempts to take over the interrogation of Isabella and, then, 'Friar Lodowick'? What is Lucio's role in this?
10 How does the Duke/friar respond to interrogation?
11 What is dramatically critical about the moment when the Duke is unveiled and the way he first behaves?
12 Does the Duke appear to be fazed by losing control when he is revealed? Why does Shakespeare make Lucio the perpetrator of this revelation?

### Lines 355–end

13 How does Angelo respond to the revelation (lines 364–372)? What is the Duke's decision? (lines 372–397)
14 How does the Duke behave towards Isabella? (lines 373–392)
15 How does the Duke use the threat of the death penalty to influence Isabella and Mariana? (lines 393–448)

16 How does the Duke lead up to the revelation of Claudio? (lines 455–484)
17 How does the Duke conclude matters? What are his final commands and judgements? (lines 488–536)

## Discussion

1 Look at the Duke's handling of the other characters and the way he plays his own role:
   • Are there any moments when he loses control?
   • Are there any hints of his feelings for Isabella before he proposes?
2 Consider the other leading characters:
   Isabella Angelo Claudio Mariana Lucio
   How does Shakespeare leave them and our attitude to them? Have they changed or developed or grown? Has our attitude towards them changed?
3 Consider the plot that the audience has been following:
   Is it fully and satisfactorily worked out? Does the play work as a whole, or is it two smaller plays joined together?

## Drama

1 Use FORUM THEATRE techniques to explore 'this moment' (line 441):
   'DUKE: *He dies for Claudio's death.*
   ISABELLA: (*Kneeling*)          *Most bounteous sir.*'
   • How domineering is the Duke ?
   • Is this his triumph?
   • How reluctantly or happily does Isabella accede to Mariana's plea?
   • Is this a moment of dignity or defeat or something else?
   (You could go on to hotseat the Duke and Isabella.)
2 • Individuals research the experiences of one of the following characters during the last scene: Isabella, Angelo, Mariana, the Provost, Lucio.
   • Each then tells his or her story including reflections and feelings.
3 Work as a group. One person plays the Duke after the end of the play, as a man who believes he did everything for the best.
   • Isabella, Angelo, Mariana, the Provost, Lucio and Claudio hotseat the Duke about his treatment of them and his motives.
   • Repeat the activity using other interpretations of the Duke.

## Close study

### 1 Lines 1–169

- What ironies can you find in the Duke's words (lines 1–19)? What is their dramatic effect?
- What rhetorical devices does Isabella use to make her plea (lines 21–62)?
- What is the irony of the Duke's words (lines 28–29)?
- Angelo offers the idea (line 35) that Isabella is out of her mind. What does he mean? How does the Duke take up this idea (lines 50–124)? What further explanation of her behaviour does he suggest?
- What is ironic about Friar Peter's words (lines 163–164)?
- What is ironic about the Duke's words (lines 168–169)?

### 2 Lines 169–258

- What is the effect of Mariana's riddles about her identity as a woman? What is the effect of Lucio's comments?
- What are the implications of the use of the word 'know' in lines 199–229?
- Is the word play in this section (lines 169–232) serious or comic?
- In what tones does Angelo request authority and the Duke grant it (lines 233–258)? What added innuendoes do you detect? What echoes are there of the start of the play?

### 3 Lines 259–358

- Contrast Escalus' attempts to deal with Isabella and Lodowick with his earlier treatment of Froth and Pompey.
- Are Lodowick's first words true (line 288)?
- Look carefully at the Duke's words as Lodowick: lines 295–301; 311–320; 339. What do we learn of him and his roles? What is his tone? Has his view of Vienna changed from since the start of the play?
- What is the effect of Lucio's intervention (lines 324–338)?
- What is the irony of Lucio's line (line 358)?

### 4 Lines 359–end

- Look at Angelo's speech (lines 364–372). What is it about the revelation of the Duke that makes Angelo confess now? What is the tone of his confession?
- The Duke is initially very commanding. How does his tone change when he speaks to Isabella (lines 380–397)?
- What verbal tactics does the Duke employ to persuade Isabella to forgive Angelo (lines 398–441)? How does Shakespeare use Mariana in this passage?
- Look at Isabella's speech (lines 441–452). What reasons does she give for forgiving Angelo? How convincing is each? What is the tone of her address to the Duke?
- How do you react to the Duke's apparent change of tack (lines 453–456)? Why is her suit 'unprofitable'?
- Look at Angelo and Escalus expressing sorrow (lines 468–475). What is the effect of this exchange at this point? Why is it placed here? What is the signficance of these last words of Angelo's, given what follows?
- How do you interpret the Duke's motives here (lines 488–491)? Does this affect your overall understanding of him?
- Since the Duke is in forgiving mood, why can't he forgive Lucio (lines 496–497)? What is his tone? What do you understand by Lucio's response that he spoke 'according to the trick'?
- Compare and contrast the Duke's judgement of Lucio (lines 505–511) with his judgement of Angelo. Is the outcome (lines 516–519) the same?
- What is the tone of the Duke's second proposal to Isabella (lines 531–536)?
- How do you interpret the fact that key characters fall silent: Isabella (from line 452); Angelo (from line 475); Claudio (all)?

## Imagery

How does each of these images fit into your reading and understanding of the play's imagery?
1 'O, but your desert speaks loud, and I should wrong it
To lock it in the wards of covert bosom,
When it deserves with characters of brass
A forted residence 'gainst the tooth of time
And razure of oblivion.' (lines 10–14)

2 ' *'Tis not impossible*
  *But one, the wicked'st caitiff on the ground,*
  *May seem as shy, as grave, as just, as absolute,*
  *As Angelo; even so may Angelo,*
  *In all his dressings, caracts, titles, forms,*
  *Be an arch-villain.'* (lines 55–60)
3 ' *This is that face, thou cruel Angelo,*
  *Which once thou swor'st was worth the looking on:*
  *This is the hand which, with a vowed contract,*
  *Was fast belocked in thine: this is the body*
  *That took away the match from Isabel*
  *And did supply thee at thy garden-house,*
  *In her imagined person.'* (lines 206–212)
4 ESCALUS '*Signior Lucio, did not you say you knew that Friar*
  *Lodowick to be a dishonest person?*
  LUCIO Cucullus non facit monachum: *honest in nothing but in*
  *his clothes.'* (lines 259–262)

## Key scene

The form of Shakespearean comedy is that it usually ends with
revelation of true identities, reconciliation and marriages. Leading
characters who have, during the play, been mistakenly opposed to,
separated from or unrecognised by each other are re-united in the
discovery of mutual love. These reconciliations are presented as
potentially permanent, and often precipitate other characters to 'pair
off'. Thus, Angelo might offer himself to Mariana, Isabella might
give herself to the Duke. The challenge of this ending is to consider
whether *Measure for Measure* is comic in this sense, or whether
Shakespeare is aiming to achieve something else.
1 Think about the extent to which Act 5 contains the comic
  elements listed above.
2 Consider carefully the ironies of this act and their effects.
3 Think about the evidence for the argument that the Duke
  manipulates the whole of the action in Act 5.
4 How much remains a mystery at the end of the play? Do you
  think this is a strength or a weakness of the ending?

# Writing

1  Compare the behaviour and language of each 'incarnation' of the Duke :
   • as the returning Duke
   • as Friar Lodowick
   • as the Duke revealed.
2  Explain the importance of Lucio's role in Act 5.
3  Use the work you did for KEY SCENE as the basis for an answer to this question: 'Is the last act of the play an intriguing success or a confusing failure?'

# Explorations

## A question of approach

When you study a play, you need to be able to see it from two different perspectives simultaneously. You need to be able to imagine and experience the text line by line, sharing the thoughts and feelings of the characters as they go through the events of the play, but at the same time you need to be able to look down on the play as a whole and see the patterns of character and relationship, of language and imagery, of themes and issues.

A play is essentially an audio-visual experience. No two members of the audience see quite the same 'play' and no two performances are ever exactly the same. Two important lessons should be learned from this. The first is that the printed text is not the play; the play is what you see when you go to the theatre. The text is a set of instructions to be interpreted by the director and the actors, artists and technicians. The second lesson is that there is no one 'right answer' to the play, only a range of possible interpretations. Your view can be just as valid as any one else's, but only if you can present it clearly and support it by valid arguments derived from the text. For this purpose you need, again, to see it as a whole **and** as a set of details.

## Thinking about the play

By the time you have discussed the text carefully you should be beginning to clarify and organize your response to the play as a whole. Most examination questions concentrate on *content* and *form*, and these are useful terms which offer you an approach and a framework within which you can prepare to write successfully.

Your first task is to establish clearly in your mind the broad issues raised by the text and the possible areas for discussion, including major characters. You need to consider and discuss some of the possible views and interpretations of these issues and lay down a sensible framework within which personal response can be convincing and well-considered. You also need to get close to the text and identify the key incidents, scenes or even quotations which will form the basis of any essay. When you come to write essays on the whole text, or even a specified passage, the appropriate textual evidence and illustrations should be noted and easily available.

### What is Measure for Measure about?
### What sort of play is it?

The action and structure of the play, its language and characters, combine to tell us that Shakespeare is exploring the exercise of power, and the theory and practice of justice and judgement in a human context.

Though these themes are undeniably serious, the play is not a tragedy: there is no single central character on whose fate and death the issues are finally focused. (Significantly, the only death in the play is that of Ragozine who never appears and who dies 'naturally', and improbably conveniently, to facilitate the plot!) Though there are comic scenes, and some of the features of Shakespearean comedy (disguise, mistaken identity, marriage in the end), the play does not conform to the comic convention in that love and marriage are not the central issues. (Significantly, although the play ends in marriages, they are decreed by the Duke, and the Duke's repeated proposal to Isabella does not receive an answer.)

What Shakespeare seems to be doing is constructing a play out of serious debate about how to administer a just, merciful and moral society (a Christian society, perhaps?) juxtaposed with more and less serious 'real' situations where law and judgement have to be exercised. Thus, whatever theoretical principles individual humans may hold about how to do this, they are challenged by the situations in which they have to put them into practice, clouded as they are by the personal motives of all involved, including those of the judges themselves. Indeed, the supreme authority in this society has the most impenetrable motives of all.

Against a comic background of seedy, street-wise and amoral characters who operate the rampant sex industry which

Angelo is determined to stamp out, we watch three judges' differing efforts to deliver justice. The Duke establishes Escalus' expertise in this field at the very start of the play (why doesn't he leave him in charge?). We see him speaking up for mercy in debate with Angelo (Act 2 scene 1), and then being both merciful and, later, firm with Pompey while Angelo's rigid approach ends in a frustrated exit. However, caught up in the emotions of the moment (Act 5), Escalus completely loses control with 'Friar Lodowick' and shows himself to be humanly fallible.

Angelo's strictness is what the Duke seems to want to enlist to deal with Vienna's moral crisis, but what we watch is the effect of his strictness on his own passions overwhelming him. Angelo can issue orders, but he can't deal with people – neither Pompey nor Isabella. As for the Duke, does he want Angelo to do his job for him or teach him a lesson ... or both? It's possible to imagine Shakespeare setting the Duke up as a character who believes he can make all come right. Yet, for all the Duke's manipulation and stage management, the Provost has to play the joker in the form of a recently severed head to get him out of a difficult situation. Though the Duke seems to act mercifully to all in Act 5 (even Lucio?), can we ignore his many earlier manipulations?

The play is a brilliant open-ended enigma: its lack of a definite interpretation is the point. The Duke is the character at the heart of the enigma. It is possible to interpret a range of different motives for his actions and behaviour. Yet he is the focus of authority in Vienna: he appears to give his authority away at the start of the play for an indefinite period and to reclaim it in the last act. Why? If you are to come to an understanding of this play, you need to address the character and actions of the Duke.

## Character

Characters in plays function in two ways:
1 They have to be written and acted in such a way that the audience (or reader) can imagine them to have a life of their own; the audience wants to make the characters 'live'.
2 They are part of the writer's overall plan, i.e. they do not, in fact, have a life of their own but are the writer's tools for exploring her/his themes in life-like form.

*Note*: Questions about character are common in A-level, but they are not best answered by writing a character analysis (however complex) as though she or he were a 'real' human being. The aim should be to explain why this complex creation is essential to the play as a whole; this is the best **literary** writing.

## Three lines of approach

Judging a character is not simply a matter of accumulating the evidence of the written word and drawing conclusions. It is more complicated, and requires some selection and evaluation to allow you to reach a coherent response to the character.

### *The evidence – 1*

Characters are revealed by:
• what they say
• what they do.

### Problems
1 Unfortunately (for examination purposes) characters are not always consistent. Major characters are subject to change because the events on which the action is based are significant enough to affect the main protagonists: the more important the character, the closer to the action and the greater the reaction to events. You must always be aware of how, and why, characters are developing and be prepared to explain and trace the changes.

**2** Characters might say or do things for effect. They might be seeking to impress or mislead someone else and not mean what they say at all.

You must always consider whether the character is being sincere or if he or she has an ulterior motive.

### The evidence – 2

Characters are also revealed by:
- what others say about them
- how others behave towards them.

### Problems

As in life, whether you accept A's opinion of B depends on how you feel about A. If you believe that A is untrustworthy or has a perverted sense of justice, then A's criticism of B might be interpreted as a glowing character reference! Alternatively, an opinion might be based on false information or might be deliberately misleading.

It is essential that you do not simply accept one character's opinion of another at face value.

### The evidence – 3

Characters are also revealed by:
- soliloquies
- asides.

These are often the most reliable evidence on which to assess a character since she/he is sharing her/his thoughts with the audience. All pretence is dropped because the soliloquy and the aside are devices which allow characters to express their thoughts and feelings directly, and solely, to the audience.

## Conclusion

These lines of approach can work very well when studying the central characters in *Measure for Measure*, for example, Angelo or Isabella, Claudio, Escalus, Lucio or the Provost; even Pompey. You only have to notice the ways in which they are **developed** to be immediately aware of Shakespeare exploring his theme.

However, the Duke presents problems for this approach – he reveals very little clear or definite information about himself in word or action; other characters differ widely in what they say about him; his soliloquies and asides are rare, brief and not clearly motivated. We shall return to him, for his impenetrability is the crux of the matter.

## Critical moments

At critical moments in the play you can begin to gain a better insight into a character by seeking answers to certain questions. Sadly, there is no formula which will apply to every situation, but you need to identify the key scenes and speeches which relate to a particular character and then ask these questions to start you off and perhaps prompt questions of your own.

- What has the character said or done here?
- Why has the character said or done this?
- What will happen as a result of this speech or action?
- How do you feel about the consequences of this speech or action?
- What does this incident tell us about the character?
- How does the character change or develop as a result of it?

What does each of these critical moments tell us about the character concerned?

**Angelo**
'*Always obedient...*
*...pleasure.*'
(Act 1 scene 1 lines 25–26)
'*Let there be...*
*...upon it.*'
(Act 1 scene 1 lines 48–50)

**Claudio**
'*Fellow, why dost...*
*...committed.*'
(Act 1 scene 2 lines 109–110)
'*From too much liberty,...*' (Act 1 scene 2 line 118)
'*I have great hope in that.*' (Act 1 scene 2 line 172)

**Lucio**

*'Grace is grace...*

*...grace.'*

(Act 1 scene 2 lines 24–26)

*'I have purchased as many diseases under her roof...'*

(Act 1 scene 2 lines 43)

*'But, after all this fooling, I would not have it so.'*

(Act 1 scene 2 line 65)

*'...and yet, to say...*

*...imprisonment.'*

(Act 1 scene 2 lines 125–127)

*'...I would be sorry...*

*...tick-tack.'*

(Act 1 scene 2 lines 179–181)

**The Provost**

*'I do it not...*

*...special charge.'* (Act 1 scene 2 lines 111–112)

**Isabella**

*'...wishing a more strict restraint...'* (Act 1 scene 4 line 4)

*'You do blaspheme the good, in mocking me.'* (Act 1 scene 4 line 38)

*'Alas, what...*

*...good!'* (Act 1 scene 4 lines 75–6)

### Character development: Angelo

The 'critical moments' approach can also be used to highlight key points in the development of a character. The Duke is a problem when using this approach and it will be more useful to consider Angelo.

Note that not all the following 'moments' are Angelo's words or actions of Angelo; they are, nevertheless, 'critical' in assessing him as a character in the drama.

1  Before Angelo appears, we know that the Duke is going to entrust him with the government of Vienna with '*all the Organs of our own power*' (Act 1 scene 1 lines 20–21). Escalus confirms that

*'If any...*

*...Lord Angelo.'* (Act 1 scene 1 lines 22–24).

2 When Angelo appears, he seems either genuinely humble or acting humbly (Act 1 scene 1 lines 25–26).

3 When the Duke has left, Angelo seems keen to examine his '*commissions*' with Escalus to discover the '*strength and nature*' of his new power:
'*Let us withdraw...point*' (Act 1 scene 1 lines 81–83)

4 Before Angelo appears again, we hear from Mistress Overdone of Angelo's proclamation that the brothels should be pulled down, and we see Claudio under arrest and threat of death for getting Juliet pregnant. Claudio speculates on Angelo's motives:
'*Whether the tyranny...*
*...fills it up*' (Act 1 scene 2 lines 153–154)
Lucio's response is to forget Angelo and appeal to the Duke (Act 1 scene 2 lines 164).
We also hear the Duke describe Angelo as '*A man of stricture and firm abstinence.*' (Act 1 scene 3 line 12) and as '*precise*', a man who '*...scarce confesses...*
*...than stone*' (Act 1 scene 3 lines 51–53).
This opinion is repeated elsewhere, especially, in comic form, by Lucio:
'*...a man whose blood...*
*...study and fast*' (Act 1 scene 4 lines 57–61) and in Act 3 scene 2.

5 When Angelo reappears, he is very '*precise*' in a discussion with Escalus about how strictly justice should be carried out; they argue theoretically, and specifically about the case of Claudio. Escalus takes a 'liberal' line, but Angelo is strict:
'*You may not......must die*' (Act 2 scene 1 lines 27–31).

6 In the comic scene that follows, Angelo's precision is frustrated by the verbal incompetence of Constable Elbow and the verbal deviousness of the crook Pompey. In exasperation, he leaves it to Escalus:
'*This will last...whip them all*' (Act 2 scene 1 lines 133–136) At the end of this scene, a very minor character (and therefore with no bias regarding Angelo) is given the strong, simple words:

'*Lord Angelo is severe*' (Act 2 scene 1 line 279).

7  In Act 2 scenes 2 and 4, Angelo himself (as well as the audience) is brought face to face with the irresistible power of his own desires. Almost every line is a critical moment! (See work focused on these scenes at the end of the text of Act 2.)

8  Angelo does not reappear until Act 4 scene 4, yet his desires and decisions dominate the action of the play. His blackmailing of Isabella produces the following critical moments:

(a) Mariana, for love of Angelo, agrees to have sex with him on Isabella's behalf

(b) after she has done so, he breaks his promise and confirms the order that Claudio must die

(c) he requires Claudio's head as evidence

(d) he orders the execution of the harmless Barnardine.

9  In Act 4 scene 4, Angelo seems rattled and guilt-ridden at the news of the Duke's return: '*This deed unshapes me quite*' (Act 4 scene 4 line 18). He seems to regret his actions: '*Would yet...we would not*' (Act 4 scene 4 lines 30–32).

10  From here to the end of the play, we see him not as the dominant cause of others' plans and actions but at the mercy of the Duke. However, there are critical moments. Lured by the Duke's behaviour into thinking that he might still escape detection, but very aware of how close the truth is coming, he tries to assert himself, ironically unaware of how true he speaks:

'*I did but smile...sets them on*' (Act 5 scene 1 lines 232–237). Compare his dismissive, bullying words before the Duke is revealed: '*Hark how...abuses!*' (Act 5 scene 1 lines 340–341) with his response to the Duke immediately afterwards: '*O my dread...I beg*' (Act 5 scene 1 lines 364–372) when he seems guilty, utterly ashamed and wishes to die. After he has been compelled to marry Mariana, he seems fixed in this desire. His last words in the play are: '*I am sorry...entreat it*' (Act 5 scene 1 lines

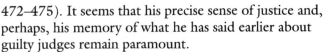

472–475). It seems that his precise sense of justice and, perhaps, his memory of what he has said earlier about guilty judges remain paramount.

- Does this give him some honour or make the audience feel sympathy for him?
- Do the reasons Isabella gives for forgiving him (Act 5 scene 1 lines 442– 452) affect our view?

11 The final critical moment is when the Duke turns to him after the revelation that Claudio is not dead: *'By this...worth yours'* (lines 492–495). What are we to make of this? Through the process of study, we can see that Shakespeare is not only inviting us to know and understand Angelo, but also to **judge** him, his motives and actions (as he judges others and himself), and to see him in the context of other characters' motives and actions.

- Do we judge him liberally or strictly?
- How do we judge his exercise of justice?

### Other characters

Shakespeare invites us also to judge other characters – Isabella especially (how similar is she to Angelo, for instance), but also Escalus, Claudio and Juliet, Lucio and the Provost.

We make our own judgement of them as the Duke deals out his justice to each of them. Apply the processes of character study suggested above to each of the characters listed here. What kind of judgements do you think Shakespeare leads us towards about each of them? Lucio is particularly interesting: compare the attitudes he expresses, his actions and reported actions. Can you discern his motives? How do you judge him?

### The Duke

Can we judge the Duke? Can we judge the judge?

The Duke is always in a role – either as Duke or friar. Both roles have authority which keeps other characters and audience at a distance.

In life, we are fascinated by authority figures: what are they really like? In other plays, Shakespeare causes the mask of authority to crack and we see the frail human being behind it.

- How does the Duke play his roles? Does he relish them or are they places to hide?
- Does his mask crack at all?
- Can we understand his motivation?
- What do we think of his exercise of authority and justice?
- Has the Duke brought about a 'happy' ending? Do we see him as god-like or as a human enjoying the exercise of power, for example, his vengeful gestures towards Lucio and his proposal to Isabella?

Here are three extreme interpretations of the Duke:

- a 'good' authority figure, guided by Christian principles, who deals out justice with mercy in a cleansed Vienna.
- a devious manipulator of people who enjoys power and is prepared to employ deception and dishonesty to get Isabella for himself.
- a character whom Shakespeare has created to be uninterpretable, as a metaphor for the idea that, to the observer, the motives of those in authority are very mixed depending on your point of view.

Whichever interpretation you develop for yourself will directly affect your interpretation of the play as a whole. You cannot judge the Duke in isolation because he is (as we have noted earlier about all characters in a play):

(a) one 'human' involved with others

(b) one element of a complex and interlocking drama.

The work in the next section on LANGUAGE will help you towards an interpretation of the Duke.

## Language

Shakespeare was an expert scriptwriter. He gave actors more than enough clues from which to create his characters and link them with the play's themes. Apart from entrances and exits, and occasional instructions to kiss, kill or die, all the clues are in the language – not only its meaning, but its imagery, form and style.

### The Duke

The Duke is a good example – he has many 'languages'.

**Act 1 scene 1 lines 3–21**

What is our first impression from the way he speaks? Look at the first sentence. What will an audience, still settling, learn from this kind of language? What kind of person and what kind of motive produce a sentence like this? Does his language change after he has sent for Angelo?

**Act 1 scene 3**

What is the driving motive in his language that makes him dominate the scene and almost prevent the friar from speaking? What are the implications of the imagery (especially lines 19–21)? What does he build up to?

**Act 3 scene 1 lines 5–41**

Look at the patterns and choices of words in this speech that give the idea of a kind of sermon. Does he act the part of friar convincingly? Is his 'sermon' sincere or is he plotting? How does Claudio react?

**Act 3 scene 1 lines 179–end**

Here, for the first time, the Duke speaks prose. What is the effect of this change of style? Why do his subject matter and motives need a change of tone? How do you think he is treating Isabella from the evidence of his speech?

**Act 3 scene 2 lines 18–26**

He is preaching again. Compare his style here with the earlier 'sermon'.

**Act 3 scene 2 lines 137–157**

He defends himself against Lucio but cannot reveal himself. What clues are there in his language as to how he is feeling?

What is his tone – is it that of a Duke or a friar?

**Act 3 scene 2 lines 181–184**

He resorts to verse for this mini-soliloquy. What is he thinking about? Does he reveal the man behind the mask? What is his tone?

**Act 3 scene 2 lines 218–227**

Now he speaks to Escalus, still in disguise. What is his subject matter and tone? In what tone does he ask the final question? What is the effect of its being placed at the end?

**Act 3 scene 2 lines 255–277**

What does this speech contribute to the drama? What special quality does the rhyming verse give? What is the tone?

**Act 4 scene 1 lines 60–65**

What emerges from this mini–soliloquy?

**Act 4 scene 2 lines 106–111**

What is the effect of this rhyming aside placed at a crucial moment in the action? What does its style reveal about the Duke?

**Act 4 scene 3 lines 92–100 and 106–110**

Here are two more mini-soliloquies. What is similar about their dramatic functions and styles? What do they reveal about the Duke?

**Act 5 scene 1 lines 1–19**

In what ways does the Duke's language indicate he is playing a public role? Is he relishing it? (He has twice said earlier that he does not enjoy public appearances).

**Act 5 scene 1 lines 311–320**

As Friar Lodowick, the Duke is vigorously charged by Escalus. How does he respond? What kind of sentences is he speaking? How does he speak after he is revealed as Duke (line 354)?

**Act 5 scene 1 lines 385–397**

He is, in effect, lying to Isabella that Claudio is dead. What is revealed by the way he does it? (Remember he has said earlier he wishes to bring her 'heavenly comforts' and will later offer her his hand.)

**Act 5 scene 1 lines 398–414**

Compare the language and style of this speech with lines 488–501 and 521–536.

### Other key characters

Now look at key speeches of Angelo, Isabella, Claudio, Lucio and Escalus. What can you learn about these characters and their roles in the play from the language they are given? Are there changes and developments? Does any of them ever seem to be acting a part?

You will notice that the Duke has many more 'languages' than the others. What does this tell us:

- about them?
- about the Duke?

## Imagery

The brief notes after each act should have given you some leads to follow up in exploring the imagery of this play. These themes have been suggested:

- the natural world, animals, birds, growth, fertility
- farming and housekeeping
- money, coinage, precious metals
- the world of borrowing, lending (usury), giving and taking
- tailoring, fashion, clothing
- appearances and reality, badges, symbols, secret signs, uniforms
- physical control and punishment
- sickness, medicine, death, mortality
- religious beliefs.

# Action and dramatic structure

A play is constructed – that is to say the action is ordered and organised – to achieve two principal aims:

- To tell the story in a way that will keep the audience wanting to know more until the writer is ready to deliver the outcome.
- To explore and develop the themes the writer chooses to bring alive through the words, motives, actions and interactions of the characters. The broad structure of *Measure for Measure* is quite simple, even though the characters and themes are complex. The play is divided about half way (at Act 3 scene 1 line 150).

First half – Shakespeare sets up the crisis:
– will Claudio die?
– what will Isabella do?
– how will the Duke become involved?
– how will Mistress Overdone and Pompey fare?

Second half – we watch the Duke's plot:
– to save Claudio's life
– to preserve Isabella's chastity
– to reveal Angelo's guilt.

How will he do it? What are his motives?

## Study suggestions

### First half

Look at the order of the action up to Act 3 scene 1 line 150. Consider the following:

1  How and when are we kept informed of the 'absent' Duke?
- **Act 1 scene 1 lines 1–end**
  What is the effect of the Duke **not** explaining why or where he's going? Does Escalus already know? If so, what are the implications?
- **Act 1 scene 2 lines 1–3**
  What does Lucio think is the reason for the Duke's absence? Why might Shakespeare want to offer this view at this point?

- **Act 1 scene 2 lines 146–161**
  What does this exchange between Lucio and Claudio imply about their view of the Duke in contrast to Angelo?
- **Act 1 scene 3 lines 1–end**
  After the brief conjectures about the Duke's absence in scene 2, how does this scene adjust the audience's view of his character and motives? How do we respond?
- **Act 1 scene 4 lines 50–55**
  How, and by what means, has Lucio's understanding of the Duke's absence changed? How does Lucio react to this new information?
- **Act 2 scene 3 lines 1–end**
  Here we are shown the Duke 'spying' on Vienna for the first time in the role of friar. How do we respond to this behaviour?
  Why is this an appropriate scene for Shakespeare to include here?
- **Act 2 scene 4 line 170**
  Notice that Isabella does not, unlike Claudio in Act 1 scene 2, think of complaining to the Duke. In what way is this ironic, considering subsequent events?
- **Act 3 scene 1 lines 1–150**
  Is the Duke behaving like one who wants to put things right?

Considering these passages, what view of the Duke and his motives for 'absence' does Shakespeare seem to be developing?

2 We are shown 'scenes' of Angelo acting as judge, and 'scenes' showing the consequences of his decisions; how are these ordered and balanced? The 'scenes' are as follows:
- **Act 1 scene 2**
  Mistress Overdone and Pompey lament the closing of the brothels at Angelo's decree.
- **Act 1 scene 3**
  Claudio is already under arrest at Angelo's decree for fornication.
- **Act 2 scene 1**
  Angelo's patience snaps when faced with having to deal with a real constable and criminals.

- **Act 2 scenes 2 and 4**

  The collapse of Angelo's integrity as judge in the face of irresistible passion.

  Why do you think Shakespeare decided to show Angelo's decrees being put into practice before we see him trying to play the role of judge?

3 How are Claudio's and Isabella's 'stories' delivered in this part of the play?

- **Act 1 scene 2**

  On his way to prison, Claudio asks Lucio to persuade Isabella to plead to Angelo for his life.

- **Act 1 scene 4**

  Lucio delivers the request to Isabella and she agrees with some reluctance.

- **Act 2 scene 2**

  Isabella argues for Claudio's life to such effect that she unwittingly arouses Angelo's passion and is invited to return.

- **Act 2 scene 3**

  The pregnant Juliet is revealed. What view of Claudio's 'crime' emerges from this scene?

- **Act 2 scene 4**

  Isabella comes to hear Angelo's decision and is drawn into further argument, unaware of Angelo's new agenda.

  When all is revealed, she is distraught and helpless. How do we react to her solution to her problem – to let Claudio die?

- **Act 3 scene 1**

  Claudio seems to accept the Duke/friar's advice to prepare to die. Why does Shakespeare want him in this frame of mind? Claudio and Isabella meet for the first time in the play (in the prison). How does Shakespeare bring their stories together so that the scene between them becomes not so much a conclusion as a starting point for the rest of the play?

  How has Shakespeare directed the audience's sympathies for Claudio and Isabella through this sequence of scenes?

**4** How is the debate about justice and morality balanced
   against moral/immoral and just/unjust actions?
   • **Act 1 scene 2**
     We gain a picture of the lax morality of Vienna at the
     same time as learning of the fatal consequences of
     Claudio's fornication, a crime which hardly seems serious
     in today's world. What does Claudio think is the reason
     for Angelo's strict application of the law?
   • **Act 1 scene 3**
     We hear the Duke condemning in violent terms the moral
     laxity of the people of Vienna – people whom, in Act 1
     scene 1, he said he loved. He then disguises himself as a
     friar. Is this honest behaviour?
   • **Act 1 scene 4**
     How does Lucio's sexual innuendo sound beside
     Isabella's strict morality of the convent?
   • **Act 2 scene 1**
     This scene contrasts the theoretical debate between
     Angelo and Escalus about how to deal with crime, with a
     comic portrayal of their efforts to judge a crime – one of
     sexual impropriety, it seems. The scene ends with Escalus
     lamenting the disproportionate sentencing of Claudio.
   • **Act 2 scene 2**
     Angelo has not condemned Juliet, but ordered what is
     'needful' for her. Isabella accepts that Claudio has
     committed a sin/crime in getting Juliet pregnant.
     However, she argues for mercy. Angelo is filled with a
     more sinful desire than Claudio's.
   • **Act 2 scene 3**
     Juliet accepts that she has sinned and repents.
   • **Act 2 scene 4**
     After further Christian arguments from Isabella, Angelo is
     forced to reveal his blatant lust. He threatens her in the
     most violent terms if she does not give him what he
     wants. How do you react to Isabella's desperate decision:
     '*More than our brother is our chastity*' (line 184)?
   • **Act 3 scene 1**
     Does Isabella's decision seem justified in the light of
     Claudio's response?

What view of sexual morality do these scenes offer?

### Second half

Through the rest of Act 3 and Act 4, the Duke, as friar, plots a situation through which he can produce a happy ending for Claudio and Isabella, and the revelation of Angelo's guilt in Act 5. He uses a false identity himself, and manipulates others, even to the extent of sometimes lying to them.

Look at this sequence of passages, and consider:

(a) whether or not they produce comic effects

(b) what the effects of the many ironies are

(c) in what light these schemes and actions place the Duke.

• **Act 3 scene 1 lines 160–167**

The Duke lies to Claudio about Angelo's intentions.

• **Act 3 scene 1 lines 179–187**

Is this a hint of the Duke's attraction to Isabella? Is it a device to test her suitability for his scheme to reveal Angelo? Is this a godly man preparing to put all right?

• **Act 3 scene 1 lines 195–196**

A repetition of what he said to Claudio. Why is he lying? Or is he himself mistaken?

• **Act 3 scene 1 lines 198–204**

How do you react to this description of a happy outcome?

• **Act 3 scene 1 lines 243–271**

How does this scheme sound: – to Isabella? – to the audience? Does it take account of Mariana's feelings?

By the end of this scene, do we see the Duke as a heaven-sent saviour in an apparently impossible situation, or as one using others' vulnerability for his own purposes?

• **Act 3 scene 2 lines 18–32**

Is this a merciful Duke/friar?

• **Act 3 scene 2 lines 83–180**

How does the Duke's disguise place him in a comic situation here? Why is it important for the Duke to hear himself misrepresented in this way?

• **Act 3 scene 2 lines 225–231**

Why is the Duke using his disguise in this way? Does the Duke now seem an all-powerful righter of wrongs?

- **Act 4 scene 1 lines 1– end**
  Do Isabella and Mariana seem to be free agents or pawns in the Duke's game? Do they seem to relish his plot? What is he Duke's concern throughout?

- **Act 4 scene 2 lines 1–58**
  If we are concerned for the success of the Duke's plot, how do we react to the comic presentation of Claudio's executioner and his assistant?

- **Act 4 scene 2 line 59 to the end of Act 4 scene 3**
  The situation of Claudio is deadly serious, and his time is running out. We are to believe that Mariana has given herself to Angelo. Re-read the page-by-page plot summaries from pages 142 to 164 to get a broad view of the action. Are these events serious, comic, or a mixture? (If the latter, which is which?) Is the Duke in control of events or just plain lucky? How do we react to his lie to Isabella? Which characters are now crucial to producing a happy ending?

- **Act 4 scenes 4, 5 and 6**
  How does the very brevity of these scenes, as well as their content, dramatise the sense that the Duke is bringing his plotting to a climax?

- **Act 5 scene 1**
  Look carefully at the way the Duke controls the events of the last act. Is he always in control? Consider:
  – his own performance as Duke, friar, and the final removal of his disguise
  – his treatment of Isabella and Mariana
  – his manipulation of Angelo
  – his use of Escalus
  – his responses to and judgement of Lucio
  – his introduction of Claudio, Juliet and Barnardine
  – his proposal to Isabella.

## Contexts

Our understanding of literature is bound to be enriched if we know and understand something about the contexts in which the play was written and performed. In A level specifications, there is the requirement to show an understanding of the contexts of literature and to be able to evaluate the influence of those contexts.

Since the time when Shakespeare wrote his plays, readers and performers have been finding them relevant in their own times and others. Productions of the plays have been set in all sorts of historical and social contexts. However, we are better able to understand the texts we have if we know something about their topicality for Shakespeare, his actors and his audience.

It is not possible in this book to provide detailed material for the wide range of contexts of a Shakespeare play. We can, however, indicate broad areas where students would benefit from making further research. We can break CONTEXTS down into four categories.

## Historical and political contexts

*Measure for Measure* first appeared soon after James I ascended to the throne of England. (He was already King of Scotland.) Although the play does not deal with a king as such, it is interesting to observe that there are several characteristics of the Duke which seem to reflect those of James I. In addition, although Shakespeare sets his play in Vienna, many of the social and political issues in the play reflect those current in England at the time. It might be pointed out that the play is in the form of a comedy (see 'What is *Measure for Measure* about?', page 229), and, as such, might not be expected to portray 'serious' public issues. However, there is no doubt that this play looks at 'deadly' serious issues of government, justice, and sexual morality.

(a) **The king**. It will be very rewarding to research what Elizabethans and Jacobeans thought about kings and their role, and the characteristics of the new king of England, to see how Shakespeare may have used them obliquely (or, even, obviously) in his creation of the Duke. For instance, it is believed that James sometimes went out into London in disguise to observe his people, and that he was not at ease with crowds. He said that he had been too liberal in his rule of Scotland. He was serious and academic, liked to influence the legal process, and wrote a book, *The King's Gift* (1603), about the ideal ruler, which contained the words 'Let the measure of your love to everyone be according to the measure of his virtue.'

(b) **Foreign affairs**. As well as introducing us to the state of the sex trade, Act 1 scene 2 presents us with opinions as to the whereabouts of the absent Duke in the context of speculation about foreign affairs. It is believed by some authorities that Shakespeare was referring indirectly to the protracted peace negotiations with Spain at that time. There are other theories, but the key aspect of the scene to understand is that it contains the colloquial style of dialogue that Shakespeare uses when he is allowing his characters to speak knowingly of topical matters.

In (a) and (b) above, and in the material that follows, we can see briefly some of the aspects of his world that he may have incorporated into his play. What is interesting is to evaluate what he may have done with them. Is the play merely using current affairs as material for a play, or do we feel the play comments or offers a particular point of view – on kingship, sexual morality, or justice? Is the play a criticism of the new king? Or a eulogy? Is it a veiled play about a shadowy king by a playwright who has basked in the sunlight of the previous monarch? Is the foreign setting and cast of characters a way of distancing critical political comment? Certainly, as the king's book shows, the issue of good government was a current affair.

## Social and religious contexts

(a) **Current affairs**. Although the new king was a Catholic, the influence of the Puritans was not dead. There would, therefore, be those who would condemn Claudio as a mortal sinner, however inclined to mercy many others might have been. Sexual offences could still be punished by death, and there was a widespread belief that mortal sin (e.g. fornication) would be punished by eternal damnation. In 1603, as a public health measure against the threat of plague, there was an order that much property in the outer parts of London should be pulled down; these were areas that contained many brothels.

(b) **The Bible**. It is clear that Shakespeare relied on his audience's knowledge of the Bible (see the section entitled THEMES). It would also be rewarding to look at the account of Christ's 'Sermon on the Mount' in St Matthew's gospel to see how that has influenced the language and moral debate in the play. Act 2 scenes 2 and 4 offer clear points of connection, but there are others.

(c) **Extremists**. Although it is not explicitly stated, the early descriptions of Angelo suggest some of the qualities of a Puritan. These suggestions are backed up by his rigorous regime when in power. It would be helpful to find out more about the social and sexual beliefs of Puritans, and how they affected the world of the theatre. Find out, too, what the audience's attitudes might have been to the portrayal of a puritanical male attempting to sexually exploit a novice nun who aspires to strictness. What attitudes, also, might they have had to a ruler who gives away his power and disguises himself as a friar?

## Theatrical context

### Contemporary

(a) Certainly, Shakespeare's audience, used to the concepts of tragedy, comedy and history (chronicle), would have recognised the comic elements in *Measure for Measure*

(see 'What is *Measure for Measure* about?', page 229').
However, they might also have been surprised by a play
in comic form which dealt with serious 'public' issues.
They would have recognised the 'street' or, so-called,
'low-life' characters and the way they complemented the
serious issues of the play. The incompetent but well-
intentioned Constable, Elbow, is a comic type, and
Mistress Overdone and Pompey provide a comic contrast
in sexual values to the central characters. However, the
audience would not have found an obvious fool or clown
character, though Lucio and Pompey have some of the
characteristics.

(b)  The educated audience would have been brought up with
a delight in argument and debate. Much of the schooling
of the day was focused on the techniques and cut and
thrust of debating – the art of 'rhetoric'. One of the
aspects of theatre that was highly appreciated was the
presentation of debate, and no better example could be
found than in the disputes between Angelo and Isabella
in Act 2 scenes 2 and 4. It is possible to imagine the
much more vocal audiences revelling in the intellectual
pleasure of these clashes, especially after the comic
frustration of Act 2 scene 1, where the rules of debate are
completely undermined.

(c)  It is also possible to imagine an audience being
challenged by the play. There is no tragic hero or
heroine, no king to study, no pairs of lovers to discover
each other or be reconciled and live happily ever after.
With whom would they have sympathised? How seriously
would they have taken Claudio's 'sin'?

### Modern

It is likely that many modern audiences will have different
attitudes to matters involving sex. Although we may not take
Claudio's sin so seriously – it is commonplace, if not entirely
conventional, for unmarried women in established relationships

to get pregnant – the play enjoyed great popularity during the 1990s. Why is this? Is it because this was the age of the sex scandal in high places – the age of sleaze? Is it because of a psychological interest in two such seemingly pent-up souls as Angelo and Isabella? Is it because we are fascinated by the motives and actions of our rulers? Is it because we like plays that embody uncertainty at their core?

## The drama of Shakespeare and the contemporary theatre

Some modern critics have labelled *Measure for Measure* a 'problem' play, along with *Troilus and Cressida* and *All's Well That Ends Well*. (You might find it interesting to read these plays and see if you find similarities.) The term 'problem' can merely mean that the play won't fit neatly into the traditional modes of drama of the day, but some use the term to indicate that the plays present the audience with problems. What is clear is that Shakespeare found the basis of his plot in Giraldi Cinthio's *Hecatommithi* (1565) and in other works of the late 16th century.

He also drew on three stock ingredients of plots which were current at the time: the idea of the corrupt judge, the disguised ruler and the device of exchanged bedmates. All of these ingredients could help focus moral and political issues in a dramatic way.

Within Shakespeare's own work, it might be revealing to contrast his presentation of Angelo with that of Malvolio in *Twelfth Night*. In the latter, we see a bitterly comic treatment of a puritanical character. In the same way, it is interesting to contrast the presentation of the Duke with the tragic presentation of the king who gives away his power in *King Lear*. Further comparisons and contrasts with the comedies may be made by looking at the way this play presents the marriages at the end and the way the comedies do it. Finally, there are obvious parallels between Elbow and Dogberry in *Much Ado About Nothing*.

## Themes

If a play is to work successfully, its themes will not seem
abstract or theoretical because they will be seen in the form of
'real' issues in the 'lives' of the characters, and will be explored
through parallel and contrasting experiences. We have already
said that *Measure for Measure* is about the exercise of justice by
human beings. This theme is explored partly in biblical terms –
Old Testament versus New Testament. Consider these two
quotations, their language and meaning:

- *'Breach for breach, eye for eye, tooth for tooth: as he hath
  caused a blemish in a man, so shall it be done to him
  again.'* (Leviticus 24)
- *'Judge not that ye be not judged. For with what judgement
  ye judge, ye shall be judged: and with what measure ye
  mete, it shall be measured to you again.'* (Matthew 7)

How have they influenced the language and thinking in
*Measure for Measure*, especially in Act 2 scenes 2 and 4, and
Act 5 scene 1 (from line 359)?

### Sex

The sexual attitudes and behaviour of Angelo, Isabella,
Claudio and Juliet focus this theme against a background of:
– Lucio's promiscuity
– Mistress Overdone's and Pompey's professional interest
– Vienna as a corrupt city.

- What are the attitudes to sex of each of those named above
  and the Duke and Mariana?
- What sexual behaviour is involved in the action of the play?
- Have Isabella's or Angelo's attitudes altered by the
  end of the play?
- Do the Duke's final instructions to marry show any sexual
  or moral concern?

### Seeming

Shakespeare, quite naturally for a playwright, was always exploring appearance and reality. Consider the ways in which the following characters are not what they seem: Angelo, Isabella, the Duke, Mariana, Claudio and Juliet. How do their 'seemings' vary – in moral terms? – in dramatic terms? Do their unveilings, exposures, discoveries, unmufflings lead to true identity, honesty and love?

### Sin

Angelo, Isabella, Claudio and the Duke are much concerned about sin and damnation. At various times, they argue about the justification or otherwise of committing a sin to achieve a 'good' end. Explore these arguments, who offers them and in what situations. Does Shakespeare offer any conclusions? Do you think the way the play ends avoids the issue?

### Punishment and torture

You should notice how often punishment, especially whipping, is referred to through the play, both in literal and metaphorical terms. It is revealing to explore why and when these references are made and by whom, and especially the emotional context in which they are expressed.

### Society

The play focuses on a very personal and private drama between a few characters. Yet the Duke is concerned about the moral and legal corruption of Viennese society, and he decrees that the last act shall be played out in public. Is there any evidence to support the Duke's and Angelo's view of Vienna? What characters represent society? Where and when are they seen? Is Vienna cleansed at the end of the play?

### Duty

Angelo, Isabella, Claudio, Escalus, Elbow and the Duke all perceive themselves as having duties and loyalties. What are they in each case? How do they react in the face of desires and pressures which put them in conflict with these duties? How does the play resolve the conflicts?

## Conclusion

*Question*: Why is enigma and open-endedness, a strength?
*Answer*: Because, in life, we are constantly drawn to judge people, actions, motives, but can never, except in a narrow legal sense, come up with definite answers. The temptation for writers is to devise endings that deliver their views. Shakespeare does not yield to this temptation and leaves his play the more true to life.

## Preparing for an examination

You will be expected to have a detailed and accurate knowledge of your set texts. You must have read your set texts several times and you need to know the sequence of events and the narrative of a text. The plot summaries in this edition should help you with this. It may seem rather unfair but you will get little credit in the final examination for merely 'telling the story'; simply 'going through' the narrative is seen as particularly worthless in an open-book examination. However, you will be in no position to argue a convincing case or develop a deep understanding unless you have this detailed knowledge.

## The questions

A-level questions are demanding but they should always be accessible and central, a fair test of your knowledge and understanding. They are rarely obscure or marginal. There is a relatively small number of questions which can be asked on any text, even though the ways in which they can be worded are almost infinite. They tend to fall into quite straightforward categories or types, as outlined below.

### Character

You may be asked to discuss your response to a particular character, to consider the function or presentation of a character or perhaps to compare and contrast characters.

### Society

You may be asked to consider the kind of society depicted by the text or perhaps the way in which individuals relate to that society.

### Themes

You may be asked to discuss the ideas and underlying issues which are explored by a text, and the author's concerns and interests.

### Attitudes

You may be asked to consider what views or values are revealed by the text, what is valued and what is attacked.

### Style or technique

You may be asked to look at the methods a writer uses to achieve particular effects. In essence, you are being asked to examine 'how' a text achieves its effects and you need to consider such matters as diction, imagery, tone and structure.

### Personal response

You may be asked to give your own view of the text but this must be more than just unsupported assertion. You need to move beyond 'I think...' to a well-considered evaluation based on close reading and textual evidence. It is worth remembering that there are a limited number of sensible responses to a text.

### 'Whole text' questions

These questions require you to consider the text as a whole. You need a coherent overview of the text and the ability to select appropriate detail and evidence.

### 'Specific' passages

These questions require close reading and analysis but sometimes the specific passage has to be related to another passage or perhaps to the whole text.

## Conclusion

A critical essay attempts to construct a logical argument based on the evidence of the text. It needs a clear sense of direction and purpose; it is better to start with a simple, coherent attitude than to ramble aimlessly or produce a shapeless answer which never gets into focus. Each paragraph should be a step in a developing argument and should engage in analysis of textual detail which is relevant to the question. You must answer the question set – as opposed to the question you wanted to be set – and you must be prepared to discuss a specific aspect of the text or approach it from a slightly new or unexpected angle. You will need to be selective and choose the material which is appropriate to the actual question. An essay which deals only in sweeping generalisations may be judged to lack detail and substance, while one which gets too involved in minor details may lack direction and a conceptual framework. The ideal balance is achieved when overview and detailed knowledge combine to allow easy movement from the general to the particular, and back again.

Although different examination boards and syllabuses have their own ways of expressing them, there are basically three criteria against which your work will be judged. They are:
- knowledge and understanding
- answering the question relevantly
- written expression.

The example and commentary on the following pages have been designed to help you in your exploration of the text and your preparation for the examination.

# Writing an essay

There is rarely a single 'right' answer to an A-level essay
question, but there is not an infinite range of sensible
responses to a text and any interpretation must be clearly
based on close reading and supporting evidence. This is a fairly
typical A-level question:

*What view of justice emerges from 'Measure for Measure'?*

```
'Measure for Measure' shows an intense and
positive concern with the properties of
government. It uses the vein of justice and
mercy throughout but also shows the
contention of divine and secular justice. It
is ridiculous to debate whether a chessboard
is considered black or white: not only is it
chequered but it is in the nature of the
game that it should be so. Similarly,
'Measure for Measure' is made up of
contrasts and antinomies that are juxtaposed
and resolved to contribute to the dramatic
form. The play explores the widest range of
responses to the concepts of mercy,
mortality and justice on the part of
governors or those governed and the tensions
provoked by them in the personalities of all
concerned. Not only are the tensions and
dischords heightened, threatening the
dissolution of all human values, but a
corresponding emphasis is laid upon the role
of true authority, whose intervention alone
supplies the equipoise needed to counter
negative forces.
     The title 'Measure for Measure' recalls a
verse in the Sermon on the Mount:
```

*'With what measure ye mete, it shall be
measured to you again'*
Closely linked in context to it is the
command:

*'Judge not, that ye be not judged.'*

However, the precept not to judge presents
a hard case for those concerned in carrying
out secular authority. It was thought that a
clear distinction had to be drawn between
private and public spheres of life. For
private persons 'Judge not' was absolutely
binding, however for rulers and magistrates
in their public capacity some qualification
had to be inferred. As human beings they
were obliged to show mercy and forgiveness
like all men. But in office they were
considered to function as deputies of God on
earth, and exercising under God the divine
right to judge and condemn.

Therefore Shakespeare introduces Angelo to
represent one side of justice - that of
divine justice and to present suddenly an
extreme way of ruling as one of the colours
on the chessboard. He is described by
Claudio:

*'Thus can the demi-god, Authority
Make us pay down for our offence by weight
The words of heaven; yet still 'tis just!*
He is set up impersonally as 'Authority' on
earth from God. The description of the state
of Vienna also exaggerates the severity of
Angelo's rule.

*'...so our decrees,
Dead to infliction, to themselves are dead
And Liberty plucks Justice by the
nose,...'*

Superficially, Claudio's offence seems characteristic of the general state of *'too much liberty'*. He is introduced as an acquaintance of Mistress Overdone and one of Lucio's circle, his arrest is linked by Pompey with the proclamation for pulling down houses of ill-repute, and the judicial proceedings are paralleled with those of Froth and Pompey. In reality Claudio's case is of
a different order.

His union with Juliet was *'upon a true contract ... she is fast my wife'* and there is a full intention to proceed to marriage. Morally indeed Claudio's conduct remains a kind of fornication, however in the eyes of secular justice it would present an obvious case for leniency and certainly not such an extreme measure as death in punishment. Therefore Shakespeare juxtaposes divine and secular justice. The conflict between the two is brought to a head when Isabella pleads to Angelo (and the second rival colour is introduced on the chessboard).

Before the two meet, Shakespeare contrasts Angelo with Escalus, a 'good' magistrate. Their brief discussion at the beginning of Act II serves to outline their attitudes.
'ANGELO: *We must not make a scarecrow of the law,*
*Setting it up to fear the birds of prey...*
*Till custom make it*
*Their perch, and not their terror.*

ESCALUS: *Ay, but yet*
       *Let us be keen and rather cut a*
         *little,*
       *Than fall, and bruise to death.'*
They demonstrate respectively the extremes
of severity and 'vain pity' and divine and
secular justice. Angelo's rejection of
Escalus's view that 'had time cohered with
place, or place with wishing', any man, even
Angelo himself, might err like Claudio, is
ironic although at this stage the audience
are unaware of such implications.

Therefore, as in a chessboard where
neither colour dominates but it is the
combination of the two that makes the game
successful, Shakespeare demonstrates that
neither extreme is 'just' and a combination
would be a more satisfactory resolution. He
illustrates this in parallel to the case of
Pompey; while Angelo's view of the law as a
machine for punishing all proven offenders
takes no account of the personal individual
case, Escalus's claim that temptation may
excuse any man, takes no account of the
necessity for laws against crime.

In the comic court scenes, 'merciful'
Escalus and 'strict' Angelo demonstrate
their concepts of justice. Here Shakespeare
can be seen to be laughing. As the
testimonies unfold, vagueness, irrelevance
and 'misplacings' distort all ethical
distinctions. 'Justice' represented by Elbow
and 'Iniquity' by the equivocal Pompey seem
interchangeable and equally meaningless.
A sharp contrast is shown between the
dismissal of Pompey by Escalus and the
condemnation of Claudio where Angelo
believes no extenuating circumstances are

meets some serious opposition. Faced with
the precept of the Sermon on the Mount,
Angelo can only reply with an evasion of
responsibility.

*'It is the law, not I that condemn your
brother.'*

Therefore it is here that tension between
personal and social ethics is stretched to
the limit. One colour on the chessboard
supports Angelo in claiming that the
exercise of private mercy must not supersede
the divinely delegated task of administering
justice. However, the other colour dictates
that justice can only be done by human
beings to human beings. The debate between
Angelo and Isabella can be seen as 'The
contention of Justice and Mercy'. Isabella's
demand for judges to practise God's mercy
is the counterpart of Angelo's claim to
practise divine justice; of both it might
be said

*''Tis set down in heaven, but not in
earth.'*

As mediator between the extremes of justice
and mercy, (and black and white on the
chessboard) stands the Duke. Without
sovereign power and sanctions to enforce his
will he has to deal as a man with men.
Therefore Shakespeare uses him to highlight
the problems involved in secular justice,
where man as man and not a demi-god judges
man, juxtaposed with Angelo's strict
authority of divine justice.

However, Shakespeare shows both sides to
have discrepancies, as human nature does not
allow any man to be faultless, and therefore
raises the question of where lies the true
authority of justice and how man should

meets some serious opposition. Faced with
the precept of the Sermon on the Mount,
Angelo can only reply with an evasion of
responsibility.

*'It is the law, not I that condemn your
brother.'*

Therefore it is here that tension between
personal and social ethics is stretched to
the limit. One colour on the chessboard
supports Angelo in claiming that the
exercise of private mercy must not supersede
the divinely delegated task of administering
justice. However, the other colour dictates
that justice can only be done by human
beings to human beings. The debate between
Angelo and Isabella can be seen as 'The
contention of Justice and Mercy'. Isabella's
demand for judges to practise God's mercy
is the counterpart of Angelo's claim to
practise divine justice; of both it might
be said

*''Tis set down in heaven, but not in
earth.'*

As mediator between the extremes of justice
and mercy, (and black and white on the
chessboard) stands the Duke. Without
sovereign power and sanctions to enforce his
will he has to deal as a man with men.
Therefore Shakespeare uses him to highlight
the problems involved in secular justice,
where man as man and not a demi-god judges
man, juxtaposed with Angelo's strict
authority of divine justice.

However, Shakespeare shows both sides to
have discrepancies, as human nature does not
allow any man to be faultless, and therefore
raises the question of where lies the true
authority of justice and how man should

interpret it on earth.

The Duke can be seen as a dark figure; not only due to his mysterious disguise and spy-like behaviour, but also due to his hypocritical side and shifting views of justice in counterpart to his good intentions of being just. He is willing to give up his authority to Angelo in order to tighten up the over-indulgent laxity in Vienna to a new severity, but goes on to undermine his deputy's authority as soon as it is used. Similarly he plans for Mariana to sleep with Angelo, just as Claudio and Juliet did, and for which they were condemned.

In parallel to these discrepancies, Angelo's authority is broken down by his personal weakening towards Isabella. His attitude of Act 2, scene 1:

'*What's open made to justice, that justice seizes. What knows the laws that thieves do pass on thieves?*'
completely turns on itself.

'*Thieves for their robbery have authority, when judges steal themselves.*'
However, finally Shakespeare uses the Duke to set an example of justice by presiding over the trial of Angelo in person. Angelo is allowed to fall into his own trap: is led to face the extreme penalty he has sought to inflict on others; and finally is saved by the Duke's act of clemency. Angelo's sin however could be looked on as part of human nature and unfairly spied on by the Duke.

But more is achieved than a demonstration of the properties of government by the Duke. The deeper moral of the trial is seen in its

effects on the consciences of those tried.
Angelo's recognition that his death is just,
removes finally the irony of his declaration
to Escalus.

> *'When I that censure him do so offend*
> > *Let mine own judgement pattern out my*
> > > *death,*
> *And nothing came in partial.'*

He has regained his lost integrity as a
judge; a necessary condition before mercy
can be exercised that is not *'vain pity'*.

Isabella's bid to save Angelo's life is
motivated by Christian forgiveness yet at
the same time the form of pleading takes due
account of the judicial approach to the
specific case. Angelo, she declares, was
sincere and uncorrupted *'Till he did look on
me'*. He had offended in thought and not in
deed, whereas her brother *'did the thing for
which he died'*. Such arguments grounded in
legalities rather than ethics are of great
importance where secular justice presides.
The Duke shapes his judgements on the minor
characters in the same way, e.g.
Barnardine's *'earthly faults'* are pardoned
because he is a special case: as *'a prisoner
nine years old'* he should have been
sentenced or set free long ago.

Shakespeare leaves the play with a *'nice'*
compassionate view of secular justice
triumphing over an attempt of a more
strictly moral society led by divine
justice.

The Duke after his initial superficial
plan to *'tighten up'* Vienna shows judicial
clemency towards those who have sinned and
requests the hand of Isabella of whom Angelo

has been robbed. This act could be seen as snide and indeed the whole underhand scheming of the Duke could have been rigged to result in this prize.

*'What's mine is yours and what is yours is mine.'*

may be seen as an ugly slant on 'Measure for Measure'.

Therefore the line between black and white and how one man should judge another is left for discussion. In the view of the radical Hazlitt, 'Measure for Measure' shows a pleasing rejection of conventional morality and a sympathy with human beings of every level and degree. More than a century ago, Gernius declared that the play's basic concern was with the idea of moderation as applied to all human relationships.

*'that circumspect equity ... which suffers neither mercy nor the severe letter of the law to rule without exceptions ... awards punishment not measure for measure, but with measure.'*

Therefore justice is not a set form dealt out to every sinner on earth, by man following laws of morality, whether divine or not. It is a flexible treatment or medicine, the amount or form of it depending on the crime. However the authority that delivers justice must not be flexible.

*'Thieves for their robbery have authority when judges steal themselves.'*

Shakespeare's way of laughing at relaxed morality and authority, and 'Liberty plucking Justice by the nose' highlights the necessity for set laws but flexible justice in a 'just' society.

## Comments

That essay was written by an A-level student, but not under examination conditions. As it was done as part of the process of studying the play, it is longer and more expansively expressed than would be possible in an exam. This is especially noticeable in the introductory paragraph which is too long and contains too many ideas abstractly expressed to provide the tight focus an exam requires.

### Strengths

1 A good introduction should attempt, simply and clearly, to offer a view of the play as a whole, its theme, action or structure. (This applies even if it is a character-based title.) Here, the very first sentence grasps one of the play's major issues, and the rest of the paragraph describes, in broad terms, how the play explores the theme. It does well to point out how the play is made up of oppositions and contrasts.

2 After the introduction, the essay immediately establishes, through reference to the play's title, that the theme of judgement and its scriptural sources was a contemporary issue for Shakespeare's audience, and that a clear distinction was drawn between public and private judgement. There follows an explanation of how Shakespeare creates the character of Angelo and his dealings with Claudio and Isabella, and contrasts him as a judge with Escalus, to bring these issues alive. Thus, the essay has moved from the outline of broad issues to the specifics of character, relationship and action – the kind of detailed work now required. It is noticeable how the quotations selected contain the language of high argument. The initial discussion of the characters places them clearly in terms of their roles in the debate about justice that Shakespeare is dramatising.

3 Just as the play offers comic perspectives on its themes, so

the essay now points this out, at one and the same time binding the 'comic' characters into the 'serious' theme and demonstrating that the contrast between divine and secular justice is not at all clear in reality. Perhaps the student's point about Escalus goes too far: 'justice dissolves easily in society's amoral nature'? Escalus does let Pompey off with a warning, and Pompey leaves, clearly not having taken him seriously, but brought before Escalus later for the same offence, Pompey is sent summarily to prison. Escalus does therefore condemn justly.

4 The scenes in Act 2 between Angelo and Isabella, nicely labelled 'The Contention of Justice and Mercy', are succinctly and purposefully handled. In tracing the process of this contention, the essay pinpoints the direction in which the play is moving: 'justice can only be done by human beings to human beings'. When describing Angelo's and Isabella's opposing positions, the essay finds a telling quotation to complete the section.

5 Though the Duke is appropriately quoted in the essay's first sentence, any discussion of his role has been delayed until now, and rightly so. The role of the Duke as judge is the key issue for an essay with this title. Discussion of the Duke should, therefore, be built up to and predominate in the 'climactic' part of the essay. (Perhaps more might have been done to establish the fallible aspects of the Duke's character.)

6 The points made about the last scene are good because they illustrate the varieties of justice. The mercy that the Duke shows Angelo is balanced by Angelo's proper remorse and self judgement; the Duke's mercy to Barnardine is based on a sense of natural justice.

7 The concluding paragraphs succeed in raising questions about the motives of the Duke, pointing out the ambivalent aspects of the play's ending, yet providing a positive concluding view in the essay.

*Aspects to question*

1 Does the use of the chessboard to symbolise a chequered view of justice actually work? Does it positively assist the discussion? Does the analogy clarify the ideas? Certainly, the essay does not fall into the trap of offering an interesting idea at the start and then forgetting it; the chessboard returns as a motif throughout.

2 Are the language and ideas of the introduction precise enough?

3 Given the specific elucidation of a biblical basis for the play's debate in the early stages, should this aspect not have been more explicitly addressed in the discussion of the Duke's final judgements, and in the conclusion?

4 Is the quotation preceding the final paragraph ('thieves...themselves') appropriate at this point? Is it clear evidence for the point being made?

## Essay questions

1 Has a cure for the corruption of Vienna been found by the end of the play?

2 What perspectives does the play offer on private and public corruption?

3 Does Angelo's fall as a result of the discovery of his corruption discredit his method of government?

4 Does Shakespeare present Angelo as an evil man?

5 What styles of government does Shakespeare explore, and which does he seem to prefer?

6 What views of Christianity are explored in the play?

7 To what extent is Isabella a sympathetic character?

8 How far is Christian morality seen to be at work in the play?

9 Do you think the Duke disguises himself as friar for Christian motives?

10 Do you think that forgiveness and redemption are the final themes of the play?

11 What view of authority emerges from Shakespeare's portrayal of the Duke?

12 Discuss the justice or otherwise of the Duke's final judgements.

13 The Duke: exponent of god-like mercy or devious self-interest?

14 'The impenetrability of the Duke's motives makes Shakespeare's point about figures of authority.' Discuss.

15 What is the significance of the Duke's choice of disguise?

16 'Angelo and Isabella are very similar characters.' Discuss.

17 Explain why you think Shakespeare did not write a final interchange between Angelo and Isabella.

18 'There are many reasons for feeling some sympathy for Angelo.' Do you agree?

19 'The character and attitudes of Isabella are a problem for the modern audience.' Discuss.

20 The scenes between Angelo and Isabella are the most dramatic in the play. After Isabella has reported their outcome to Claudio, the play loses our interest.' Discuss.

21 Is Lucio a benevolent or malicious character?

22 'Lucio flits erratically in and out of the play. It is hard to understand his role.' Do you agree?

23 Discuss the view that Lucio's role is like that of the clown or fool.

24 'The issues of the play are too serious to be treated in comic form'. Discuss.

25 'Only comedy could provide a humane solution for the problems dramatised in the play.' Discuss.

26 Do you agree that the play is a comedy about love and sex?

27 Do you think an audience can be satisfied at the end of the play?

28 'The final act of the play reveals Shakespeare's uncertainty about the value of authority.' Discuss.

29 Does Shakespeare bring his plot to a satisfying conclusion?

30 Is there a clear plot for an audience to follow?

31 Do you imagine Shakespeare had a problem resolving the plot of *Measure for Measure*?

# Glossary

**Alliteration**: A figure of speech in which a number of words close to each other in a piece of writing begin with the same sound:

'*Mortality and mercy in Vienna*
*Live in thy tongue, and heart.*'
(Act 1 scene 1 lines 44– 45, page 5)
Alliteration helps to draw attention to these words.

**Antithesis**: A figure of speech in which the writer brings two opposite or contrasting ideas up against each other:

'*Blood, thou art blood.*
*Let's write good angel on the devil's horn –*
*'Tis not the devil's crest.*'
(Act 2 scene 4 lines 15–18, page 77)

**Apostrophe**: When a character suddenly speaks directly to someone or something, which may or may not be present:

'*O place, O form,*
*How often dost thou with thy case, thy habit,*
*Wrench awe from fools*'
(Act 2 scene 4 lines 12–14, page 77)

**Aside**: A speech which can be long or, more usually, short, made by one of the characters for the ears of the audience alone, or for the benefit of another, named character. As with a soliloquy (see below) we rely on an aside to express the true feelings of the character.

'ISABELLA  *Let it not sound a thought upon your tongue*
*Against my brother's life.*
ANGELO [*Aside*]  *She speaks, and 'tis such sense*
*That my sense breeds with it. – Fare you well.*[*Going*]
ISABELLA  *Gentle my lord, turn back.*'
(Act 2 scene 2 lines 141–144, page 69)

**Assonance**: The repetition of vowel sounds within words in a line, sometimes for poetic effect or, as here, to reinforce a point:

'*Our natures do pursue,*
*Like rats that ravin down their proper bane.*'

(Act 1 scene 2 lines 121–122, page 17)

(Here there is alliteration as well, to emphasise the point.)

**Double meaning**: see *Pun*.

**Dramatic irony**: A situation in a play when the audience (and possibly some of the characters) knows something that one or more of the characters does not know. Act 5, with its twists and turns and contradictions, is riddled with dramatic irony.

**Epilogue**: A speech at the end of the play summing up and commenting on the play; also the character who delivers such a speech.

**Exeunt**: A Latin word meaning 'They go away', used for the departure of characters from a scene.

**Hendiadys**: A figure of speech expressed by two nouns joined by 'and' ('...*the fault and glimpse of newness*', Act 1 scene 2 line 148, page 17) rather than by an adjective and a noun ('*the faulty glimpse*').

**Hyperbole**: Deliberate exaggeration, for dramatic effect.
'...*it is certain that when he makes water, his urine is congealed ice*'
(Act 3 scene 2 lines 105–107, page 123)

**Irony**: When someone says one thing and means another. For example, Escalus describes Elbow as '*a wise officer*' in Act 2 scene 1 line 57 page 45, when he is clearly nothing of the sort.
See also *Dramatic irony*.

**Onomatopoeia**: Using words that are chosen because they mimic the sound of what is being described:
'*For every pelting petty officer*
*Would use his heaven for thunder; nothing but thunder.*
*Merciful Heaven,*
*Thou rather with thy sharp and sulphurous bolt*
*Splits the unwedgeable and gnarled oak,*
*Than the soft myrtle.*'
(Act 2 scene 2 lines 113–118, page 67
Here the sounds (and movements) of the storm,
'*thunder...thunder...sharp and sulphurous bolt Splits the unwedgeable and gnarled oak*', contrast with the soft sounds of '*soft myrtle*' and the preceding, rather feeble sound of '*every pelting petty officer*'.

**Paradox**: an apparent contradiction introduced for a striking effect:

> '*If thou art rich, thou'rt poor,*
> *For, like an ass whose back with ingots bows,*
> *Thou bear'st thy heavy riches but a journey,*
> *And Death unloads thee.*'

(Act 3 scene 1 lines 25–28, pages 99–100)

**Pastiche**: A piece of writing done in imitation of the form and style of another writer or literary period.

**Personification**: Referring to a thing or an idea as if it were a person:

> '*Thus can the demi-god, Authority,*
> *Make us pay down for our offence*'

(Act 1 scene 2 lines 113–114, page 15)

**Play on words**: see **Pun**.

**Pun**: A figure of speech in which the writer uses a word that has more than one meaning:

> 'LUCIO    *Behold, behold, where Madam*
>           *Mitigation comes!*
> *I have purchased as many diseases*
>           *under her roof as come to –*
> 2ND GENT.    *To what, I pray?*
> LUCIO    *Judge.*
> 2ND GENT.    *To three thousand dolours a year.*
> 1ST GENT.    *Ay, and more.*
> LUCIO    *A French crown more.*'

(Act 1 scene 2 lines 42–49, page 11)

See the notes on page 10 for an explanation of this punning talk.

**Soliloquy**: Spoken apparently to herself/himself when a character is alone on stage, or separated from the other characters in some way. When Angelo is left alone on stage at the end of Act 2 scene 2 page 71, for example, we see for the first time how easily and how powerfully he can be tempted by Isabella's beauty and purity.